A SLOT MACHINE,
A BROKEN TEST TUBE

THIS BOOK IS PUBLISHED AS PART
OF AN ALFRED P. SLOAN FOUNDATION PROGRAM

S. E. LURIA *(Salvador Edward), 1912 -*

A SLOT MACHINE, A BROKEN TEST TUBE   *An Autobiography*

HARPER & ROW, PUBLISHERS, New York
Cambridge, Philadelphia, San Francisco, London
1817   *Mexico City, São Paulo, Sydney*

A SLOT MACHINE, A BROKEN TEST TUBE. Copyright © 1984 by S. E. Luria. All rights reserved. Printed in the United States of America. No part of this book may be used or reproduced in any manner whatsoever without written permission except in the case of brief quotations embodied in critical articles and reviews. For information address Harper & Row, Publishers, Inc., 10 East 53rd Street, New York, N.Y. 10022. Published simultaneously in Canada by Fitzhenry & Whiteside Limited, Toronto, and simultaneously in Great Britain by Harper & Row Limited, 28 Tavistock Street, London WC2E 7PN, and simultaneously in Australia and New Zealand by Harper & Row (Australasia) Pty. Limited, P.O. Box 226, Artarmon, New South Wales, 2064.

FIRST EDITION

Designer: Sidney Feinberg

Library of Congress Cataloging in Publication Data

Luria, S. E. (Salvador Edward), 1912–
    A slot machine, a broken test tube.

    (Alfred P. Sloan Foundation series)
    Includes index.
        1. Luria, S. E. (Salvador Edward), 1912–
    2. Virologists—United States—Biography. 3. Virologists
    —Italy—Biography. I. Title. II. Series.
    QR31.L84A37 1984   576′.64′0924 [B]   83–48366
    ISBN 0–06–015260–5 (U.S.A. and Canada)
    ISBN 0–06–337036–0 (except U.S.A. and Canada)

84 85 86 87 88 10 9 8 7 6 5 4 3 2 1

To Zella and Dan with love,
To Bernie with gratitude

Contents

Acknowledgments

I am indebted to the Alfred P. Sloan Foundation for support in the preparation of this book as one of a series of autobiographical works by scientists; to the Rockefeller Foundation for hospitality at the Villa Serbelloni, Bellagio, in August 1982; and to the Center for Advanced Study in the Behavioral Sciences, Stanford, for a fellowship funded by the Henry J. Kaiser Family Foundation.

I thank my editor, Aaron Asher, and his colleagues at Harper & Row for their wise handling of the manuscript. Margery Colten, my unique linguist-philosopher-typist, raised many cogent questions of logic and aesthetics, thus demonstrating that even a word processor cannot stifle a good mind.

Finally, I thankfully acknowledge the essential contribution of my novelist friend and colleague, Ilona Karmel, whose patient advice guided me throughout my effort to write on a subject and for a public that were beyond my previous scope of experience.

S.E.L.

Preface to the Series

The Alfred P. Sloan Foundation has for many years included in its areas of interest the encouragement of a public understanding of science. It is an area in which it is most difficult to spend money effectively. Science in this century has become a complex endeavor. Scientific statements are embedded in a context that may look back over as many as four centuries of cunning experiment and elaborate theory; they are as likely as not to be expressible only in the language of advanced mathematics. The goal of a general public understanding of science, which may have been reasonable a hundred years ago, is perhaps by now chimerical.

Yet an understanding of the scientific enterprise, as distinct from the data and concepts and theories of science itself, is certainly within the grasp of us all. It is, after all, an enterprise conducted by men and women who might be our neighbors, going to and from their workplaces day by day, stimulated by hopes and purposes that are common to all of us, rewarded as most of us are by occasional successes and distressed by occasional setbacks. It is an enterprise with its own rules and customs, but an understanding of that enterprise is accessible to any of us, for it is quintessentially human. And an understanding of the enterprise inevitably brings with it some insights into the nature of its products.

Accordingly, the Sloan Foundation has set out to encourage a representative selection of accomplished and articulate scientists to set down their own accounts of their lives in science. The form those accounts will take has been left in each instance to the author: one may choose an autobiographical approach, another may produce a coherent series of essays, a third may tell the tale of a scientific community of which he was a member. Each author is a man or woman of outstanding accomplishment in his or her field. The word "science" is not construed narrowly: it includes activities in the neighborhood of science such as technology and engineering as well as such disciplines as economics and anthropology as much as it includes physics and chemistry and biology.

The Foundation wishes to express its appreciation of the great and continuing contribution made to the program by its Advisory Committee. The Committee has been chaired since the program's inception by Robert Sinsheimer, Chancellor of the University of California—Santa Cruz. Present members of the Committee are Howard Hiatt, Dean, Harvard School of Public Health; Mark Kac, Professor of Mathematics, University of Southern California; Daniel Kevles, Professor of History, California Institute of Technology; Robert Merton, University Professor Emeritus and Special Service Professor, Columbia University; George A. Miller, Professor of Psychology, Princeton University. Earlier, Daniel McFadden, Professor of Economics, and Philip Morrison, Professor of Physics, both of the Massachusetts Institute of Technology, and Frederick E. Terman, Provost Emeritus, Stanford University, had been members. The Foundation has been represented throughout by Arthur L. Singer, Jr., and Stephen White, and Harper & Row, principal publishers for the program, by Winthrop Knowlton, Simon Michael Bessie, and Edward L. Burlingame.

—ALBERT REES
President, Alfred P. Sloan Foundation

Introduction

An aged man is but a paltry thing,
A tattered coat upon a stick, unless
Soul clap its hands and sing, and louder sing
For every tatter in its mortal dress.
                    W. B. YEATS, "Sailing to Byzantium"

Over the years I have read many biographies and some autobiographies and have been struck by the differences between these two literary genres. With few exceptions, such as the Boswell of the *Life of Samuel Johnson,* biographers are chiefly historians. The individuals they dissect interest us as prototypes, that is, as historical figures rather than as unique human beings. In a sense, they are too big for average human breeches.

Biographies are mainly history, then, and like all history they deal with facts and events and the relations among them. Personalities emerge through the actions they perform or in which they share. The skill of the biographer is to crystallize these facts and events around a protagonist. Few people today, especially in the United States, know or care in which century Henry VIII acted out his marital and religious capers, yet most people know of him as a powerful historical figure. Every time a book about that king appears on the bookstalls readers expect to be both stirred by the beauty of Anne Boleyn and secretly titillated by fantasies of her brutal demise. A biography of Henry VIII will stir readers with images of *terribilità* (to borrow a word from his contemporary Machiavelli): the *terribilità* of a king who, for the sake of his personal desires—for sex and for power—was willing to consign all the English, present and future, to the possibility of eternal damnation.

If the biography of a king must deal with a life of power, the biography of a scientist must inevitably deal with science. Yet, just as a king's biography limited to the story of power would be nothing but a tale of battles and intrigues, a scientist's biography confined to his or her scientific work would turn into popular science. There is seldom any *terribilità* in a scientist's life. Even the moments of greatest excitement in science can hardly be conveyed to the lay public. Though everybody has heard of Albert Einstein's equation $E = mc^2$, very few readers can grasp its meaning, no matter how much their own lives are affected by it. A scientist's biographer deals with much duller material than does a chronicler of kings.

I have found most biographies of scientists remarkably uninteresting and their autobiographies even more so. Biographies are essentially history written for broad consumption rather than for the professional journals. As such, they should convey elements of struggle and intensity: if not kings dealing with popes, at least figures in a milieu of well-defined, committed personalities. Twentieth-century physics has produced, for better or for worse, such a milieu, and some physicists' biographies have conveyed a satisfactory sense of drama, ambiguity, and controversy. But these are exceptions. It may be a fault of my taste that most biographies of scientists, even of great scientists such as Darwin, Pasteur, or Einstein, leave me indifferent. One reason, to which I shall return later, is that the scientific narrative, a necessary part of such biographies, deals with science of the past, which belongs to the canon of scientific knowledge and not to literature. The science that can be made vivid by a storyteller is science in progress, the struggles and anguish and triumphs of discovery. We may be amused by Archimedes running naked through Syracuse yelling "Eureka," but an explanation of his discovery of buoyancy would kill even a science-fiction story.

Somehow, the biographer of a scientist should find a way to

integrate the scientific content of the story with the more human, more controversial, more intimate aspects of the subject's personality. This is not an easy task. In the shadow of their enormous achievements, even Pasteur's religious faith, Darwin's neurasthenia, Newton's mental illness and his tyrannical rule over the Royal Society tend to become minor features instead of being keys to understanding these powerful personalities at their work. Yet any biography worth reading should ideally turn around a personality, not around a "poet," a "painter," or a "scientist." The personality should emerge as a landscape composed of many vistas, like a fourteenth-century life of a saint or a Breughel panorama of peasant life. Pasteur's religiosity and Einstein's fiddle would not in themselves justify biographies, but accounts of lives that lack serious exploration of such aspects are truncated. To examine Pasteur without his roots in French provincial bourgeois life or Einstein without his relation to Judaism is to diminish them.

A child, visiting a cemetery for the first time, is said to have asked, "Where are the bad ones buried?" This may be applied to scientists' biographies. Not that we should have more biographies of professionally bad scientists, although these too might be illuminating. But some scientists have had disagreeable personalities and have been disliked by their colleagues. History would gain from their biographies a more complete picture of the kind of people that make science.

If biographies of scientists make them appear rather too good, their autobiographies often make them outright milksops. I can think of three people I have known, a mathematician, an astronomer, a biologist—interesting, dynamic, decisive persons involved in many activities and responsibilities—whose autobiographies are nothing but shy chronicles, destroying their liveliness and mischievousness and masking the emotionally complex aspects of their lives. These autobiographies are dull; the authors were not. Why the incongruity? One reason, I believe, is the tradition of humility fostered in academic science (less so in the social sciences) by the pervasive veneration of the subject matter—science seen as some sort of a *summum bonum* before which one genuflects.

Sometimes age corrects the excessive illusions, and scientists begin to look upon their enterprises with a cooler, more existential eye. But this attitude rarely appears in books. The doubts and inner struggles of scientists, unlike those of novelists, are more often converted into inner turmoil than into print.

It is characteristic of scientists to transfer from their work to their lives a deep respect for rationality, the essential element in the structure of science. In Jacob Bronowski's words, "a mode of knowledge not formalizable is an exploration."* "Not formalizable" here means that the knowledge cannot be organized in sets of formulae or relations that are parts of a comprehensive theory. Most scientists distrust those aspects of their personalities that drive them away from the domain of the formalizable. Thus they tend to distrust romantic love and abstract art, poetry and politics. Since enthusiasm is a potentially dangerous weapon in the laboratory, scientists also tend to avoid fervor in other areas of activity. No one is more aware of this than one who like myself has worked at stimulating scientists' participation in public affairs. Distrust of the nonformalizable would tend to make scientists avoid expressing in their autobiographies the anguish of doubt they must certainly feel. Even in recounting their relations with power centers —as members of or advisers to government—scientists tend to be studiously technical. Social scientists, whose subject matter is mostly nonformalizable and who might therefore be more wary of their ground, exhibit no such reserve.

The academic tradition itself is a handicap for the scientist attempting to write an autobiography. The tradition of humility fosters fear of self-aggrandizement, and conformity hides the most interesting aspects of interpersonal relations: ambivalence, jealousy, manipulations. Perhaps humility and conformity are a reflection of the very motives that have driven the autobiographers to a life in science. The psychologist Anne Roe, herself the wife of an eminent biologist, concluded from a study of members of the National Academy of Sciences that many of them had had child-

*Science and Human Values (New York: Harper & Row, 1956), p. 72.

hoods marked by serious family conflicts.* She suggested that these individuals may have sought in science a protective, uncontroversial, conflict-free profession both in terms of subject matter and of social relations. The relative solidity of scientists' marriages may also reflect a wish for stability or a deficient spirit of adventure outside their own field of work. The same may be true of the timid, middle-of-the-road political stance of most scientists.

Be that as it may, autobiographies of scientists (except those of a few physicists) have failed to convey the sense of adventure that is intrinsic in the work of science itself. Attempts to explain scientific methods and ideas in full to a broad public either leave readers baffled or cause the writing to sink to the level of newspaper science. What best conveys the sense of science as adventure is not the substance but the process of discovery. Did the scientist use a screwdriver, or break a test tube at a critical moment, or find crystals in a solution? And how did these events lead to discovery? Just as insights into the process of literary creation illuminate the workings of the minds of poets and novelists, so do insights into the scientists' day-by-day operations tell us more about the humanity of their trade than does the packaged final output.

If an autobiography is to be more than a superficial record of events, it must be something of a confession. It must be a study of the author's personality, a dissection of action and motives, a revelation of the self. Even if such revelation can never be completely candid because of emotional restraints or of insufficient insight, still a confessional autobiography is more illuminating than a purely narrative one. It is candor that makes Boswell's journals worth reading, the confessional content being unself-consciously exposed, without judgment or anguish. The result is a picture of a superficial man of high sensitivity. One may go a step further and suggest that an autobiography is valuable if it shares with the reader even those budding insights of which the writer is still

The Making of a Scientist (New York: Dodd, Mead, 1953).

uncertain. In fact, it ought to reveal the effort of self-creation through self-exploration.

True autobiographies are bound to be ambiguous in character. Opening up the self exposes its many sides, some of them sources of pride, others of embarrassment or guilt. Self-exposure may also require the overcoming of humility, either through irony or through arrogance. It may require admission or justification of failures of the will. Actual infractions of socially accepted rules of behavior—social sins—may be easier to reveal than transgressions of one's canons of decency or virtue—sins against the Holy Ghost. Yet such revelations may be valuable biographically as well as for emotional catharsis.

Autobiography provides opportunities for self-justification as well as for concealment. The confessional mode may hide an arrogant assertion of the author's personality. Rousseau's *Confessions* is an interesting prototype, crowned by the statement, "I am not made like anyone I have seen; I dare believe that I am not like anyone in existence." Arrogance, rather than the few transgressions of his youth and the not so few of his mature life, is the true subject of Rousseau's confession.

James Watson's *The Double Helix* is a wonderful book, because the discovery of the structure of DNA is a great story and it is told with style and verve.* It is also a confessional book because, with a smile that is never a sneer, the author unburdens himself of a variety of transgressions: insensitivity in dealing with colleagues, arrogance inappropriate to his age at the time of the discovery. Some scientists were offended by Watson's light tone and his failure to prostrate himself before the goddess Science. Knowing that few people are as completely dedicated to science as Jim Watson, I believe that he has done a service to science by demystifying it in a literary work of distinction. In *The Double Helix,* at any rate, confession is not contrition: whatever sense of guilt existed is dissolved. The arrogance of course persists.

Confessional features of this kind are important in a scientist's autobiography because the revelations are intimately related to

*New York: Atheneum, 1968.

the professional aspects of the personality. They illuminate choices, achievements, and relations with colleagues. The revealed emotions often turn out to have been the driving forces of a successful life. *The Double Helix* tells us more about the mainspring of Watson's career and social life than one could discover in a straightforward account of his achievements.

Prescribing to her fellow historians Barbara Tuchman writes: "One should resolve one's doubts, examine conflicting evidence, and determine motives behind the scenes, and carry on any disputes with one's own sources in the reference notes, not in the text."* Blessed historians! They can choose a great moment or a great man or woman in history and shape them as a sculptor shapes a monument. But the autobiographer's task is not greatness but self-revelation. In an autobiography, the process of definition recommended by Tuchman would eliminate, not confusion of fact, but shades of personality. It would hide those ambiguities whose disclosure justifies the writing.

Yet one cannot paint a good picture of a life totally in chiaroscuro. The problem for an autobiographer—at least for this autobiographer—is to achieve a reasonably coherent portrait of the self with all its arrays of certainties and uncertainties, strengths and weaknesses, failures and achievements, without falling into the trap of reducing a personal life to a chaos of self-contradictions. A principle of order must be introduced, though different from that prescribed by Tuchman for her fellow historians. The principle I have adopted is a sectorial approach, in which different areas of significant involvement—professional, political, artistic, emotional —are dealt with separately and in a developmental way. The sectorial arrangement makes it possible to examine a sequence of events and choices within a certain area without, for example, breaking into the story of research activities with "At that time I became interested in the poetry of Wallace Stevens." The interactions among sectors should, I hope, become evident in the unfolding of the narrative.

Practicing History (New York: Knopf, 1981).

Equally important, I believe, is to replace the chronological with the developmental mode. The growth of a person occurs at different rates and in different ways in different sectors of personality. The developmental process of the self is something different from a biological developmental process. The latter is the unfolding of a program intrinsic to an organism because it is inscribed in its genetic material. The instructions of the genes are obeyed according to a temporal and topographic schedule—make a brain here, then make a heart there—that can be modified only by major disruptions. The developmental instructions of the human self, on the contrary, come mostly from the outside world, from contacts with the social and physical environments. Filtered through the network of consciousness and language, these instructions are the raw materials of the self. Acting in response to these instructions, the individual functions in society and in so doing creates itself as a unique being, thereby also creating a personal world. In existential terms, we can say that the individual defines itself by existing in the world, not passively but actively, creatively —by acts of the will.

This brings me to my next thesis. The developmental process of self-definition is neither automatic nor smooth. At some point in life, different for different areas of activity, one faces significant choices between alternative paths or activities or devotions. Some of these alternatives are so preposterously unequal in value as to make the choices almost automatic, but this is the exception rather than the rule. It is easy, for example, to choose between a Harvard chair and a job as a post office clerk. But choosing between Harvard and Yale may be hard. It involves a balancing of many subtle factors and ultimately performing an act of the will—an existential choice.

Such existential choices may simply be isolated occurrences, but they illustrate a general class that I include within the collective category of commitments. At some points in life, in some specific areas of activity, an individual, I believe, performs a specific, conscious act of the will, deciding that from that time on, barring cogent reasons, he or she will act in that sector of the self according to a certain line of conduct, almost a system of virtue. For example, a commitment to science is not only a decision to do scientific research rather than business management. It is a commitment to act as if the rational structure of science were a valuable, reliable guide to action in the material world. To be committed to the rationality of science means, for example, to reject the possibility that a pack of cards can be influenced by the will of the dealer.

In his influential book *The Structure of Scientific Revolutions* Thomas Kuhn suggests another useful application of the commitment concept.* He points out that scientists, in carrying out the business of science, make a commitment to the assumption that the approaches and procedures currently effective in research—the current paradigm—will continue to be effective. Such commitment extends necessarily to situations not yet comprised within the paradigm, just as a social or political commitment does.

Commitment as here defined is a consciously chosen device that facilitates active performance in a certain sphere, preventing the individual from being immobilized by every resurgence of conflict or ambiguity. Commitments do not eliminate doubts or questioning, but provide a certain measure of reactive automatism. They enable one to act in a reasonably consistent way in ambiguous situations. In existential terms, a commitment is a self-pledge to act in one or another sphere as if a certain set of propositions were at least provisionally valid. Even the reason why most people do not commit suicide may be because of a commitment to act as if life had this or that meaning.

Tracing the origins and timing of one's specific commitments is a fascinating operation. As I shall mention further on in this book, for example, I can trace with reasonable precision how and when I became committed to a socialist view of society, to being an American (as distinct from just being a U.S. citizen), and even to personal decency (and thereby learned the difference between decency and routine truthfulness). Such insights are illuminating

*Chicago: University of Chicago Press, 1962.

because they point out discontinuities in personal development.

Some degree of conflict between various commitments is always present, precisely because most commitments are made separately and not as parts of a single guiding principle. Tolerance of such conflicts is part of the achievement of maturity. It protects the self against inner chaos and inaction. Sticking by one's commitments until the conflicts become acute is a source of predictability and dependability in social life. Lightly shifting one's commitments may be evidence less of crisis than of superficiality. One may say of commitment what a physicist once said of theories: Don't rush to abandon a good theory just because of a few facts. Theories and commitments are operating tools, not ends in themselves.

A set of functional commitments keeps life from dissolving into chaos and makes possible an effective existence in reasonable freedom. Yet each lasting commitment is something of a restriction of pure existential freedom. By preventing unrelieved existential despair, like that of Beckett's characters, a commitment pledges one to perform some kind of activity. The resulting loss of freedom is but a loss to the inner self; it is different from a relinquishment of freedom to the external world. If I decide to be a socialist I make a commitment to myself to act in certain ways; but if I were to join a political party my commitment would be to an external structure. It would become a loyalty.

In the chapters that follow I have tried to identify the time and motive of the key developmental events in my life as they affected various aspects of my personality. I have called these events commitments, both because of my existentialist bias and because I wished to emphasize their active rather than passive nature. Such commitments are guides to action and remain valuable as long as they lead to effective and honest activity. They are in a sense the condensate of life's purpose. I am reminded of a statement by Bernard Shaw (in the Preface to *Man and Superman*): "This is the true joy in life, the being used for a purpose recognized by yourself as a mighty one; the being thoroughly worn out before you are thrown on the scrap heap."

1

The Younger Years

> I wake to sleep, and take my waking slow,
> I feel my fate in what I cannot fear.
> I learn by going where I have to go.
> THEODORE ROETHKE, "The Waking"

I was born in 1912 in Turin, the capital of Italian Piedmont, a stern industrial city nestled at the foot of an oppressive range of hills and surrounded at some distance by the Alps—snow-covered, spectacular, and forbidding. In Turin mountain climbers are an admired elite, the best among them usually dying before middle age on some impossible slope. Nonclimbers like me felt rotten with shame and envy.

Turin in my young years contained three leading socio-cultural structures: the clerical aristocracy, traditionally tied to the disreputable House of Savoy; the liberal academic intelligentsia, including famous lawyers, mathematicians, and art historians; and the "red" elite, which led the great workers' movement after the First World War and out of which was founded in 1921 the Italian Communist party. One of its founders, along with Antonio Gramsci, was a philosophy professor in the school I had then just entered.

Most of the intellectual and political ferment touched me only peripherally. Although the Luria tribe is one of the oldest and proudest Jewish families, including innumerable rabbis and famous mystics, my own immediate family was Italian lower-middle class trying to emerge into a better-off stratum of society. My father, David, an accountant by training and the manager of a small printing business, was vaguely liberal but too timid to act on his beliefs. My mother, Esther, who had had only the equivalent of some junior high school education, was widely read and a witty ghost writer of students' theses (some of "my" best homework on literature was written by her), but had no consistent world view beyond the achievement of economic well-being. Her overriding concern with illness tended to turn the entire family into valetudinarians. Against this influence I reacted violently, struggling to deny my vulnerability to disease.

My only sibling, Giuseppe, six years my senior, was a strong influence on my childhood, providing a model of serious scholarship and active social life. He was kinder to me, I suspect, than I was grateful to him. We diverged in the way we reacted to our family's concerns, he sharing them and even identifying physically with the parental concern for health, while I was, at least in attitude, the rebel. We also diverged professionally, Giuseppe becoming an engineer and later a dealer in electrical hardware, while I strove for an academic career. We drifted apart in our early adulthood only to find ourselves close to each other again in our mature years.

My brother and I went through school at the time when Fascism was clamping down on open independent political activity, reducing it, at least in Turin, to conspiratorial initiatives involving small numbers of workers and intellectuals. Yet while living passively in Fascist society, I was not totally sheltered from the underground political ferment. My high school, the Licèo d'Azeglio, by tradition one of the great schools of Italy, had on its staff in the 1920s some brilliantly independent personalities and was destined to produce some of the future leaders of post-Fascist Italy. Politics never openly entered the classroom, of course, and good teachers were respected for their work. Two superb teachers, who roused my interest in mathematics and history, were committed members of the Fascist party.

The man who influenced me most in learning as well as in intellectual growth, however, was a teacher of Italian and Latin literature, Augusto Monti, the author of several novels and other books, a liberal socialist who was later to spend several years in jail for anti-Fascist activities. His impact in the classroom was not political but personal. One felt confronted by a personality of deep intellectual and human integrity, a teacher who demanded and extended respect and who treated adolescent students as equals in rights if not in knowledge. He was the only one of my teachers whom I visited again whenever I went back to Italy after the war. Both he and I recalled how his eyes filled with tears when in the classroom he recited to us, without comment, poems of liberty; and how our band of fifteen-year-olds watched with some emotion this show of courage. The lesson was not just literary. It was a lesson in sincerity.

I must mention an oddity in my secondary education: I was always on the verge of failing natural-science courses. Then as now, it is impossible for me to learn and recall names and hierarchies of objects—plants, animals, rocks—in which I am not actively interested. It may have been the fault of the teachers; I had no trouble learning by heart all the irregular Greek verbs or, later, the names of anatomical particulars. I guess I learn that for which I have either a use or a motive. At any rate, an unconfirmed rumor circulated that my literature and math teachers had threatened a poor natural-science teacher with exile to some savage Sardinian city unless she passed me. She did.

Throughout the school years I was one of the shortest and therefore least athletic students. My own lack of physical aptitude was unfortunately encouraged by my family's exaggerated concern about physical health and by their anti-athletic bias. Laziness and fear of failure on my part conspired to make me eschew any serious effort to participate in sports—a situation that I bitterly regretted later, especially when chronic dorsal pains made me unable to do what I had earlier avoided.

My lack of athletic disposition brought me close to a group of schoolmates who were also for some reason the most studious ones. Among them, one friend, Ugo Fano, was destined to play a major role in my later career. The son of a mathematics professor at the University of Turin, he is now a professor emeritus of physics at the University of Chicago. Brilliant of mind and somewhat awkward in manner (he was nicknamed *Urangus fanoides* by his physicist colleagues), Ugo from the beginning was absolutely dedicated to science and, later, to assisting other scientists. He more than anyone else encouraged and helped me to become a scientist.

His influence, however, was not only scientific. Through our friendship I acquired, while still in my middle teens, a longing for the academic life. I felt the attraction of an existence centered on intellectual rather than economic pursuits. It was of course a naïve view: my friend's family, like many other academic families in Italy, was backed by enough private income to provide comfort as well as leisure for intellectual pursuits. Yet for me the identification of academic life with the good life has persisted.

I emerged from high school with a good store of knowledge (except for chemistry and biology; and the irregular Greek verbs were soon forgotten) but without any real passion for learning, only with a good ability to learn when I had to. In the continental system, high school led directly to specialized university courses, almost free of cost but forcing a professional choice at age seventeen or eighteen. The choice was hard: I had neither the guts nor the conviction needed to choose an academic, nonprofessional career, such as mathematics or physics. I went into medical school, because of my parents' wish and my own lack of alternative inclinations.

The medical-school years were troubled ones, despite my more or less steady academic success as measured by grades. My family's financial situation declined because of the depression, and my mother's chronic illness became increasingly troublesome. More and more I felt eager to escape from home life, but medicine turned out not to be the solution; I never fully identified with it as an activity. I was perhaps too immature to integrate myself into the confusing structure of the hospital, and lacked the initiative, even eagerness, required in an Italian medical school to gain access to practical expertise beyond the formal lectures. Thus, although I graduated in 1935 near the top of my class, I felt totally inadequate as a doctor and not at all eager to practice. Yet I had found excitement in patient examination and diagnosis (which constituted the center of medical practice in those pre-miracle-drug days) and in seeing patients improve. I recall two striking episodes. One was a case of pernicious anemia, a woman who entered the ward white as a sheet, was treated with the first available preparation of liver extract, and a few weeks later left the hospital laughing. The other case was a man with slow endocarditis, hitherto an inevitably fatal disease, who was cured by prontosil, the forerunner of sulfonamides, just arrived from Germany. These were exciting moments, unfortunately rare among much drudgery.

My lukewarm attitude toward medicine as a profession was fed by my interest, first vague then more serious (although with many misgivings), in becoming a research scientist. I shall explore later in this book the emotional aspects of my shift of careers. Here let me recount only how the actual opportunity developed, over a number of years, through a peculiar series of accidents and other circumstances. These included, first, my need to learn some mathematics beyond high school trigonometry; next, the poor performance of Rome's electric trolley cars; then, Mussolini's persecution of Italian Jews. Mixed with these was the role of my friend Ugo Fano as a catalyst and at times as instigator. When we entered the University in Turin, I chose medicine, he physics. But in the evenings, as we walked the streets and parks of Turin, he started giving me peripatetic lessons in elementary calculus, using the starry sky as a system of coordinates to explain limits, derivatives, and integrals. And while teaching me calculus he told me about physics. Those were the years, 1929–1930, when the new, revolutionary ideas of physics—quantum theory, wave mechanics—were filtering down to undergraduates, at least to the best ones, and with them, names like Bohr, Heisenberg, Schrödinger, and especially Enrico Fermi, the already legendary young star of Italian physics. Listening to Ugo's exciting tales of quanta and positrons and neutrons, I came to think of physics as a romantic landscape whose magic was enhanced by my almost complete lack of understanding.

I suspect my romantic view of physics and of science in general was heightened because I was then entering a period of sentimental education, in both my personal and literary life. In studying German I read Heine, responding to his cosmopolitan romanticism. Also at that time I discovered (in translation) the German neo-romantic novelists of the 1920s—Mann, Wassermann, Feuchtwanger, and Arnold and Stefan Zweig—whose stories stirred in me the desire to strive for something out of the ordinary. This something became the dream of being a scientist.

I was, in fact, doing some science. Throughout the years of medical school I worked rather seriously in the laboratory of an eminent histologist, Giuseppe Levi, an international authority on nerve tissue and an outspoken anti-Fascist. Out of his laboratory there emerged several other well-known scientists. But in those years I acquired little scientific training. My teacher was immensely learned in the field of histology, but histology was not very exciting. Some of my experiments on muscle and nerve cells were published in Italian and German journals, but none of them dealt with fundamental problems. What I learned from Levi that served me well later was a solid attitude of professionalism: how to take experiments seriously and bring them to conclusion. I learned the importance of writing and publishing: when a set of data made sense, said the master, write it up for publication. And when the manuscript was written he mercilessly rewrote it from scratch. The other lesson that I learned from him and have practiced throughout my career was not to put my name on my students' articles unless I had actually contributed a significant part of the work.

Such lessons on how to do science were effective because of the respect that the master's personality commanded. His integrity, his gruffness, his absent-mindedness, and his anti-Fascist stance made him an almost legendary figure in university circles. For, strangely enough, in Fascist Italy the anti-Fascists, although sometimes harassed or worse by the authorities, were looked up to by the educated public, including the many who lacked the courage to imitate them. I can think of similar situations in other countries.

Histology was not for me. And in the medical school I found no other source of intellectual inspiration, nothing that appealed to a mind full of dreams of physics. But an exciting plan was maturing in my mind. I decided to find a medical specialty that could bring me close to physics and then use it as a bridge to what might be called "biophysics." I must admit I was totally ignorant of what might be going on in biophysics in the rest of the world. The specialty that could provide the bridge was obviously radiology. Hence, disappointing my family (who dreamt of my becoming a famous surgeon) as well as my teachers (who saw in me a potentially good internist), upon finishing medical school I joined a radiology department in Turin and registered for a course there.

My disappointment and sense of loss were profound. Both radiotherapy and diagnostic radiology turned out to be the dullest of medical specialties, lacking even the full responsibility for patient care. And the so-called specialization courses turned out to be a farce: the chief professor could not write the simplest equation correctly even when copying from a manual. And the scheduled physics course for radiologists was not taught at all.

But soon enough I was in the army. Italy of course had a system of universal military service, with doctors required to serve five months in training and thirteen months as junior medical officers. I could easily have been exempted, partly because of my borderline physical aptitude, partly through the good offices of a colonel uncle—the use of influential connections being a rather common practice in Italy, at least at that time. But I insisted (again against my parents' advice) on going into the army. My motive was not patriotism; in fact, I was by then a convinced if silent anti-Fascist. Yet I had a romantic feeling (to which I shall return later) that I should not take advantage of special protection. Moreover, military service was an excuse to delay the choice between medicine and science.

Army life was not inspiring, although my women friends thought I looked rather good in the olive-green uniform of a second lieutenant, complete with boots and a borrowed saber. I myself had not a bit of martial spirit or pride of uniform. In the process of taking the formal oath of allegiance to the King of Italy, I was unable to return the unsheathed saber to the scabbard and was ignominiously dismissed from the colonel's office. On another occasion, having to accompany a battalion on a training exercise, I was offered a horse, confessed to my lack of horsemanship, and traveled by bicycle, to the cheers of the troops. The main gains from my military life were: studying calculus, and changing from a fastidious to an omnivorous eater. More importantly, experience as a medical officer confirmed my desire not to practice medicine. I was acutely aware that I was not adequately trained to deal with emergencies. Also, while I was eager to help the young soldiers under my care, I realized that dealing with medical problems was for me a chore rather than a vocation. At times I panicked at my responsibilities; when I did not, I worried that maybe I should.

But while I was supposedly defending my country (my military service fortunately came too late for me to participate in Mussolini's Ethiopian adventure), the wheels of destiny were working, lubricated once more by my friend Ugo. The idea we concocted together was that I should finish my radiology courses in Rome and at the same time study physics at the University of Rome, where Fermi and his closest colleagues were working. This idea Ugo sold to the physicists, the clinching comment being Fermi's laconic "It sounds reasonable." Thus in the fall of 1937 I stepped out of my uniform and moved to Rome, an arrangement made possible by the hospitality of my aunt and uncle (the colonel, who happened also to be a fine mathematician). In the happy home of these beloved relatives I was received like a son, fed like a gourmet, and relieved of daily contact with the many worries that were continuing to beset my own family.

Rome in 1937 was as beautiful as ever, even for one like myself who does not greatly appreciate Roman baroque. The hideous architecture of Fascism, trying to recapture the imperial greatness by cutting huge stern malls through the ancient center, could not undo the beauty of the ocher walls of Piazza Navona, the enchanting views on Monte Celio, or the glory of Trinità dei Monti. Yet I discovered then for the first time a side of my personality that was to assert itself again later. I was impressed by the luminosity of Rome and yet I recoiled from the city, recoiled from its expansiveness, its crude openness, and from the easy familiarity of the Roman people—qualities that contrasted with the hazy grayness of my northern Turin and the restrained manners of the Piedmontese, truly the "Protestants" of Italy. Years later the contrast between the restrained atmosphere of Boston or the Middle West and the narcissistic aspects of California life evoked similar emotions in me.

Professionally speaking the Rome experience was a torment, although a delicious one. My rather perfunctory duties in radiology were probably sufficient to give me the training I would have needed if I had entered that practice. But physics was something else again. It soon became clear that my ability to deal with physics was weak, especially because mathematics was not my "natural language." I struggled along with the undergraduate students and gained some confidence when studying thermodynamics and electromagnetism. Most interesting and later useful was a course in spectroscopy, elegantly taught by Franco Rasetti. Rasetti was a remarkably encyclopedic man, with innocent hobbies such as a complete knowledge of all Italian roads. Years later, out of disgust with atom bombs, he turned into a Cambrian paleontologist and became a leader in that field. I actually had the opportunity to learn something of experimental work when I was taken in as a helper—rather, a handyman—by another professor, Edoardo Amaldi. My main accomplishment there, as I recall, was to polish by hand a series of aluminum counters for protons; but in the process I acquired some idea of the principles of particle physics.

At the end of my year in Rome it was clear to me that my interest in physics was bound to remain amateurish rather than professional. Yet that year among physicists proved to be the critical turning point in my life. It taught me to think a bit in the way physicists do, a way more analytical than the way of biologists. Also, life among the stern Rome physicists reinforced my natural streak of puritanism. I remember, for example, Amaldi's horrified reaction when someone mentioned "playing bridge in the afternoon"—clearly a sign of irretrievable corruption.

Most important, that year among physicists introduced me to

radiation biology. This came about when Rasetti, an omnivorous reader, discovered and gave me a set of articles by Max Delbrück in which this German physicist formulated the concept of gene as molecule. These papers seemed to me, however ignorant of genetics I then was, to open the way to the Holy Grail of biophysics— and there and then, I believe, I swore to myself that I would be a knight of that Grail.

Yet oaths are easy to make but paths hard to find. How was I to pursue that knightly goal? Here another event came into play, which I may call the trolley-car accident. The tram I regularly took to work was almost as regularly stopped by electrical failures. One day, sitting in the paralyzed conveyance, I engaged in conversation with a fellow whom I knew by sight. He turned out to be a bacteriologist named Geo Rita, now professor of virology in Rome. My head that day was filled with Delbrück's articles, so we talked of bacteria and genes and radiation, and when the tram's electric current returned I went with my new friend to his lab to chat some more. He was at the time sampling the water of the Tiber for dysentery bacilli, using as a test the presence of something called bacteriophage, a viruslike parasite of bacteria whose name I had never even heard. Between bacteriophage and myself it was love at first sight. All week I played with test tubes and petri dishes, devising new ways of growing and counting bacteriophage, even using some of the simple statistical methods I had learned in physics—making all possible mistakes but for the first time in my life getting excited about research.

Thus bacteriophage, Delbrück, and I were somehow brought together in that winter of 1938. I had been looking for some biological object on which to test Delbrück's ideas on the gene, something small enough to be like a gene and yet easy enough to work with. Bacteriophage was just that. One could raise billions of copies in a few hours and enumerate them with a precision and sensitivity even higher than for any chemical. And, as I was to discover some years later, bacteriophages are actually beautiful: each has a head and a tail, and whiskers, and legs like a spider's; but all this at the molecular level, so small that it can be seen only in electron micrographs. But until then bacteriophage, like any other group of viruses, could be detected and counted only by observing the damage they produced on living cells or bacteria. Adding to the excitement of my meeting with bacteriophage came the discovery that Delbrück, who by then had moved from Germany to California to escape the Nazi regime, had also found out about bacteriophage and was actually working with these exciting things. That meant I was on the right track. As in a troubadour romance, the love triangle among Delbrück, bacteriophage, and me had come into being at four thousand miles' distance and without mutual awareness of each other.

Before I read Delbrück's first article on bacteriophage I had applied for an Italian government fellowship to work for a year at Berkeley, where there was supposed to be some radiation biology going on. One day I heard that the fellowship had been approved. Immediately I decided that I would go to Pasadena instead and work with Delbrück. That day was July 17, 1938. The next day, Mussolini proclaimed his notorious "Racial Manifesto," aligning Fascist Italy fully with Nazi Germany and excluding Jews from the "pure" Italian race. The identification of Italians as a nordic race was left for sycophantic journalists to complete. The manifesto was especially preposterous because Italy was undoubtedly the least anti-Semitic of European countries. Jews were few and mostly belonged to the middle class. They had produced patriotic leaders in the Risorgimento, and after the unification of Italy Jews had been a strongly nationalistic group; some had been ministers and one, prime minister. The impact of the manifesto and of the racial laws that followed displayed the usual features of political events in Italy—a mixture of farce and tragedy. While the Fascist militia was arranging, for a price, to help wealthy Jews to export money and jewels, the newspapers searched their files to find evidence of the evil infiltration of Jews into the national life. I was myself discovered several times as having been an assistant (without pay) in a few hospital departments. And my fellowship, like an ephemeral flower, had lasted *l'espace d'une nuit.*

The impact of the racial laws was, of course, felt more strongly by the least secure groups. It is a tribute to Italians, both Jews and Gentiles, that outside the official press there was an almost general persistence of mutual trust. In fact, even during the worst period of German occupation, the Italian people, including police and soldiers, tried, often successfully, to save Jews from deportation.

My family was hurt, my brother losing his job in industry and my father most of his business. They had neither the means nor the energy to emigrate. Later, during the German occupation, they spent almost two years in hiding and were saved by the admirable devotion of Gentile friends, who probably risked their own lives to protect them. Both my parents and the relatives who had been my hosts in Rome survived many years after the war.

I was torn in 1938 between the call of duty to my parents, which meant for me to stay with them and return to medicine, and the call of freedom, driving me where I could be a scientist. The latter won, I must say, with the full approval of my parents, who felt that once abroad I would be safer myself and might also be of help to them. The news from Germany—the *Kristallnacht* later that year as the outstanding example—made clear to me that the persecution of Jews was not likely, even in Italy, to remain merely a nonviolent humiliation.

It proved easy for me, alone, without money, but also without responsibilities, to leave Italy. I wound up in Paris. Sergio De Benedetti, a physicist whom I barely knew then, was working in the Institute of Radium in Paris and wrote me that France was still, as always, the home of persecuted intellectuals and that I should try my luck there. Thus, on a November morning, having said good-bye to family and to physicist friends (my friend Ugo was preparing to emigrate to America; Fermi and his Jewish wife Laura had just left for Stockholm to receive the Nobel Prize, and thence for New York), I found myself in foggy and chilly Paris.

There my extraordinary luck held. Fernand Holweck, a physicist renowned in the field of high-vacuum physics and also an expert in radiation biology, was so surprised at meeting a physician who knew a bit of physics and had even read some of his articles that within a week he got me a fellowship from the National

Research Fund, a brain child of the left-wing Front Populaire that was destined to revive French science and later became the Centre National de la Recherche Scientifique. Holweck was a jolly giant of a man, a wonderful experimenter and inventor. In his laboratory I gained some confidence in instrumentation, although neither then nor later was I ever really adept at devising or using instruments. Holweck even introduced me to the aging glory of French physics, Jean Perrin, who later submitted to the *Comptes Rendus de l'Académie des Sciences* a research paper of mine. In fact he asked me to read it to him and slept peacefully while I did so.

The shadow of Hitler, the threat of war, and sharp class enmities made Paris a tense city. With its human resources depleted by World War I France was a tired country, uncertain of its own vitality. Yet even in its weakened state the French Third Republic tasted of freedom. What I discovered in Paris was politics, not the whispered underground politics of Fascist Italy but the politics of democratic processes, with political parties, political newspapers, political rallies and marches. Left and right made sense because of their comparable strength and because they stood at least in principle for dialectically opposed classes of society, not just for divergent interest groups. France taught me basic lessons about the structure of a modern society. Helping loyalist refugees from Franco's Spain who reached Paris without clothes or shelter was the first contribution I could make, almost token amends for my long political silence in Italy.

My home was a couple of tiny rooms near the Val-de-Grâce hospital, conveniently close to the Curie Laboratory, where I worked. (It was also near the Closerie des Lilas of Hemingway and Henry Miller fame, both of whom, however, I was then unaware.) Walking to work through the ancient Rue St. Jacques was pleasant, and the work itself was exciting and demanding: the laboratory was suited for physics rather than biology, and it was a challenge to organize it for my labors with bacteria and bacteriophage. I felt pleased with myself, discovering in my own personality an element of adaptability and efficiency that until then I had not been called upon to exercise. I also discovered, in succession, first that I could darn my own socks, and next that there is no need to darn socks at all: two stages in my liberation from a past dependence on exploited labor.

Socially, Paris was a dull experience. I have never been fun oriented and while in Paris I was not even capable of taking full advantage of the sexual freedom so much greater in France than in Italy, being then still emotionally tied to a past relationship. Except for two Italians—De Benedetti, who was also in the Curie Laboratory, and another physicist, Bruno Pontecorvo, who was to acquire notoriety when he defected to the Soviet Union around 1950—my friends were few. I therefore spent most of my time working, using my free time to discover French poetry—Baudelaire, Verlaine, and the difficult Mallarmé—and French art—the Impressionist, Post-Impressionist, and modern painters.

My work on the effects of radiation on bacteriophage brought me in contact with an interesting man, Eugène Wollman, who was chief of bacteriophage research at the Pasteur Institute and had written some prophetic articles on the biological role of bacteriophage. Short, belligerent, but kindly, he had a sharp, acid wit. One day I told him that I thought one of his colleagues seemed a bit dulled by age. "Nonsense," he replied, "he is just as bright now as he was at thirty." In 1940, the night before I left Paris as the Nazi army approached, Wollman took me to his home and made me listen to some Beethoven "to preserve my faith in humanity." I was never to see him again. He and his wife and lifelong co-worker disappeared in a Nazi extermination camp in 1943. Holweck too fell victim to the German invaders. A non-Jew, he was arrested for helping British parachutists and perished in a Nazi jail.

During my time in Paris I was for the first time, so to speak, on my own in the laboratory. I started exploring in a variety of directions, generally without much luck. One episode of failure is worth mentioning. Upon a suggestion from an Italian bacteriologist, Federico Nitti of the Institute Pasteur, I tried to apply a method I had devised to the analysis of survival of bacterial cells in sulfanilamide, the first wonder-drug antibiotic (a derivative of the prontosil I had seen used while in medical school). I obtained a clear-cut result: each bacterium multiplied in sulfanilamide from 1 cell to about 100 and then stopped. Not being a good biochemist I failed to see the implications of this finding—that the cells could multiply in sulfanilamide as long as they had a store of something whose production was inhibited by sulfanilamide. This could have led me to explain the mode of action of sulfonamides, a discovery made a year later by the British biochemist D. D. Woods. It was the first—not the last—lost opportunity in my scientific career. It is a risk that faces the naïve scientist venturing into a new field without the required knowledge of the background.

I was touring Brittany on a borrowed bicycle when World War II started in September 1939. (I don't mean to imply that I could have prevented it had I been in Paris.) Back in the city I went to a military recruiting office and, after some arguing, persuaded the *fonctionnaire* in charge to take my name. I never heard from the army. My war-related activities consisted, first, in helping Holweck in an abortive attempt to make rhodium-coated mirrors for French tank periscopes; and second, in working with a group of physicists on devices for the protection of ships against magnetic mines. My single achievement on this project was to rig up a gadget to demagnetize the watches of colleagues who forgot to remove them before handling the magnets.

A few months after the beginning of the war I was approached by a businessman interested in patenting a new additive for airplane fuel. The claim was that a mixture of lead shavings and ethyl alcohol irradiated with ultraviolet light would produce an additive that increased fuel efficiency. I was asked to check the claim and Holweck agreed to let me try on a consulting basis. A few weeks' work were enough to convince me not only that the claim was false, but that it was probably part of a rather sinister swindle. My samples had been secretly replaced with a known additive, lead tetroxide, by the messenger who brought them to the test lab, as I discovered by marking them in a secret way. This first experi-

ence with the industrial world contributed to my budding radicalism, but also promoted my safety: my earnings from this consul-
tantship were to pay for my travel to America.

The German army entered Holland and Belgium in May 1940
and rolled unopposed toward Paris, entering the city on the 14th.
By then Parisians had been leaving for days—by train, by car or
cart. The scene of Paris being emptied of its people was heart-
breaking. The absence of chaos or real pain made it even more
dismal—recalling one of those animal migrations that start accidentally and spread through an entire herd. I recall going to the
Place Montmartre on the 12th of June with Frida Stewart, a British friend who had driven an ambulance in loyalist Spain and had
then settled in Paris. We marveled at the emptiness of the streets
and, walking around the Sacré-Coeur, heard the cannon rumbling
from the direction of Chantilly.

Being present at a major social dislocation such as the evacua-
tion of Paris is a peculiar experience. To a historian such an event
represents a nodal occurrence of causes and effects; to a journalist,
a mosaic of vignettes with human interest. In the hands of a great
novelist—the plague of Milan for Manzoni or the retreat from
Moscow for Tolstoy—the great dislocations of human life become
inspiration for revealing the human condition at its worst and its
best. But for the individual participant who is not in any of these
literary classes the great event translates itself into a composite of
minor occurrences, each of which amounts to problem solving—
making do. While a great city bleeds out its people, while the
places of work slowly grind to a halt, while carts loaded with
mattresses make an unusual appearance on the Boulevard St.-
Michel, one finds oneself busy looking for a monkey wrench to
tighten the nut on a borrowed bicycle or deciding which book to
put into one's rucksack or worrying whether a friend has enough
money to last maybe a couple of weeks. Not that one misses the
forest for the trees: the trees are the forest. Such incidents, in my
mind more than forty years later, are the fall of Paris.

That evening I left, by bicycle. For a couple of days I managed
to keep just ahead of the German troops. I was twice the target

of ineffectual strafing from planes, once while on the bicycle, once while on a freight train. My excursion from Paris through Southern France took me to Limoges, Bordeaux, Toulouse, and Marseilles, a month through a hallucinating summer landscape under a sun whose improbable glow contrasted with the deadly reality as in a surrealist painting. In my peregrinations I met all kinds of people, from gruff, hostile peasants to tender landladies. By chance or by referral I also met some interesting people: the famous Italian writer Carlo Levi—the author of *Christ Stopped at Eboli*—who was living in princely fashion with his beautiful mistress near Bordeaux and with whom I escaped by taxi just before the Nazis arrived. We spent three days in a farmhouse playing cards, till I got impatient and left, having no mistress to keep me there. In Toulouse, having found hospitality in the home of an Italian agronomist, I met a remarkable man, Carlo Dozza, a Communist who had fought in Spain and was destined after the war to become the almost legendary reform mayor of Bologna.

Marseilles was the Mecca of my travels, of course, because it was the seat of a functioning American consulate. To obtain an American immigration visa, even if one was eligible, could take one or two months or longer. Meanwhile one had to be ready with a French exit visa, Spanish transit visa, Portuguese transit visa, and these required an entry visa for some overseas country. Catch-22 —except that any overseas visa was good. So one went from consulate to consulate exploring opportunities. The battle of the visas was in fact the only protracted ground battle to be fought in France that year. A motley crew of European scholars and anti-Fascists and Jewish refugees fought against a redoubtable crew of bureaucrats: crassly insensitive French *fonctionnaires;* tiny dignified Portuguese; an exquisitely courteous Chinese, who promised a reply in two or three years; an understanding Belgian aristocrat, who gave me a visa for the Belgian Congo (could I have become another Kurtz?); a set of rude Spanish officials; and finally the helpful, mafia-like Italian black-shirt officials. For me, alone and young, the battle of the visa was just one more experience, exercising my talent for survival. But for the survivors of earlier persecutions it was tragic. Some could not take it, and committed suicide in front of the often closed doors of the consulates.

The scene at the American consulate, located in a lovely suburban villa, was worth a sociologist's attention. In the waiting room dozens of petitioners, some shabbily, others elegantly dressed— among them I recognized a Nobel Prize–winning biochemist— were icily ignored by the staff, except when, one by one, perhaps two a day, they were called into the inner offices. There each victim was questioned in a casually inquisitorial way as to his or her personal, political, and sexual conformities. But when your beribboned visa papers were finally ready and you had acquired the ultimate right to apply for American citizenship, you suddenly became a human being with all the privileges of that condition. In fact, I was even allowed to shake the vice-consul's hand.

Crossing Franco's Spain in four days, I managed to witness a bullfight in Barcelona and visit the Prado Museum in Madrid. The bullfight left me indifferent. I have never been romantic about animals, whether bulls or whales, and simply reacted to the actual bullfight as I later reacted to the only baseball game I ever attended: I did not grasp what was skill and what display. But the frenzied enthusiasm of the crowd made me shiver with the discomfort I always experience in the midst of any mob. Large numbers of excited, clamoring individuals frighten me even when they are political demonstrators on my own side of an issue. My temperament is more like that of the sedate cricket fan than that of an Italian or Spanish or American sports enthusiast, just as my political activity is more effectively carried out on the phone than in the street.

At the Prado I discovered Goya in all his moods: the titillating but insipid Majas, the Bourbon portraits full of the artist's contempt for his models, and the black paintings that mirror the horrors of one's own nightmares. The "Horrors of War" were not then shown in the museum.

After a few days and nights in dreary Spanish trains, Lisbon, an island of light in blacked-out Europe, was delightfully peaceful, with its contrasts between the incense-scented quarters of the poor and the cologne-sprayed upper-class neighborhoods. No adventure there except a good swim in the Tagus estuary. By luck, a place was available on an excellent Greek ship sailing for New York in a couple of weeks. Thus I left Europe on the S.S. *Nea Hellas,* fancying myself Odysseus beyond the Pillars of Hercules. In first class, besides a few South American officers shining in their macho uniforms, was a lonely civilian, the composer Paul Hindemith, for whom the saloon piano was reserved part of each day. In third class were eight hundred refugees, mostly journalists and writers. With fifty-two dollars in cash and one suit bought in Lisbon I was one of the better off. On September 12, 1940, while entering New York Harbor in the early-morning mist, the good ship *Nea Hellas* hit a Norwegian freighter, carving a deep cut in its side. We had left our first mark in the promised land.

2

The Promised Land

Turn away no more;
Why wilt thou turn away?
The starry floor, The wat'ry shore,
Is giv'n thee till the break of day.
WILLIAM BLAKE, *Songs of Experience*, Introduction

New York glowed in the cool September sun. With the hundred spires of its skyscrapers, Manhattan's center was like a gray-and-rose cathedral. No city, before or after, has ever conveyed to me a similar sense of power. From the first day I felt I had come home. This feeling of belonging in the new world increased as days went by, despite my uncertain future and some language problems. I had studied English while in junior high school and had read quite a bit, including some of Shakespeare and Shelley, but the English spoken in New York's buses and luncheonettes was not poetry. Somehow, I managed.

My professional future started looking up almost immediately. Enrico Fermi, whom I visited at Columbia University soon after my arrival, suggested that I approach the Rockefeller Foundation. There I found out that he had, unsolicited, given me a powerful if laconic recommendation, something like, "I believe he will make good use of whatever help you may give him." This from Fermi was better than a four-page letter from someone else, and worked like magic. Moreover, to my good fortune Professor Leslie Dunn of Columbia University had read and liked a short note that my French colleagues and I had recently submitted to the prestigious British journal *Nature*. Within a few weeks

I was installed at the College of Physicians and Surgeons—the P & S of Columbia University—under a complex arrangement of minifellowships. I had a desk, a lab bench, an incubator, and a spectacular view over the Hudson River and the George Washington Bridge. I also felt a deep gratitude to Fermi, not unmixed with suspicion that my excursion into physics in Rome had misled him into thinking too highly of me. I thought of this again one evening some twenty-five years later, when Fermi was already dead and I was back at Columbia Medical School to give a dinner speech to the graduating class. I wondered whether or not I had let him down, whether he would be pleased with me or think me a shallow man who went around giving after-dinner speeches. As I was so musing and looking down along the Hudson River in the golden twilight, suddenly before my eyes the lights of the city failed: the great blackout of 1965. It seemed a rather exaggerated response to my questioning.

At P & S, I worked in collaboration with Frank Exner, a physicist with a missionary background, who had taught in Peking for many years and was currently building a million-volt x-ray machine, a monster suitable only for research purposes. The x-ray output was low and the machine capricious; Frank and I had plenty of time for long talks and for brewing mint tea. We became fast friends and remained so, even though thousands of miles soon separated us. Frank's serenity, candor, and lack of conceit gave me my first close look at the Protestant personality. At its best, the Protestant tradition produced much of what attracted me to American society: personal reliability, respect for privacy, and concern for social welfare, traits that seemed so different from the unpredictable human behavior and hierarchical structure of the society in which I had grown up. Yet Frank's lack of aggressiveness was in part responsible for his leaving an academic career for a successful industrial one.

My first months in America were not all pleasure and wide-eyed excitement. After the first impact of novelty started wearing off I realized how lonely I was in this huge new world and how precarious my life's adventure still was, even though survival was assured. Fortunately, I soon found more friends, whose welcome eased my adaptation to the new life. At first these were mostly Italian refugees like myself, or recent émigrés from other European countries. An unexpected Santa Claus role was played by a geneticist, Salome Schonheimer, whom I met at Columbia University on my second day in New York. Salome wore a solemn hairdo —a flat bun on top of her head—and a mischievous smile. She also had a knack for organizing other people's survival through channels which I came to think of as the German refugee mafia. Within a few hours after we had met, and without my knowledge, she had put her mafia machinery in motion. Next day I was installed as house guest of her future husband, Heinrich Waelsch, who also lent me a raincoat and clean trousers while my only ones were being cleaned. A housekeeper appeared, a German lady who washed my shirts, surveyed my clothing when I left the apartment, and before leaving brought me Freud's selected writings in German from Heinrich's shelf, presumably to put my mind in line with my newly laundered clothes. Heinrich himself unearthed one of the foundations that came through with part of my salary, and even coached me on how to behave at the critical interview. When we meet now, Salome and I still recall with relish those days when survival was an interesting game, a problem-solving activity not unlike scientific research.

Another event of those first American weeks had a permanent effect on my name if not on my life. When I went to register for future citizenship I was told that I could change or alter my name as I wished; afterward that would forever be it. On the spur of the moment I decided to split my first name, Salvatore, which I had never liked, into Salvador E. The Spanish version pleased me: Salvador, toreador, conquistador. But the immigration officer wanted more: what did E. stand for? So I asked the person next in line to come up with a name starting with E. Being an Englishman and perhaps thinking of kings, he said Edward. So there I was and am to this day, Salvador Edward Luria.

Two days before the New Year of 1941 I finally met Max Delbrück. He was then teaching physics at Vanderbilt University in

Nashville. We had arranged by mail to meet in Philadelphia at a meeting of the American Physical Society. We met and talked, compared notes, planned some experiments, and spent January 1 in my New York lab playing with bacteriophage. On our first evening together Max took me to dinner with two other scientists, one of them the great physicist Wolfgang Pauli. I was properly intimidated, but Pauli simply asked me *"Sprechen Sie Deutsch?"* and without waiting for a reply proceeded to eat and speak German so prodigiously fast that I understood not a word. I would have been even more scared had I known of Pauli's classic remark concerning a young colleague: "So young, and he has already contributed so little!"

From the start Delbrück struck me as a dominant personality. Tall, and looking even taller because of his extreme thinness, moving and speaking sparingly and softly but with great precision, he conveyed the impression that whatever he said had been carefully thought out. His seriousness was occasionally broken by sparks of amusement, often produced by unexpected contrasts, and especially at the expense of someone's pretentiousness. His humor was usually gentle but could be deflating, although never cruel. I recall a morning when a young colleague walked into his office and announced: "Max, I have thought of a wonderful experiment." And Max, immediately: "The experiment to end all thinking?"

He was certainly not lavish with approval. When I published my first book, *General Virology,* he never mentioned it to me except to point out a misprint in a footnote. Later, mellowed by age, he wrote me warmly about another book and about a lecture I had given before the American Academy of Arts and Sciences. By then, although pleased, I had less need for approval.

Delbrück, who worked hard in a disciplined way, also liked fun: parties, cookouts, tennis, camping trips. Here we were badly matched: my idea of fun has always been centered on conversation, while Max became restless when talk involved more than two people. The difference in our personalities constituted the attraction at the base of our friendship. Our collaboration, which lasted for many years, was for me an apprenticeship as well as a friendship. It is painful for me to write about him in the past tense. He is a vivid presence in my heart as in my mind.

In our first few days together Max and I made plans for the following summer and for the next year. The seeds of what was to become the "phage group" were planted then. We arranged to spend the summer of 1941 together at the Biological Laboratory of Cold Spring Harbor on Long Island. This institution, a center of genetics about to play a central role in the history of molecular biology, was then being revitalized by its new director, Milislav Demerec. Demerec was a shy but extremely energetic man, whom I came to know well and to admire for his unshakable belief in science and in the virtues of laboratory research, even as a treatment for emotional depression or high blood pressure. He had recently brought my old friend Ugo Fano to Cold Spring Harbor as a biophysicist to work on the genetic effects of radiation, and thus in the summer of 1941 I was reunited with my oldest as well as my newest friends.

That summer was a remarkable season in many respects. In June, some of the world's great geneticists and biochemists assembled at Cold Spring Harbor for a symposium, each recounting his or her discoveries and exhibiting unique peculiarities. H. J. Muller, the discoverer of radiation-induced mutations, was there with his irrepressible wit and somewhat tentative giggle. Later he and I were to be colleagues at Indiana University. There was Barbara McClintock, a tiny but formidable scientist, speaking as fast as anyone I knew and packing years of work into a one-hour lecture. Her discoveries in maize genetics had to wait decades before being appreciated as opening new paths in biology. Many other geneticists became my friends that summer. Despite my limited knowledge of their subject, I began to feel like one of them.

After the symposium Delbrück went to California to marry and then brought his radiant, fun-loving bride, Manny, to Cold Spring Harbor. Thereafter the summer was truly a movable feast. We worked, swam, square-danced, and held daily seminars. At the time, the place was something of a hermitage. The living quarters were monastic, some on the verge of physical collapse (one of the springs for which the place is named flooded one of the houses whenever it rained, and in one apartment water spouted around the light bulbs, whose sockets had been adapted to old gas lines). The tennis court, always overgrown with weeds and pitted with large holes, was not, however, bad enough to excuse my poor game. One day Max exploded: "Why don't you learn enough to play with grownups?"

The laboratories were less than primitive: one had to bring or scrounge around for each piece of equipment. But the view of the harbor, the near seclusion, and the common interests of the summer denizens, and especially their youth—all combined to make us feel that Cold Spring Harbor was a perfect setting, for fun and for work. There for many years we spent summers working and teaching—on bacteriophage at first, then on other exciting topics in molecular biology. In that summer of 1941 Delbrück and I did the first experiments that attempted to probe the question how bacteriophage multiply within bacteria. The collaboration between us continued for years not only at Cold Spring Harbor but also at Vanderbilt University, or by mail.

In December 1941 I was again in Philadelphia, this time for the purpose of photographing bacteriophage. RCA had perfected an electron microscope, and a biophysicist, Tom Anderson, was in charge. He and I worked many hours with the prototype instrument, Tom calm and unflappable, I all excited (Tom saw in me a typical ebullient Italian), and we succeeded. We had pictures good enough for us to write a definitive article on the subject. While we were working, the Japanese struck at Pearl Harbor, so that one day coming out of the photographic dark room I found myself an enemy alien. Would I be deported? Or jailed? Would our results be published? This illustrates the range of my worries. Fortunately, the U.S. government behaved generously toward resident Italians (and Germans; not toward Japanese Americans). All I had to do was to register as an enemy alien (I was already registered with Selective Service). And our paper was published.

The electron micrographs of phage (as they inevitably were nicknamed) brought me not only the pleasure of seeing my favorite microorganisms in all their naked beauty, but also a much coveted award. When I showed the photos to Michael Heidelberger, the grand old man of immunochemistry and one of the gentlest scientists I have known, he encouraged me to apply for a Guggenheim fellowship. He told me to see René Dubos, who in turn showed the photos to Peyton Rous, the discoverer of cancer viruses. Someone in turn, probably Alfred Mirsky, showed them to the eminent chemist Linus Pauling, who was then the chairman of the Guggenheim committee. In one day those few pictures had made the tour of the very highest luminaries of biology and biochemistry. The fellowship was for a bit less than a full stipend, a proper reminder that I had as yet accomplished nothing much. When I met Pauling the week of the award at Mirsky's home he gave me a piece of advice I never forgot (though I occasionally violated it): "To do biochemistry you must know a lot of chemistry. If not, stay away from it."

My career as an enemy alien was unspectacular if not completely uneventful. One night, upon returning to Cold Spring Harbor from New York City and walking the two miles of highway from the train station under a glorious full moon, I was startled by multiple siren sounds and searchlight beams seemingly focused upon me. If I had realized that the military were searching for a band of Germans that had landed from a submarine I would have panicked. I could have been shot, or at least arrested and deported. Fortunately, I thought it was some sort of midsummer revel and went on my way.

After I was awarded a Guggenheim fellowship, several well-meaning friends and self-appointed advisers worried about my intention to go to Vanderbilt to work with Max. A German and an Italian? And Max not even Jewish? In a Southern town, supposedly full of prejudices? Why not go learn some biochemistry instead? My adviser at the Rockefeller Foundation raised such questions in the characteristically cautious and judicious way of that institution. He then approached someone in Nashville for advice, and finally gave me his blessing: "We believe you are not the kind of person that will get into trouble there." True—not there. Nashville proved in fact to be exceedingly pleasant, the hospitality abundant and the people friendly. So friendly in fact that I almost married a local young woman. I learned about the Fugitives, the Nashville-centered group of Southern poets, and even met one of their last disciples. A most instructive experience, and the first step toward dispelling whatever New York provincialism I had absorbed in my first American years. Work in Max's lab was interesting, although it was devoted mostly to drafting manuscripts of our earlier work. We explored, without much success, a number of possible approaches to phage multiplication.

My stay, however, lasted less than a year because in January 1943 I moved to Bloomington, Indiana, a place I had never heard of before. When the Rockefeller Foundation had given me a fellowship in 1940 they had committed me to accepting the first "respectable" academic position offered to me. In summer 1942 Indiana University offered me an instructorship at $1,800 a year, which the Rockefeller officer advised me to decline. They bounced back with $2,000; I was advised to accept and I did. The threshold of respectability was apparently defined within rather precise limits.

And so in January I arrived in Bloomington, the seat of the university. Bloomington was probably the smallest town I had ever been in for more than a few days. It was an ugly town, but not an uninteresting one. In 1943 it was a bit of a depression town, with an invigorating if sometimes startling strain of the American frontier. For example, the newspaper's editor executed her straying boyfriend in the center of town with a shotgun blast, and then came back after one or two years in prison to be greeted by welcoming headlines. It was also a prejudiced town. When Marian Anderson sang at the university, no hotel would take her. She slept at the house of the dean of women, where I was then renting a room, so that I had the chance of attending her after-concert reception.

The campus of Indiana University was attractive, with lovely trees and lawns and a superb auditorium. The surrounding countryside was agreeable, with forests not too different from those of

New England. The hilly neighborhood invited the outdoor-minded to easy or strenuous walks. My fellow geneticist Tracy Sonneborn and his wife, Ruth, enticed me a few times into this pastime, till they realized my general indifference to exercise. By some historical anomaly the university was then a leading center of genetics, prominently represented by Ralph Cleland and Tracy Sonneborn, with H. J. Muller himself joining them in 1946. This pride of geneticists was brought together by a remarkable dean, Fernandus Payne, a splendid administrator who took a liking to me and from whom I learned many valuable lessons.

So there I was in Bloomington, Indiana, on January 1, 1943. The next day I taught systematically and for a living for the first time in my life—fourteen hours a week of bacteriology, of which I knew very little: one bacterium and two or three phages. But I discovered then, and confirmed later, that the best way of learning a subject is to teach it. The students were sometimes baffled but never really bored. This can probably be said of all students I have had in forty years of teaching. During my years at Indiana my teaching and therefore my knowledge broadened, extending to virology on the one hand and to bacterial physiology on the other. These are subjects I still like to teach. At first I was concerned about my accent, which I have never lost, but it did not prove to be a serious impediment. Fortunately, I had taken some lessons in phonetics before going to Bloomington, and my teacher had impressed upon me the importance of concentrating on pronunciation, especially of consonants and, in her words, "to hell with the accent." The accent stayed with me, the flat nasal accent of Turin, identifiable by Italians in any language I speak.

Soon after arriving in Bloomington I visited Chicago and had dinner at the Fermis'. After dinner I asked what I thought was a perfectly innocent question: "Would it be indiscreet to ask whether one may hear of some great discovery in physics when the war is over?" Fermi, always precise and deliberate, thought for about two seconds, then said, "Yes—it would be indiscreet." How could I have guessed that a few days earlier he had set the first chain reaction going under the stands of the University of Chicago's football stadium?

Fermi was not as wise in sociology as in physics. Soon after Pearl Harbor, in his Columbia University office, he had told me: "Once we win this war, technical progress will be such that all problems of society will be easily taken care of." Even genius can underestimate human folly.

In Bloomington, shortly after arriving, I did what is probably the most significant piece of research in my life, the demonstration of spontaneous mutations in bacteria. (The details will be recounted in the next chapter.) All excited I wrote to Delbrück, who replied, "I believe you have something important. I am working out the mathematical theory." The theory came a week later, when more experiments were already at hand, and everything checked. I was walking on clouds, just from the pleasure of the discovery. Later, after the appearance of the "famous" Luria and Delbrück paper of 1943, there came also the sweeter if less pure pleasure of recognition.

I had expected to spend one semester at most in Bloomington and then be taken by the army or by a military radiation laboratory. But the army did not call me and the laboratory never got me security-cleared. So I stayed on in Bloomington for several fruitful and happy years, both in research and in personal growth. There I met Zella Hurwitz, and in 1945 we were married in the old Monroe County courthouse by a jolly Republican judge. My father-in-law, a lifelong Democrat, never quite believed our marriage was legal. I feel to this day that my emotional adulthood began when Zella entered my life. Our marriage has been full of love and respect. I shall say more about it later.

Our courtship had some odd moments. A few weeks after meeting Zella I called her to say I had two tickets for a football game, would she like to go? She said yes, so I explained that a colleague of mine would go with her. I never even thought she might assume that I would go to a football game on a gray fall day. She changed her mind about the game, of course, but fortunately not about me. My orneriness was matched by her naïveté. She complained to a mutual friend that I, obviously an Italian Catholic, told Jewish jokes to her, a Jewish girl from the Bronx. We had a laugh at her expense before we enlightened her.

Zella's background was Eastern European working class. Her father went to work as a house painter's helper at twelve upon arriving from Minsk and retired from house painting at seventy-eight. His family had contributed some political prisoners to Czarist Russia, including a formidable sister who raised twelve siblings before being sent to Siberia. Zella's only brother, Jerry, has become a distinguished biochemist.

When we married, Zella was just twenty-one and was working toward a master's degree in psychology; she did not get her Ph.D. from Indiana University until 1951. By that time, we had a two-year-old son, Daniel, who was disgusted at finding out that the doctorate Zella was bringing home was not some sort of sweet.

Immediately after our wedding we spent a year's leave of absence in Cold Spring Harbor, where I directed a government research project on bacterial resistance to antibiotics while Zella commuted to a teaching job at Brooklyn College, her alma mater. For the only time in our lives we had a vegetable garden—a victory garden—and grew enormous amounts of vegetables, especially eggplants, enough to provide each of Zella's fellow commuters with at least one eggplant a week. I decided then that gardening, like any other perversion, should be tried once and once only in one's lifetime.

Before our marriage I had shared in Bloomington the home of a colleague, Kenneth Cameron, a scholar of English literature. That association influenced me in many ways. Ken was (and is) a foremost authority on the romantic poets, especially Shelley, with whom he identified to such an extent that he developed the symptoms of every illness he believed the poet to have had. He was a knowledgeable Marxist and also a gourmet, with a robust enjoyment of life, like someone out of Defoe or Fielding. From him I learned about American radical history, so different from official history as well as from the history of the European left. I also learned to enjoy substantial meals and even hard liquor. Most importantly, in a home lined with scholarly books, I acquired the habit of reading English and American literature, past and present, more systematically in fact than I had ever read Italian or

French. It was a significant step in my transformation from a European refugee into an American intellectual. The transformation was not just literary. It was also connected with working in a Midwestern university in a Midwestern semirural community, an experience that lasted for sixteen years, first in Bloomington and later in Urbana, Illinois. I have never regretted my Midwestern years, and believe that the lack of similar experiences was a real loss for those European refugees whose Americanization stopped at the Eastern Seaboard. It is not easy to express the essence of this aspect of American life; perhaps it is a mixture of directness and homogeneity, a lack of concern for sophistication, a respect for certain traditional values and communal emotions.

A significant contribution to my Midwestern assimilation as well as Zella's came from Bess Cameron, Kenneth's wife. Indiana-born and a first-class sociologist, she combined with her knowledge of social science an unfailing devotion to issues of human rights, from racial and sexual equality to the rights of students. And to these she added enormous energy and *joie de vivre.* From her Zella learned to cook, and from her I learned to translate my longing for justice into almost immediate political commitments. I can't forgo telling an anecdote, perhaps apocryphal but certainly characteristic of Bess. During the Spanish Civil War, while seeking funds in support of the Loyalists, Bess is supposed to have gone for money to her father, an old-time Indiana Klansman, and when all other entreaties failed, she brought him around by boasting to him that the Loyalists, bless their souls, were killing priests and raping nuns!

To the period in Bloomington, where I stayed until 1950, belongs my discovery of the reactivation of bacteriophage killed by radiation, a finding which was to open the field of DNA repair studies. And my very first graduate student in Bloomington, in 1947, was a thin young man named Jim Watson, of twice double-helix fame—for his discovery of DNA structure (for which he shared a Nobel prize with Francis Crick) and for the excellent book he wrote about that discovery. With me Jim worked on the reactivation phenomenon. My role in arranging Watson's fateful move from Copenhagen to Cambridge has been recounted many times in books on the DNA story. That I arranged the move is true; that it was arranged when I met the British spectroscopist John Kendrew, and that John and I were congenial because we both were socialists is also true. Watson later developed into a shrewd administrator (he is now head of the Cold Spring Harbor laboratory) and a rambunctious statesman of science.

In 1947 Renato Dulbecco came to my Bloomington lab from Italy, an arrangement suggested by Rita Levi-Montalcini, whose immigration to Washington University in St. Louis I had promoted a few months earlier. That was the first step in Rita's extraordinary career as a great neurobiologist, collector of honors and prizes as well as of the nickname "the queen" because of her impeccable dresses and regal manner. Dulbecco stayed with me two years before moving to Cal Tech, where he started his marvelous work on culturing viruses and tumor cells that was to win him a share of the Nobel Prize in 1975. Watson and he are the only two of my many disciples to get the Stockholm accolade, but many others have had brilliant university careers. Only two went wrong: one is vice-president of a university, the other president of a company. My former students keep in touch with me at least sporadically; there is much affection between us. Yet, my relations with students, although cordial, have seldom been as intimate as those that develop in the laboratories of some of my colleagues. This is partly a reflection of my reluctance to establish close ties with the young. About this I shall say more later.

Alfred Hershey, who was to do the most seminal and elegant experiments in bacteriophage genetics, and who would share with Delbrück and me the Nobel Prize in 1969, came into our lives in 1943, visiting Vanderbilt and Indiana, and immediately became a partner in our phage adventure. Al is a remarkable person, so silent that even Delbrück appeared garrulous by comparison. His writings like his experiments have a spare elegance that I greatly admire and envy. They often represent the last word on a subject. Once, asked for his idea of Heaven, he replied: "To find a perfect experiment and do it every day for the first time." Al formed with

Max and me the nucleus of the "phage group," a nucleus that grew slowly at first, then at an almost catastrophic rate as more people realized the remarkable opportunities of bacteriophage as a research object. But Al always remained something of a lone wolf in his research. He was also the first one to retire from research work.

In 1950 our family moved from Indiana to the University of Illinois. My political activities—nothing more than working in the 1948 Progressive party campaign and helping the union that organized the university workers—had attracted the unfavorable attention of the Indiana University administration and caused them not to match an offer from across the state line. Urbana, the seat of the University of Illinois, was another sample of Midwestern life and landscape, but different from Bloomington. The flat plain, where one drove between interminable hedges of cornfields, made us miss the lovely hills of southern Indiana. The campus itself was more citified, less interesting, despite a few gigantic trees in the quadrangle. Next to the Noyes Chemistry Building, where my office was, stood a huge female ginkgo tree, unwisely planted not far enough from male ginkgos across campus. When fall came the stench of butyric acid from the decaying fruit more than matched the worst concoctions of the chemists.

The university campus was also more sedate than Indiana's. Indiana's faculty, especially during the war, had included a rather bohemian crowd, fond of entertainment: young Eastern intellectuals, drowning in rum and riot their feeling of being cut off from where the action was. Contributing to Indiana's veneer of sophistication was the presence of Alfred Kinsey, the entomologist turned sexologist and a rather prepossessing personality on campus. Anecdotes, mainly apocryphal, about his Institute of Sex Research abounded. But the very fact of Kinsey's presence and that of his co-workers influenced campus attitudes toward sexuality. Hundreds of students and faculty members were interviewed, and they and their friends learned more and faster about the reality of American sexual life than the public at large, which was presented with the same stuff packaged in ponderous professional form. If our society lost its illusions of chastity after Kinsey, improbably Bloomington, Indiana, was the first to lose them.

Indiana's faculty also had pretensions to intellectual sophistication, which sometimes expressed themselves in the most unexpected ways. I recall a remark by a charming and intelligent woman, the wife of a psychology professor, whose lovely daughter had just married a very eligible young man: "It breaks Roland's heart to know that his daughter has married a student in the School of Business!" The Illinois faculty was more family-oriented and achievement-minded. Zella and I, by then a sedate couple, fitted readily into the new pattern.

Professionally, at least for me, the change to Illinois was a plus. A superb biochemist, Irwin Gunsalus, who had come from Bloomington at the same time as I, was in my department. A worker of prodigious energy, he dips into problems and often also into people without restraint or mercy, leaving things either shattered or more solid, but never unchanged. With us also was Sol Spiegelman, a brilliant geneticist-biochemist, one of the early heroes of molecular biology, who before almost anyone else had visualized the relative roles of gene and environment. A short man with the mind of a mathematician, he impressed me by his ability to deliver a lecture without an incomplete sentence or a split infinitive. The three of us must have been a rather formidable presence in the midst of a large but diffuse population of biologists on campus. In fact, we were the only ones to be accepted socially and professionally by the infinitely more formidable Chemistry Department, led by the great Roger Adams and socially controlled by two redoubtable ladies, Mrs. Adams and Mrs. Rose. We were even invited to the Chemistry Department parties, along with the president and provost and no other outsiders. Once, when Zella and I forgot the invitation to one of these command performances, we were discreetly advised to choose between suicide and eternal opprobrium.

The years in Urbana were fruitful. I had a large laboratory through which passed a number of brilliant and successful scientists—Gio Bertani, Dorothy Fraser, Edwin Lennox, and several students, including George Streisinger, Robert De Mars, Seymour Lederberg, and Jane Adams. All aspects of phage genetics were explored; most notable was the discovery of the "restriction modification" phenomenon, which I made in 1952 and which was soon generalized by Bertani, Jean Weigle, and others. It became the foundation of so-called genetic engineering.

Meanwhile Zella was training as a clinical and child psychologist, doing research and publishing with some of her senior colleagues. Her analysis of a triple-personality case with Charles Osgood was even reprinted in a *Reader's Digest* volume, a fact that gained her the wide-eyed admiration of our neighbors. When we first moved to Illinois, Zella had inquired of Civil Service about psychologist jobs open in the area. A few weeks later she received an application for the border patrol, requiring "unusual physical strength, perfect horsemanship, and preferably a high school diploma." Since Zella lacked the qualifications required to defend Illinois from its threatening neighbor states, she let the matter drop. Meanwhile Dan was growing, making friends, riding a bicycle to school, and learning a few French words. When we gave him an electric train, I realized that at the age of seven he already had my lack of interest if not distaste for things mechanical. After about an hour, he paid no more attention to the train, while Ed Lennox, a physicist friend, spent the rest of the day excitedly running the silly little locomotives.

Although work was fruitful and life pleasant in Urbana, by the late 1950s we felt restless. McCarthyism was supposedly on the wane, but the Truman-ignited Cold War, carried out with religious zeal by John Foster Dulles, was going strong. A president of the university, George Stoddard, came under attack from the lunatic fringe of Illinois politicians and was forced to resign, although a large part of the faculty including me came to his defense. Stoddard was neither a great president nor a true liberal. It was my first realization that in fighting for a principle of justice one often has to defend victims whose liberal credentials are less than impeccable.

In 1951 I was refused a passport, presumably because of old

radical associations in the Italian community of New York. For me this was an excellent excuse for turning down invitations to European meetings, but the incident was somewhat embarrassing to a jittery and insecure university administration. Also, I was actively involved in organized opposition to the Broyles bill, a piece of McCarthyite state legislation. Later I would be one of the initial signatories of the famous Pauling statement that was the first salvo in the successful campaign to outlaw nuclear bomb tests. Among the politically sedate Illinois faculty I stood out as a somewhat deviant figure.

Added to the political factors was the question of Zella's career. After receiving her doctor's degree she had gone from fellowship to fellowship to an occasional one-semester teaching job, without succeeding in cracking the preposterous nepotism rule excluding two members of the same family from the faculty. In 1958, while spending a sabbatical year at M.I.T., Zella and I were debating an attractive offer from the University of Wisconsin when a better one came from M.I.T. itself. M.I.T. won, aided by an offer of a position to Zella at Tufts University, where she still is today, an influential member of that faculty and an authority on the psychology of human sexuality and gender identity. If we had needed extra reasons for not returning to Illinois, they were provided by a long letter to Zella from the dean and former head of the psychology department there, asking her to persuade me to return because *I* was needed—not a word about her being wanted. Those whom the gods plan to use to destroy universities they make deans!

The M.I.T. offer was accompanied by earnest protestations from the president that I was needed not just as a professor but as one whose counsel on all matters of life sciences was going to be asked for and valued. The same statement has since been repeated by four successive presidents, whenever I have considered offers from other institutions; but over the next two decades my counsel was never sought. It was probably better that way. I could and did concentrate on building the Biology Department into one of the best in the world and, later, assembling in the M.I.T. Center for Cancer Research a superb group of scientists whose successes have been my greatest reward.

So in 1959 we became neo-Bostonians, living on top of a hill in Lexington (where Zella and I are still today), working respectively in Medford and Cambridge, and getting resettled culturally and professionally. My father-in-law's reaction to our move to Boston was peculiarly encouraging. Upon hearing the news he told Zella: "That's fine. If Salva works harder someday he'll get a job in New York."

The New England landscape and Boston's cultural sophistication more than made up for certain deficiencies, such as lack of the courtesy and efficiency in public places to which we had been accustomed in the Midwest. At first the absence of signs at most street corners was a challenge; but soon one learned that in the Boston area one goes only where one has been before, unless one is given a detailed map, like those used to find lost temples in Cambodian jungles. Streets in Boston itself proved hard to learn; I still get lost when I venture downtown. Over the years, driving to work on Memorial Drive, I have seen rising one-by-one the belt of skyscrapers which now form the backdrop of the State House on Beacon Hill, like giants watching over the sleep of a golden-haired maiden.

A host of new colleagues and friends entered our lives, some of them actually becoming the intimates that constitute the true family of one's mature years. Closest to us have been Ray and Doris Siever, whom we had met in Urbana before Ray joined the Harvard faculty. They have become family to us, family people whom one depends on almost instinctively and whose affection is infinitely secure. With Irwin Sizer, the head of my department, and his wife Helen we have had many pleasant times, even being seduced into taking some reasonable walks, made delightful by Helen and Irwin's inexhaustible knowledge of birds and trees. Noam and Carol Chomsky became our friends in a peculiar way. At a party someone introduced me to Carol, mentioning that I was an M.D. Carol wondered what I was doing at M.I.T., to which I replied in a whisper that since M.I.T. physicists were doing secret research and were very neurotic, I had been sent by the Pentagon to be their "security-cleared" psychiatrist. She was completely taken in and I continued to spin my yarn, but a few minutes later Zella and Noam joined us and my story collapsed. I admire Noam for his brilliance, his political integrity, and his almost terrifying store of information. I find it uncanny that on practically every political issue we reach the same conclusions, I on first principles, he on the solid ground of enormous knowledge. I cannot claim to match his physical courage in political actions, just as I could never share his passion for sailing, swimming, or gardening. Other valuable friendships soon developed in Boston, especially among Zella's colleagues, who, being social scientists, tend to be lively conversationalists, less inclined to the shoptalk that excludes nonprofessional people.

Dorothy Fraser, a close friend and the most senior of my coworkers in Illinois, moved with me to M.I.T. and was responsible for helping the transition and for much good work we accomplished in those years. Dorothy and I set up our lab at M.I.T. and were soon joined by a large group of colleagues: Naomi Franklyn, Helen Revel, both superbly trained scientists, and many graduate students, almost all of whom went on successfully to their doctorates and to university careers. One of my tasks was to develop microbiology in the Biology Department and in fact make it central. I sometimes wonder if I may not have succeeded too well. Boris Magasanik, a microbiologist whom I attracted from Harvard, later became the next head of the Biology Department. Harvard and M.I.T. had a nonraiding understanding, which worried me in the Magasanik case, until I found out that M.I.T. President Julius Stratton was angry because Harvard had just tried to steal Paul Samuelson, the great M.I.T. economist. So he told me to go ahead with my own steal. Boris is one of the few scientists with whom I can exchange cryptic literary or historical references without drawing a blank.

A very special role in my life at M.I.T. has been played by Nancy Ahlquist. This remarkable friend, who can do anything from building a cottage to solving hard puzzles, both crossword and those presented by life, applied to M.I.T. for a secretarial job on the very day I started. I shudder at the thought that someone else might have grabbed her. Nancy has made my professional life possible and easy. She has also been a model of a superior person, helpful, straightforward, and willing to put me in my place when I become discourteous or unreasonable. In more than twenty years of association, no one has failed to have for her the respect and affection she deserves. Her remarkable linguistic facility enables her to greet any of our foreign visitors—French, Israeli, Japanese, or Finn—with the appropriate welcome in their own language. Biologists on four continents call her Nancy and share my affection for her.

Political activity in Boston was more lively than in Urbana, less provincial because closer to the centers of power, which were in fact soon to be filled by Cambridge academic technocrats. My first activity was to help organize and publish a *New York Times* advertisement in which sixty Harvard and M.I.T. professors denounced the Bay of Pigs invasion for what it was—a violation of international morality rather than the tragic misfortune bemoaned by our press and government.

Soon we had another opportunity to use the advertisement technique, when the Kennedy administration launched a nonsensical drive for civil defense, promoting mass hysteria and commercial speculation on home shelters. A group of us at M.I.T. organized and published an advertisement, which the *New York Times* accompanied with a sensible news article. Our actions contributed to the killing of the shelter program. They also led to the formation of BAFGOPI, the cacophonic acronym for Boston Area Faculty Group on Public Issues, which remained active throughout the Vietnam War.

Between shelters and Vietnam, Zella, Dan, and I took off in 1963 for a year in Paris. We arrived exhausted from two weeks of teaching in Israel, where I worked at the frantic pace of Israeli life, with temperatures around 100° F. and the notorious food of the

Weizmann Institute cafeteria. We had been in Israel two years earlier, at a less trying time of the year, and had enjoyed the warm hospitality and general *Gemütlichkeit* of the Israeli scientists and other acquaintances, including the kibbutzniks whom we visited near Lake Kinneret. Hospitality was still as warm as the outside temperature, at the time of our 1963 visit, and the pleasant atmosphere compensated for the discomfort. A later visit in 1969, after the Six-Day War, left me with a very different impression of Israel and of my friends and colleagues, most of whom seemed to me to be prey to a bellicose euphoria. "If they attack us again," a famous chemist and statesman told me, "we shall simply dictate Arab unity from Cairo." May the Lord forgive those whom hubris deceives!

Cool Paris and an apartment in the Quartier Latin seemed like heaven. I had visited Paris for a few weeks in 1959 while the Algerian struggle was still on and Paris was again an armed camp, sadder than in 1939. By 1963, however, Paris was serene, beautiful, the Paris of songs and dreams, the only city besides New York where one feels what a city truly means—something created by generations of human beings to be their permanent assertion of communal pride.

Zella and Dan soon mastered the French language and became Parisians, especially Zella, who, while walking in the Quartier, was often hailed from café tables by her fellow students at the Alliance Française. As for myself, my knowledge of French literature proved sufficient for me to hold my own in the literary sparring that characterized the conversation of the young *normaliens* and *polytechniciens* at the Pasteur Institute. There I made or renewed some valuable friendships, with Jacques Monod, François and Lise Jacob, Agnes Ulman, Adam and Suzanne Kepes. The institute was then a busy hive of research. Jacques Monod and François Jacob had recently put forward the "operon" theory, a powerful model of gene regulation that was to guide molecular biology for the next twenty years. Biologists from all over the world were in Paris, exploring the implications of the new theory and creating a stimulating scientific atmosphere.

On the personal plane the experience at the Pasteur Institute was rewarding, particularly in cementing my friendship with Jacques Monod. Many hours spent with him—a truly universal man: musician, writer, political activist, and mountain climber, a courageous fighter in the French Resistance and later again in the days of student revolt—taught me to cherish his friendship and his witty, allusive conversation with its wonderfully trenchant remarks. We both admired the French existentialists and considered existentialism the most appropriate philosophy for scientists. We agreed on most fundamentals, and Jacques, a generous friend, was liberal with approval and affection. Our friendship continued to grow in later years, and his death was a great personal loss.

The atmosphere of Paris gave me courage for a venture I had wished for many times in recent years without the occasion or opportunity of putting it in practice. I took sculpture lessons from a tiny but strong young woman, Piera Rossi, now a well-established Paris artist. Years before I had done a bit of painting, but the sculpting bout, which continued for only a few years after I returned to the States, was more serious—too serious to last, as I'll explain later.

In Paris my research work took a new turn. Having been for some time intrigued by problems of membranes, for reasons I shall explain elsewhere in this book, I decided to study a group of membrane-active proteins. I have continued that line of work to this day, discovering a number of interesting properties of these molecules. This research is only now being recognized as a significant field. It is a small twig on the tree of biology; perhaps it will grow into a large branch.

Our return from Paris coincided with the phony Gulf of Tonkin crisis that led the United States into the shooting war in Vietnam. Soon the Boston Area Faculty Group on Public Issues, chaired now by the Harvard philosopher Hilary Putnam, was in action with a series of ads, at first against the bombings, then against the war itself. Anti-war activities became much broader than BAFGOPI's followers, involving masses of students and other people, and many faculty members including myself gave speeches and marched in demonstrations. Student participation declined when the government decided no longer to draft students, and the increasing frustration of the diminished antiwar groups led to a number of attacks on the universities themselves. The pretense of normalcy on the part of universities and their official unwillingness to face the moral disintegration of the country, which was a direct product of that immoral war, did, in my opinion, more than justify the minor outrages committed by the student movement. The students represented the conscience of the nation.

My son, Dan, a student at the University of Rochester, debated whether to register as a conscientious objector but, after consulting the American Friends Service Committee, decided he could not be a CO because he did not object to wars as such. He registered for the draft, drew a high number, and was never called.

As a member of the peace movement I met a number of politicians, among them Senator Edward Brooke. A few weeks after his election, Brooke switched from (mildly) antiwar to (mildly) prowar. When Jerry Grossman (a Boston antiwar leader), I, and several ministers confronted Brooke after his switch, we encountered the infuriating argument: "If you knew the things I know but cannot tell you . . ." I heard this non-argument several times from colleagues who had become hawks upon joining government agencies. Some of them later expressed regret at having been wrong—about the war, not about their way of arguing.

Possibly because of my opposition to the Vietnam War, or at least notwithstanding that opposition, in 1966 I was elected vice president and then president (in 1968) of the American Society for Microbiology. I was surprised and pleased by this honor, which somehow reassured me that I had in fact become a microbiologist. I even caused a minor tempest when I spoke against cooperation by the society with the armed forces in the field of biological warfare. Some members were shocked but the council rallied strongly to my support. Later, in 1970, as a delegate of the Society to the International Panel on Biological Warfare, I had the pleasure of helping achieve the unanimous recommendation of the panel against the use of biological weapons, in line with President Nixon's unilateral decision to renounce such weapons.

In the midst of the Vietnam War the year 1969 brought a series of pleasant happenings. In the spring I was invited by Jacques Monod to give a series of lectures at the Collège de France. The pleasure of returning to Paris for such an occasion more than compensated for the effort to create a set of lectures out of material that was probably not very exciting. I suspect that the relief of listening to an American who spoke French was the main pleasure for my audience. In the classroom next to mine the Harvard philosopher W. V. O. Quine was also lecturing in French. Paraphrasing Socrates's comparison of his fate with that of his judges, "which students were luckier only God knows."

In October of the same year Max Delbrück and I shared the Luisa Horvitz Prize of Columbia University, and a few days later we received the announcement of the award of the Nobel Prize for Physiology or Medicine, jointly with Alfred Hershey. By then, of the three musketeers of bacteriophage Hershey was the only one still active in that field of research.

For me, the Nobel Prize was not what T. S. Eliot called "a ticket to one's own funeral." On the day the prize was announced the press in Latin countries highlighted the fact that I had received the news while washing the breakfast dishes. My macho image, if any, received a death blow in Italy and Brazil. The *New York Times* found more interesting copy: my name was on the political blacklist of the National Institutes of Health. Such blacklists were supposed to have died in the fifties, but this one was still in use in 1969 (and may still be now). This discovery warranted having my picture in the *Times* twice: on an inside page for the prize and on the front page, two days later, for the blacklist. A tangible result of the Nobel Prize is that my record of letters to the editor published by the *Times* has soared by a substantial factor. The other tangible benefit, the prize money, makes me wish the Nobel committee had waited a bit longer, since the prize money doubled the following year—a clear case of premature recognition.

Stockholm in December was cold and beautiful. Dan with his

long hair was portrayed by the Swedish newspapers as a snobbish beatnik who, at the airport, announced he wanted to discuss economics with Gunnar Myrdal. The festivities were grand and tactful. The Swedes have the remarkable ability to be formal and warm at the same time. Least formal was the Prime Minister, Olof Palme, who after the banquet instead of dancing spent a couple of hours talking politics and sociology with Zella. They became good friends, and renewed their acquaintance years later when Palme visited M.I.T. Zella also stole the show at the Royal Palace, where His Majesty was supposed to spend ten minutes with each laureate. The King turned to Zella, saying, "I understand you are a psychologist," and spent nine and a half minutes talking to her. Al Hershey, speaking for the three of us biologists at the banquet, made the simplest and most touching remarks, quoting from an old man's letter that said simply: "You are working for knowledge and for the good of mankind. God bless you."

After the banquet, which had been heralded by the sound of golden trumpets, *Aïda*-style, I told Zella I'd find it hard from now on to sit down to eat without the sound of trumpets. On our first evening at home there was a trumpet on my plate—plastic but mine to keep.

The excitement of Stockholm—"the infirm glory of the positive hour"—coming in the middle of the Vietnam War added a note of excitement to our already busy but interesting lives. Dan came back from a year at the University of Manchester—a year full of pot and protests—to become a graduate student in economics at the University of Michigan, a school always rife with political activity. Then, as the Vietnam War ended, our lives remained busy, full of involvements but not turbulent. Zella pursued her career at Tufts, an institution to which she is strongly attached. My work at M.I.T. continued and became more complex when in 1972 I was asked to organize and direct a Center for Cancer Research. I accepted, without giving up either my teaching or my research, a decision that may have been unwise but at least insured me against idleness. The Cancer Center has been an exceedingly successful venture. I chose for the center an old building, owned by M.I.T. but rented to the Brigham chocolate factory. We converted it and turned it into an outstanding laboratory building. Although I have not myself undertaken any program of research on cancer, I have assembled in the center a distinguished group of scientists who have already contributed major findings and received much recognition. The highlight came in 1975 when my colleague David Baltimore, a brilliant young scientist whose career I closely followed and nurtured until he joined us at M.I.T. for good, shared with Dulbecco and Howard Temin the Nobel Prize for their work on tumor viruses.

As director I learned of the joys and frustrations of administration. The hardest part is to have to say no to perfectly reasonable requests from colleagues when funds are either not available or in limited supply. I find decision making easy, but often have a hard time afterward wondering whether the decisions were right or wrong. A difficult duty of a Cancer Research Center director is to handle the stream of requests for help from cancer patients and their relatives. It is painful to have to explain how far research still is from helping the patient. Fortunately Nancy Ahlquist, with her exquisite tact, can write sensitive and comforting letters.

In the last twenty years Zella and I have traveled much, both in the United States and abroad, enlarging our range of acquaintances and experiences and gaining friends in many countries. We are, however, neither eager travelers nor experienced tourists, preferring usually to return to familiar places and friendly companions. We loved Mexico City, that most European of American capitals. An initiative taken when I was president of ICBO (International Cell Biology Organization) located the executive committee meetings in several different countries, so that we visited and made friends in Athens, Madrid, and Yugoslavia. These sessions were in fact fruitful in establishing new international research activities.

In 1977 I was asked to give the Fermi lectures in Pisa at the Scuola Normale, a venerable remnant of Napoleonic days where an elite of young philosophers, mathematicians, and physicists—

less than one percent of the applicants—are paid, fed, pampered, and diligently taught, while a few blocks away at the university twenty thousand students, with little hope of jobs and little incentive to learn, degenerate into an unruly crowd. I had neither group at my lectures. The "normalists" would not dream of listening to a biologist, and the university students were on one of their interminable vacations. My classroom was full, nevertheless, of faculty and researchers from Pisa and Florence. I lectured in Italian, which was hard at first both because of lack of habit and because any Piedmontese in Tuscany is aware of the barbarous quality of his accent compared with that of the local people. I was pleasantly surprised, however, at how my presentation of some biochemical principles from the point of view of elementary physical chemistry pleased my audience, accustomed to more traditional teaching in medical or biological courses.

Since 1966 I have spent some weeks each year at the Salk Institute, where I renewed my friendship with Jonas Salk as well as with my former colleagues Renato Dulbecco and Ed Lennox. The Salk Institute was the product of the vision of Leo Szilard, the physicist famous for writing the Einstein letter to President Roosevelt concerning neutron chain reactions and atom bombs. Szilard's vision was of a biological Nirvana where great minds would flourish through mutual stimulation. Szilard did not live to see his brain child in action. My more cynical view used to be that the Salk Institute was like a foundling whom nobody wanted, but whom one must still help to live and grow. Since coming under the financial stewardship of Fred de Hoffmann the Institute has in fact grown and prospered.

My most amusing recollection from my association with the Salk Institute is of a fund-raising banquet when Zella and I were seated at the table of a prodigiously wealthy, prodigiously garrulous lady. After describing her cruises on her fifty-meter yacht, she told of her embarrassment when once, on that yacht, she caught a fish bigger than the one caught by her guest of honor, John Wayne. As she paused for breath, I turned sweetly to Zella: "Darling, who is John Wayne?" End of conversation.

At the Salk Institute I greatly enjoyed my friendship—still another cut short by death—with Jacob Bronowski, the eminent mathematician, philosopher, and literary scholar. This chubby, encyclopedic man could bring to life almost any author, living or dead, with a few comments, in the same way that he could demolish a colleague with a single remark. His mastery of any subject from psychology to poetry to science to linguistics made for many delightful evenings in La Jolla.

Linguistics was for a time a serious interest of mine. Reflecting on my friend Noam Chomsky's ideas on the innateness of the fundamentals of grammar in the human mind, I saw that any innate features of the language capacity must be a set of biological structures, selected in the course of the evolution of the human brain from that of some primate ancestor. This led me for a while to explore the possibilities of research in the biology of language. But I soon realized that the subject was not ready for a biologist of my kind, so my interest petered out.

Another interest stimulated by travel was poetry. While at Stanford University for a sabbatical semester I sat in a poetry seminar taught by a lovely teacher, Diane Middlebrook, who introduced me to the work of Wallace Stevens, Theodore Roethke, Charles Olson, John Ashbery and other contemporary Americans. My interest in modern poetry has continued to grow and has been the source of much pleasure.

After 1970 an increasing part of our family's activities has been the writing of books. Before then my writing had produced *General Virology,* which has remained the more-or-less standard textbook on the subject. The first few chapters of the first edition were dictated in the summer of 1949 to Manny Delbrück, precariously balancing a portable typewriter on her enormously pregnant lap. We hoped her baby would be born on August 13, my birthday, but we had time for a few extra pages since Nicola Delbrück waited until the 19th to emerge. A year earlier my son, Dan, had punctually been born on September 4, Max's birthday. The book itself had a longer gestation, appearing only in 1953. A second edition, with Jim Darnell as a co-author, appeared in 1967, and a third—by Luria, Darnell, Baltimore, and Campbell—in 1977.

By then my range of subjects had become more catholic. In 1970 a suggestion by Theodosius Dobzhansky led me to accept Scribner's request for a book on molecular biology for the general public. It was flattering to be asked by Dobzhansky, himself a superb writer, and it was a bit titillating to write for Hemingway's publishers. The result, published in 1973, was *Life: the Unfinished Experiment*, which won the National Book Award for Science in 1974. Translated into many languages, it sold better in Japan and Germany than in the United States. Since the most interesting sections are in the last few chapters, I suspect Japanese and German readers and critics are the only ones who read a book through. My friend Gunther Stent used his review of the book in the *New York Times* to take a few cracks at Monod's *Chance and Necessity*, which didn't prevent Monod from writing a brief preface to my French edition.

Meanwhile Zella was working on a book based on her very successful course on human sexuality. She and her colleague Mitchel Rose produced a lovely volume, well written and superbly illustrated with drawings inspired by Picasso's erotic art. When it was published, Zella and I had to learn to ignore the snide comments on our sex life made by some of the readers of *Psychology of Human Sexuality*.

The appearance of *Life: the Unfinished Experiment* whetted the appetites of textbook publishers. A set of thirty-six lectures, recorded by two students and revised by me, was published by M.I.T. Press. The book was illustrated by hundreds of sketches by Nancy Ahlquist. The challenge of writing a real text, as well as financial greed (or rather, the hope of assuring an income in old age) made me accept an offer from Benjamin Publishers. Writing a biology textbook is like Pascal's wager about the existence of God: the chances of financial success are few, but if they work out the reward is worth the bet. The product of my wager was *A View of Life*, co-authored by Stephen Jay Gould, the eminent paleontologist, writer, and chorus singer, whose writing I admire although we differ somewhat on the subject of evolutionary theory. A third author, Sam Singer, revised a set of my chapters on physiology. The book was good but proved a commercial failure.

A good part of my writing has been done on weekends or on vacation. Soon after moving to Boston we acquired the habit of vacationing on Cape Cod and ultimately acquired a cottage in Woods Hole. I never liked the place. Since I don't sail or play tennis, and avoid libraries whenever I can, I felt a stranger among ardent biologists dividing their vacation time between library and tennis court and affecting an insufferable air of marine outdoorishness, complete with ragged trousers and unkempt beards. But we built our cottage next to those of Zella's brother and of the Isselbachers, a family very close to us. Come August, each year our three families formed an extended family, which we jokingly call the Kibbutz McGregor, as it came to be known even to our postman.

Nevertheless, my son Dan has never cared for Woods Hole nor spent more than a few days there. His college and graduate-school years have been—he moved from Michigan to the University of Massachusetts for his Ph.D.—heavily oriented toward politics. Political economy is his field of work and his vacations have been spent with friends of similar interest. With some of them Dan organized a musical combo that wrote and recorded spoof songs on economics, some of which became very popular. After receiving his doctorate Dan joined the research department of the United Automobile Workers in Detroit. To his and my surprise, this young man who had never wanted to take a serious course in science found himself in charge of energy policy for the union. This forced him to learn lots of physics and chemical engineering and brought him into contact with the top energy agencies of government.

Zella's father, for over sixty years a member of the painters' union and an ardent trade unionist, was delighted to learn, shortly before his death, that his beloved grandson had become a union man. Among the many discontinuities that fragment our modern lives, grandfather and grandson had established a new continuity, through the medium of organized labor. Such continuities are witness to the structure that the social world provides to our otherwise barren individual existences. They give to our declining years some reassurance and a comforting peace of mind.

Thus this chronicle pauses with some measure of serenity in the life of the writer. In the words of Denise Levertov,

> Twilight has come, the windows
> Are big and solemn, brimful of the afterglow.

3

The Science Path:

I. *Toward the Sunlit Heights*

> Think of all the men who never knew the answers
> think of all those who never even cared.
> Still there are some who ask why
> who want to know, who dare to try.
> ROD McKUEN, "Here He Comes Again"

In Stockholm in 1969 a journalist asked me the question "Precisely when did you become a scientist?" My answer, after a couple of seconds of reflection, was "When I moved from Turin to Rome in 1937. That night, on the train."

The train itself—the passengers packed on the green leatherette seats of the third-class compartment—marked a break in my life. As a bourgeois, a young M.D., and lately an officer in His Majesty's army, I had always traveled second class. Now I had burned the bridges behind me; I was an adventurer. Adventurers travel first or third class. I also felt like a traitor: I had dashed the fond hopes of my family to see me a successful doctor, a famous man, one who would travel only first class. The third-class compartment was an assertion as well as a rejection.

In retrospect, my adventure was even more preposterous than I was then willing to admit to myself. I was leaving a promising career to pursue a rocky path that might well lead nowhere. I wanted to "go into physics," which I did not understand, in order to land upon some utopian branch of biology that did not yet exist.

A few days before leaving I had told Giuseppe Levi, my old histology teacher, what I had decided to do, and he had bellowed, "Preposterous! You know nothing of genetics! You are not a biologist!" Perfectly true, but as useless as telling Gauguin not to paint. I was escaping from current reality at least as much as I was plunging into wonderland or jumping through the looking glass. It might not make sense to Levi, but it made sense to my friend Ugo Fano, whose commitment to science as the most desirable activity never failed. And, according to Ugo, it made sense to Fermi.

In the gloomy light of the blue night lamps of the train I realized that fear is part of adventure, and fell asleep. I woke up when the train had reached the outskirts of Rome. I was desperately hungry, a bit light-headed.

My plan was to learn some physics, at first by studying and hanging around physicists, watching for some research opportunity to open up. Meanwhile, I was to complete my training as a radiologist at the University Hospital. The second task was easy enough. The people in charge liked having a trainee from Turin, the city reputed to have the best medical school in Italy. They also were impressed by the idea of a doctor being accepted among physicists. They were eager to help me. A year later, just as I was on the point of quitting Italy for France, they actually offered me a coveted clinical job in radiology. They were surprised when they learned that I was Jewish, ineligible, proscribed.

Physics was as expected a never-never-land. In the beautiful building, the most modern laboratory I had ever seen, with color coding of the floors and machine shops swept clean as parlors, I was at first utterly lost. I sat in the reading room with my beginning physics text, talked with fellow students several years younger than I, and occasionally approached one of the teachers to ask advice, usually in the professors' shop. Fermi himself was considered the king of the shop, almost as good as a professional mechanic. He had an unfair advantage, it was said, because as a consultant for a big industrial company in Milan he spent his consulting time in their shops learning metal-working tricks from the pros. In the physics building he always wore a mechanic's gray lab coat. I was present one day when an important-looking fellow entered the building, approached a group that included Fermi, and asked peremptorily: "Where is Professor Fermi's office?" "Third floor, end of the corridor," answered Fermi in his soft voice without batting an eyelash. The chap reappeared a few minutes later, shepherded by a janitor and obviously nonplused. Fermi made no comment.

One day a few months later, when I had finally been given something to do in the lab, I needed some melted paraffin and took a little pyramidal chunk of it that lay on a window sill. As I prepared to cut it, it was ripped from my hands by Edoardo Amaldi, the professor I was helping. "Don't touch that!" he screamed. It was a holy relic, this paraffin chunk, matching a similar chunk of lead that Fermi years before had shaped one morning with his pocket knife and then used in his famous experiments showing that neutrons are slowed by collision with the hydrogen atoms in paraffin but not with the heavy atoms of lead. It turned out to be the basis for nuclear fission and chain reactions, and ultimately nuclear bombs and power.

To a nonscientist such an episode may seem trivial. To me then it had the thrill of greatness, an objectification of science greater than seeing Galileo's telescope or Leeuwenhoek's microscope in a museum. Here was the thing itself, on a window sill right in the room where the experiment had been conceived and done.

The opportunity for me to work in the laboratory was arranged by the indefatigable Ugo Fano, who returned to the Physics Institute in mid-year. I was to be *garzone,* that is, helper to Professor Amaldi. The son of an eminent mathematician and only a little older than I, Amaldi was already a well-known physicist, a great mountain climber, and a frightfully hard worker. Working for him was a good discipline. My job consisted in helping him set up experiments, bending aluminum sheets, smoothing the walls of proton counters with sandpaper. I learned by watching and helping. According to the lab tradition everyone had to have a nickname. Mine was Signor Garzone, since as an M.D. I was too distinguished to be simply a *garzone*. Once I happened to locate some screws that had been misplaced; I was promoted to *primo garzone*. But this accolade was short-lived. One day, having complained that my future was dim—what will I do after this year? how will I make a living?—I was demoted on the battlefield to *terzo garzone di Ciociaria,* the latter word referring to the most benighted region of central Italy. It was all in fun, but what Amaldi really meant, as I was later to find out, was that no one who worked seriously in that group needed to fear being left stranded.

What else was I doing besides learning to do some measurements? The meatiest parts were talks with Franco Rasetti, the encyclopedic man whose course in spectroscopy I was taking. Tall, gaunt, almost spectral, with all sorts of odd hobbies and curiosities, Rasetti had just finished building a cloud chamber, a beauty of glass and bronze gleaming like a science-fiction instrument, in the center of a spotless room. Everything around Rasetti was spotless. We talked, and he educated me on sophisticated aspects of genetics, which I was then studying and which he knew well. Most important, he had a physicist's viewpoint on biology, especially on the problems of evolution and heredity. It was he who gave me to read H. J. Muller's papers on x-ray-induced mutations. And it was also he who one day gave me the articles by Max Delbrück on genes and gene mutations that had the most profound influence on my own research.

Biological science has progressed so much since the times I am describing—the late 1930s—that the reader may not easily realize the status of biology at that time. One knew about genes, which determined specific traits of plants and animals, and one knew that genes were in the cell nucleus. In fact, they were strung in some unknown way along filaments called chromosomes. Genes underwent changes called mutations, and H. J. Muller had shown that x-rays and other kinds of radiation could cause such mutations. One also had an idea that somehow genes functioned by controlling the chemical reactions that take place in cells; but one knew mighty little about these reactions except that they were catalyzed by enzymes. Enzymes were proteins but the structure of proteins was not known. Most of the fundamental problems remained unexplored: how large molecules (including possibly genes) were built; how the functioning of genes was regulated so that some genes, for example, work in brain and others in liver cells; and how cells influence each other.

In 1935 at Princeton Wendell Stanley had succeeded in crystallizing a virus. Since viruses like organisms have the ability to reproduce true to their own kind, Stanley's discovery suggested that an organism could have an organization simple and orderly enough to form crystals. Stanley's virus consisted of protein and nucleic acid. But the chemistry of proteins and nucleic acids was still a mystery and so was the relation of either to the genes. Geneticists had, although with little success, tried to explore the chemical action of specific genes, for example, those that control the eye color in the fruit fly. But this approach still had to wait some few years before it succeeded. It was not an empty wilderness that I was entering. It was like a newly opened gold field where a few promising nuggets had been found. What one had to do was to stake a claim and go to work.

I have already mentioned that a major event in orienting my research career was the reading of Max Delbrück's articles on the idea of the gene as a molecule, based on the physical interpretation of the mutagenic action of x-rays on fruit flies. My first reaction was to think of some suitable material on which Delbrück's theory could be tested experimentally. It had to be an organism on which effects of radiation could be measured with precision; it had therefore to be an organism that could be handled in large numbers, preferably a microorganism, so that even small effects would be detectable. I thought of bacteria, about which I knew very little, and of protozoa, about which I knew nothing at all. My idea was to expose the cells of some such organisms to x-rays or other radiation and study quantitatively the killing of the cells. If killing by radiation was due to damage to the genes, presumably their most vulnerable parts, the relation between dose and type of radiation could provide information about the genes themselves. This is the essence of the target theory, made precise in Delbrück's articles.

The target theory may be illustrated by an analogy. Imagine a cherry tree with only a few cherries on its branches. You take a BB gun and, blindfolded, shoot repeatedly at the tree. The chance of hitting a cherry will depend, of course, on how many pellets you shoot and on how many and how big the cherries are. If the tree were an apple tree the targets would be bigger and the same number of shots would produce more hits. From the number of pellets that have been shot and the number of apples or cherries that have been hit, one can calculate the relative sizes of the two fruits. The analogy is, of course, a bit silly: shooting blindfolded at fruit trees is not sensible; nor is it necessary to go to such complicated methods to measure cherries or apples. But put the invisible, submicroscopic genes in the place of cherries or apples, and x-rays in place of the BB gun. A beam of x-rays is like a gun delivering lumps of energy that can produce chemical changes in genes or other molecules. Since one such lump of energy can mutate a gene or make it nonfunctional, from the amount of x-rays that an organism receives and the number of mutations produced we can calculate the size of the gene. We can also compare the size of different genes, as we did for cherries and apples.

There are many refinements to the theory: for example, if instead of x-rays, which deliver small lumps of energy far apart from each other, we use α-rays, which deliver energy in large, tightly packed lumps, we will need more energy to get the same effect since each α-ray hit on a gene will waste extra energy compared with x-rays. The analogy would be shooting apples with the usual BB gun vs. a BB shotgun that delivers ten clustered pellets at each shot. If one pellet is enough to "kill" an apple, the extra nine pellets are wasted. In the same way, for comparable amounts of energy delivered α-rays should be less effective than x-rays in their action on genes.

A further refinement is to establish whether a single x-ray or α-ray hit is enough to alter a gene or whether two or more hits are needed: if more than one hit is required, the number of genes that are altered will increase more rapidly with increasing doses of radiation.

It is easy to invent experiments with cherries and apples and BB guns. It is not so easy to do experiments with genes and x-rays or α-rays. Mutations, such as changes of eye color in a fruit fly, are rare, even after exposure to radiation. One needs to examine thousands and thousands of flies in each experiment. Moreover, the experiments are complicated because the flies have two copies of each gene, so that a gene altered by x-rays may remain undetected when the irradiated flies are properly bred for one or two generations. When I read Delbrück's articles I realized that one would need a simpler system than the genes of a fruit fly if one wanted to verify experimentally the predictions of the theory. And just about at that time I discovered the existence of bacteriophage through meeting Geo Rita in a trolley car in Rome.

Today we know that bacteriophages are a large group of viruses that prey on bacteria. A given bacterium may have hundreds of these enemies. And each species of bacteriophage is different from all others. The electron microscope has revealed the beautiful architecture of the phage units or *virions,* each of which can attack a bacterial cell, reproduce within it, and after fifteen to thirty minutes dissolve the cell, releasing hundreds or even thousands of new virions. The virions of different phages are characteristically different, some perfectly polyhedral in shape, others with tails and filaments and spikes. Each of these little devils has, we now know, not one but many genes, as few as a handful or as many as several hundreds, depending on their species. And when a phage attacks a bacterium the phage genes take over from the genes of the bacterium and turn the machinery of the bacterium from making bacterial proteins to making bacteriophage proteins.

In Rita's lab I witnessed the dramatic effects of the bacteriophage upon bacteria. One drop of a one-to-a-billion dilution of a phage solution could completely dissolve a culture of bacteria in a few hours! One phage virion attacks one bacterium, produces a hundred virions, these attack a hundred bacteria, and so on till after a few rounds of attack there are no bacteria left. Since bac-

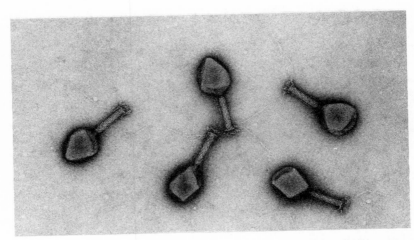

Five virions of bacteriophage T4, one of the most investigated species, photographed in the electron microscope. Enlargement 200,000 ×. *(Courtesy Dr. E. Kellenberger)*

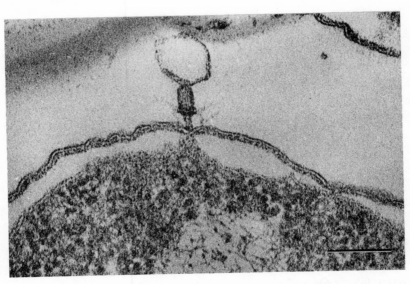

A virion of bacteriophage T2 has attacked a bacterium; its DNA has entered, leaving the phage shell outside. *(Courtesy Dr. Manfred Mayer)*

teriophage reproduced exactly its own kind it seemed reasonable
to assume that they had genes. In fact, I thought naïvely, they
might even *be* genes. If so, they were the ideal material with
which I should work. They were easy to handle, easy to prepare,
and, most important, easy to count with great precision. One milli-
liter of phage may contain one billion virions, and each one can
be counted because it forms a nice round spot of destruction on
a layer of bacteria. If radiation kills phage, I might be able to do
the apple and cherry experiment with great precision. Using radiation as a means to explore the vital substance of a virus was a
novel enough approach to make me very excited. It was a break,
or at least a potential one.

For some months Rita and I spent time doing huge experiments to persuade ourselves that a single phage virion (no one had
photographed virions or measured them yet) was responsible for
killing a bacterium. We used thousands of test tubes in statistical
experiments inspired by the little mathematics I had just learned.
In the rather sleepy Institute of Microbiology no one had ever
worked so hard or given so much work to the dishwashers. The
only interesting experiment under way besides ours was a test of
the bacterial killing activity of classical Italian wines. The attractive young woman who did this for her thesis took five milliliters
of wine from each bottle; the rest we drank.

By the time our experiments were successful and I was beginning to look around for suitable sources of radiation—x-ray tubes
and the like—for my apple-cherry experiment, Mussolini struck.
The racial laws were on the books and I found it advisable to move
on, to Paris.

There I found a group of people already interested in the same
problem I wanted to tackle. Professor Fernand Holweck, who
became my boss, had done radiation work with yeasts and protozoa, trying to identify the cellular targets where radiation produced various kinds of damage. And at the Pasteur Institute, Wollman, collaborating with the eminent oncologist Antoine
Lacassagne, had started to irradiate various bacteriophages to
compare their radiosensitivities. After some hesitation we got to-

gether. I persuaded the others that the urgent thing to do was to follow Delbrück's analysis and compare the action of x-rays of various energies with that of α-rays on one bacteriophage. This could produce a precise estimate of the vulnerability of the phage as a target. I worked hard and made some mistakes, the worst being that I once wafted a bit of radon from the radium source into the Paris air—a one-man fallout source. By the time I had the result I was after, France, at war since fall 1939, was falling apart. Holweck, Wollman, and I decided to send a brief article to *Nature*, reporting the conclusion that the size of the radiation target of a phage was nearly the same size as the (estimated) size of the phage itself. That was the article that pleased Leslie Dunn and caused him to help me get my first job in America.

My first research project at the medical school of Columbia University was a continuation of the Paris work. Frank Exner's x-ray machine was located in a basement, but I had a desk and a bench on the fifteenth floor, higher than I had ever been except in the mountains. I had a glorious view of the George Washington Bridge and, often, of ships anchored almost at my feet. Exner's machine was frequently under repair, and I had time to explore all sorts of sidelines. One of them proved fruitful. Bacteriophage is much more sensitive to x-rays when it is in a dilute salt solution than in a broth rich in organic substances. Exner and I showed that the organic materials protected the phage from toxic stuff generated by x-rays in water; the real, direct damage to phage was that measured in a solution rich in organic compounds. This finding settled a controversy that had been going on in radiology of enzymes. A similar finding was obtained at the same time by a student of the pathologist Peyton Rous, who in 1910 had discovered the first cancer virus. When Exner's and my paper was published, Rous believed we had plagiarized his student's work, and got angry enough to try to have me fired. Twenty years later, when mutual respect had grown between us, Rous told me, with evident effort, "Dr. Luria, I like you more the more I get to know you," which might be taken as a double-edged compliment.

Meeting Max Delbrück on New Year's Eve 1940 marked a

critical turn in my research path. As I have said, Delbrück had also turned to bacteriophage, but had taken the biological rather than biophysical path. The question he raised was: how does one phage make a hundred or more phages in twenty minutes or so inside a bacterium? This was very different from asking how big the essential part of phage was, and required different tricks. The trick Max and I worked out was to attack the same bacteria simultaneously with two different phages and see what would happen. I was excited about the plan and about the idea of working with Max. It was like being again in Rome among my physicist friends; but now I was really working. When in the summer of 1941 we got together in Cold Spring Harbor and set up a laboratory in the old Davenport lab (now Delbrück Laboratory), we were ready to go and the work went well from the start. We soon discovered that if two different phages attacked the same bacterium only one of them could multiply: there was a complete mutual exclusion. But what of it? We proposed hypotheses but could not verify or disprove them.

The difficulty was the same as in the experiments with radiation. We could by radiation experiments estimate the specific portion of a phage that was needed for reproduction; and we could by mixed infection with two phages define a limit to their individual ability to multiply in a bacterium. But we could not translate these observations into terms of function. The missing link between the hereditary material of any organism and the functions of that organism, including its ability to reproduce, was the nature and activity of the genetic material. These were essentially chemical problems, and their solution had to await the discovery, twelve years later, of the DNA double helix and the biochemical interpretation of protein synthesis under gene control.

Yet our experiments on mixed infection of bacteria with two phages proved to have a seminal role in the rise of molecular biology. They focused attention on the possible mechanisms of phage multiplication—and more generally of virus reproduction—and shifted the interest of virus workers from the problem of cell damage by viruses to the life cycle of viruses themselves. Not without an eye to this possible fallout, Delbrück and I in our first set of published papers referred to bacteriophages as bacterial viruses, and were gratified by the interest evinced by specialists in viral diseases. As for the mutual exclusion we had discovered between different phages, the explanation became clear years later: each phage attacking a bacterial cell reprograms the biochemical machinery to obey the phage genes. The programs of two different phages are generally as incompatible biochemically as are the program of a phage and that of the bacterium; hence they exclude one another.

While we struggled with bacteriophage growth, the attack on gene action was already under way. Late in 1940 at Columbia University I had heard a thrilling report of the work of two West Coast scientists, George Beadle and Edward Tatum, on the common bread mold *Neurospora*. The question that had obsessed Beadle for years was the central one: how do genes control specific traits of an organism? For example, how do two alternate forms of a human gene produce one blue eye, the other brown? Beadle with Boris Ephrussi had earlier tackled this central problem of genetics by working with fruit flies, trying to figure out how genes presided over the synthesis of the pigments of the fly's eye. But the problem had proved too difficult. As was learned later, at least twenty genes were involved, controlling as many steps in a complicated series of chemical reactions.

Beadle's shift to the bread mold—which incidentally illustrates the opportunism of scientific research, shifting from one material to another in pursuit of the solution of a general problem—was an astute and brilliant move. The bread mold is a fungus that grows and multiplies with nothing more than a bit of sugar, some salt, and a pinch of a vitamin. Thus, reasoned Beadle, its genes must give it the enzymatic machinery to manufacture all the thousands of chemicals that its cells are made of. The genetics of the bread mold had been studied in almost as much detail as that of the fruit fly. It should be possible to find (or induce by x-rays) mutations of genes that preside over individual steps of the chemical machinery, that is, over the making of individual enzymes. Then one would be a step closer to the Holy Grail: how a gene controls a chemical reaction.

This time things worked. Beadle and Tatum obtained some of the mutations they wanted, mutations that made the mold unable to grow in the usual solution of sugar and salt. Each mutated mold now had to receive one or another of the chemicals that make up proteins or other essential cell materials. The interpretation was unambiguous: the normal mold had all the catalysts, that is, all the enzymes, needed to manufacture its organic molecules; each mutated mold lacked one of these enzymes and could not manufacture the corresponding substance. It could not grow unless it received that substance. The mutated molds resembled human beings, who like most animals must get in their food a number of essential substances that their cells cannot synthesize.

Beadle and Tatum pithily summarized their interpretation of the bread mold experiments in the aphorism "One gene—one enzyme." Each gene works by directing the production of one of the protein catalysts of the cellular machinery; several such catalysts must function, stepwise, to synthesize each of the essential cell substances. Later this slogan had to be qualified as more became known about enzymes and proteins; but it still stands as a major insight into gene function. Surprisingly, the same conclusion had been reached thirty years earlier by a British physician, Sir Archibald Garrod, in a book on inherited human diseases of metabolism. But Garrod's book had remained unread by geneticists.

The outline of the origin of biochemical genetics I have presented is not just a digression from the story of my scientific life. It is tied closely, if indirectly, to my next undertaking. This goes back to the work with a mixture of two kinds of phage that Max Delbrück and I did our first summer together. One step of that work was to count the two kinds of phage separately in a mixture. Counts of phage are made by spreading samples of phage on agar plates covered with a layer of sensitive bacteria, on which each phage virion gives rise to a circular zone or colony where phage has dissolved the bacteria. For our mixture of phages we needed two different bacterial strains, each sensitive to one phage only, so that only that phage would produce colonies. Such bacteria are readily obtained. One spreads about a billion phage-sensitive bacteria with about as much phage on a plate of nutrient agar and by the next day all except a few bacteria have been killed and dissolved. The few bacteria that remain alive grow into colonies, and the cultures derived from these colonies contain bacteria that are specifically and permanently resistant to that phage.

I used this well-known technique to produce bacteria resistant to our two phages, which I called α and γ (the symbols were chosen because they were available on my Olivetti typewriter). But I soon started wondering, how do the phage-resistant bacteria originate? Are they produced by a direct action of phage on a few bacterial cells, about one in a billion? Or do they originate spontaneously by mutations, like those of the fruit fly or the bread mold? If so, the bacterium must have a gene that makes it sensitive to phage α and a different gene that makes it sensitive to phage γ. When one of these genes mutated, the bacterium became resistant to one of the two phages. Traditional wisdom among bacteriologists in those days had it that bacteria had no chromosomes and no genes. This idea was bolstered by the authoritative opinion of an eminent British physical chemist, Sir Cyril Hinshelwood, who through mathematical models explained all hereditary changes in bacteria as due solely to altered chemical equilibria. I have often noticed in later years that biologists are readily intimidated by a bit of mathematics laid before them by chemists or physicists. It was one of the blessings of my too short stay among physicists to be immunized against mathematical humbug.

Despite the strength of public opinion and Sir Cyril's authority denying genes to bacteria, I favored a gene mutation origin for my phage-resistant cultures—an arrogant David pitted against the Goliath of physical chemistry. My reasons were several. My interest was in genes and genetics, and I could not conceive of an organism without them. And where there are genes there are mutations. Also, the extreme stability of the resistant bacteria spoke for a mutational mechanism. And, finally, I could not really understand Sir Cyril's mathematics.

Bias apart, how could the problem be attacked? How could I try to decide which of the two mutually exclusive hypotheses was correct? What I needed was some way of establishing whether or not the exceptional, phage-resistant bacteria were already there in a culture of sensitive bacteria before they came in contact with phage. If they were, then clearly it was not the phage that made them resistant. Note that, in the absence of good evidence either way, I was not at all impartial. The image of the impartial scientist uncommittedly weighing the various alternatives is a gross simplification. Scientists, like everyone else, have opinions and preferences in their work as in their lives. These preferences must not influence the interpretation of data, but they are definitely an influence on the choice of approaches. Someone who was not betting on the mutation side would probably never have thought of the test I finally used.

I struggled with the problem for several months, mostly in my own thoughts, and also tried a variety of experiments, none of which worked. The answer finally came to me in February 1943 in the improbable setting of a faculty dance at Indiana University, a few weeks after I had moved there as an instructor. Faculty dances at Indiana were held at the Bloomington country club. I am not a passionate dancer, but the dances had other attractions for a young bachelor. I was certainly glad to have gone to that one, but not for any romantic reason.

During a pause in the music I found myself standing near a slot machine, watching a colleague putting dimes into it. Though losing most of the time he occasionally got a return. Not a gambler myself, I was teasing him about his inevitable losses, when he suddenly hit the jackpot, about three dollars in dimes, gave me a dirty look, and walked away. Right then I began giving some thought to the actual numerology of slot machines; in so doing it dawned on me that slot machines and bacterial mutations have something to teach each other.

A slot machine, if honestly programmed, returns, say, 90 percent of the money it receives, but it returns in a very uneven distribution: most trials yield nothing, some yield small amounts, and a few trials, the jackpots, yield relatively large amounts. Whatever the average yield may be, the actual yields vary much more than at random. This is why gamblers usually lose if they do not have enough coins or patience to keep playing until one or more jackpots arrive. The gambler who wins is the one who by chance hits the jackpot early.

What struck me was that the pattern of slot-machine returns had a lesson to teach me about bacteria. I stated earlier that, when a billion bacteria are exposed to an excess of bacteriophage, only a few resistant bacteria survive and grow. And my problem was to decide whether the resistant bacteria were spontaneously arising mutants or were cells that became resistant as a result of an action of the phage on otherwise normal bacteria. A key difference was that, if bacteria were made resistant by contact with phage, the number of resistant ones should depend only on the number of bacteria exposed to the phage; if instead the resistant bacteria were spontaneous mutants, they should be clustered in "families" within each culture, because each mutant could divide and produce a group of resistant siblings. The idea the slot-machine problem gave me was to compare the numbers of resistant bacteria in each of, say, twenty bacterial cultures with the expected returns from different kinds of slot machines.

Consider first a completely unprogrammed slot machine with a small pool of dimes in it. When one puts in a dime, the machine returns money at random, mostly zero, or one, or more rarely two, exceptionally more. (This is called technically a Poisson distribution of rare independent events.) The returns are very different from those of a programmed machine with its excess of zeros and a certain number of jackpots.

Consider next many separate cultures of bacteria each containing one billion bacteria. Upon testing with phage we find a few resistant bacteria in most cultures; say, an average of three resistant colonies per culture. How are these colonies distributed among the many cultures? This depends on how the resistant bacteria are made. If it is the contact with the phage on the test plates that makes some cells resistant, then before that contact all bacteria in all cultures are similar and sensitive; the phage acts independently on a few bacteria at random, making them resistant, and the resistant colonies will be zero, or one, or two, or three, or four, according to the well-known distribution of rare independent events.

Consider the alternative situation, in which during the growth of bacteria a few of them mutate to phage-resistance spontaneously, at random. As already mentioned, these bacteria and their descendants will be resistant. When the bacteria in each of our similar cultures are tested with phage, the resistant colonies will generally be clustered: there will be one, or two, or four, or eight, or sixteen . . . resistants, depending on when the mutations have occurred. A mutation that occurs just before the testing will register as one colony; a mutation that occurred four generations earlier will produce a cluster of sixteen resistant colonies; and so on. The average of resistant colonies per culture may still be three, but the actual numbers will now be zeros, ones or twos, plus some larger clusters—the jackpots, each due to a mutation that happened some generation earlier than might be expected by pure chance.

Realizing the analogy between slot-machine returns and clusters of mutant bacteria was an exciting moment. I left the dance party as soon as I could (I had no car of my own). Next morning I went early to my laboratory, a room I shared with two students and eighteen rabbits. I set up the experimental test of my idea— several series of identical cultures of bacteria, each started with very few bacteria. It was a hard Sunday to live through, waiting for my cultures to grow. I still knew almost no one in Bloomington, so I spent most of the day in the library, unable to settle down with any book. Next day, Monday morning, each culture contained almost exactly one billion bacteria. The next step was to count the phage-resistant bacteria in each culture. I proceeded to mix each culture with phage on a single test plate. Then I had again a day of waiting—but at least I was busy teaching. Tuesday was the day

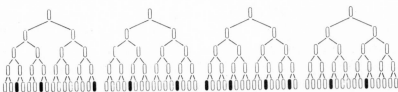

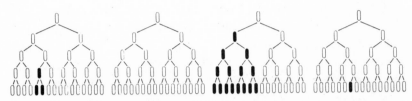

Upper part: If the resistant bacteria (filled ovals) became resistant by contact with phage, their numbers should be more or less similar in all comparable bacterial cultures.
Lower part: If the resistant bacteria are mutants originating from spontaneous mutations that occur during bacterial growth, there should be families of resistant siblings in some of the cultures.

of triumph. I found an average of ten resistant colonies per culture, with lots of zeros and, as I hoped to find, several jackpots. I had also set up my control: I had taken many individual cultures and pooled them all together, then divided the mixture again into small portions and counted the resistant colonies in each portion. Complete success: this time the average number of resistant colonies was again about the same, but the individual numbers were distributed at random and there were no jackpots.

The explanation was evident. In the individual cultures there were clusters of sibling phage-resistant mutants; in the pooled cultures all mutants were mixed together, their family relations were lost, and the resistant mutants had landed at random in the various portions. The results fully supported the idea that the resistant bacteria originated by spontaneous mutations.

By Tuesday afternoon I had my results. I was excited, elated, but not completely sure that there was no catch in my reasoning. There was no one around I could consult: the reasoning behind my experiment was a somewhat subtle one, the kind that physicists would understand more readily than biologists, at least until it was all worked out in writing. Delbrück was the obvious resource. I dropped him a note explaining my idea and describing the first set of experiments. (Why did I not call? Those were not yet the days of long-distance phone calls paid for by research grants; in fact, there was no research grant except, I believe, $300 from the Graduate School. Also it was easier to explain my idea in writing rather than orally to Max, who was wont to get impatient and say something like "Why can't you speak decent English?")

Four days later I received a postcard: "I believe you have something important. I am working out the mathematical theory." A few days later the theory arrived. It did something more than rationalize my results: it showed that my experiment, which came to be called the "fluctuation test," also provided not one but two methods to calculate "mutation rates" from the number of mutants actually observed. That is, the analysis of the numbers of mutants in a series of parallel bacterial cultures made it possible to estimate rather precisely the probability that a given mutation occurred in the brief life of a bacterium.

This was a major step forward in genetics. With no other organism had it been possible to calculate the spontaneous mutation rate for one specific gene, or in fact, for all genes. If genes of bacteria were the same kinds of structures as genes of other organisms, bacteria became overnight a choice organism for genetic research. Bacteria can easily be raised in test tubes, billions of bacterial cells per spoonful of culture. Their mutants can be scored in experiments lasting less than a day instead of weeks as with bread mold or fruit flies. Soon after my experiments with phage-resistant mutants were published, geneticists jumped onto our bacterial bandwagon. All kinds of bacterial mutations were studied. Those that caused bacteria to become resistant to antibiotics such as penicillin or streptomycin were the easiest to find since, as for the phage-resistant ones, the agent—phage or antibiotic substance—wipes out all sensitive bacteria, leaving only the resistant ones alive.

Then Joshua Lederberg had a breakthrough and discovered a clever trick that made it possible to isolate mutants that *fail* to grow in a culture medium where the normal bacteria grow: an antibiotic such as penicillin, which kills only growing bacteria, preserves the mutants that cannot grow. Most of these mutants are like the few that Beadle and Tatum had found in the bread mold: mutants in which a gene mutation had blocked one chemical step in the synthesis of some essential cellular constituents, which, therefore, had to be supplied from outside. These mutants had led Beadle and Tatum to formulate the one gene—one enzyme hypothesis. But in bacteria such mutants could be obtained by the thousands, so that biochemists, working on our favorite organism, the bacterium *Escherichia coli,* an innocuous resident of the animal gut, soon identified the chemical reaction steps catalyzed by each one of several hundred enzymes. Each enzyme was the product of a gene, and each mutation in a gene caused a corresponding change in that enzyme, usually a loss of function. (If you wonder why most mutations should cause loss of function, think of the analogy of a delicate and complicated piece of machinery like a fine watch: almost any change will impair its operation. Proteins, the gene products, are such pieces of machinery. More of this later.)

The opening up of bacterial genetics proved to be one of the key steps in the growth of molecular biology—the fusion of biochemistry and genetics. To me the development of bacterial genetics was not only a rewarding outgrowth of my study of phage-resistant mutants. It was also a strong reinforcement of the choice I had made years earlier, choosing to approach biological problems through a paradigm resembling those of physics. The fluctuation test was directly related to the way of thinking I had absorbed from physicists—from Ugo Fano, Franco Rasetti, Max Delbrück—thinking in terms of individual spontaneous events, be they radioactive decay or mutations. The commitment had been a gamble; and the gamble had proved successful.

The fluctuation-test work had another distant sequel. In 1979 the oncologists James Goldie and A. J. Goldman realized something that I had unsuccessfully tried to explain to oncologists many years earlier: if cancer cells became drug resistant by mutation this would profoundly affect the formulation of cancer chemotherapy. Goldie and Goldman in fact developed a formalism for chemotherapy based on the "prehistoric" Luria and Delbrück analysis. Besides being an ancestor of molecular biology I found myself a forerunner of cancer chemotherapy. Alas, Max Delbrück had not lived to share in this belated recognition.

Soon after the paper with the fluctuation test was published I made another discovery, equally exciting even if not reached at a faculty dance. I discovered that bacteriophage itself undergoes mutations. Specifically, a bacteriophage culture will contain a few individuals that by mutation have become capable of attacking bacteria that are resistant to the normal phage. This observation opened up another area of work, the field of genetics of bacteriophage, just as the fluctuation-test experiments had done for bacteria.

In the next chapter I will try to place the observations on bacterial and phage genetics into the framework of molecular biology. Here I must turn briefly to bacteriophage and medicine. On Thanksgiving 1943 I went by bus and train from Bloomington to St. Louis to visit Al Hershey and tell him about the phage mutations. He was as excited as his nearly silent manner would express and soon took up the study of phage mutation, to which he was to make the most important contributions. I returned to Bloomington. It was a cruel trip, one of the coldest Thanksgiving weeks on record. I became a bit ill, then more ill, then deadly sick, and was on the critical list with pneumonia and phlebitis for almost two months—punished, maybe, for working on Thanksgiving, but definitely 4-F for Selective Service. It has been, I may add, the only serious illness of my life. Under my physically unimpressive appearance I hide a stubbornly healthy constitution.

In contrast with the misery of illness, another personal consequence of bacterial and phage genetics was wonderfully pleasant. The publication of the Luria-Delbrück paper on the fluctuation test excited Theodosius Dobzhansky, the eminent Columbia University geneticist, to direct some of his students to study the genetics of bacteria. One of them was Evelyn Witkin, a brilliant young woman who later became an authority in the study of gene repair mechanisms. Evelyn and I met one summer in Cold Spring Harbor and became friends. Her husband, Hyman, a psychology professor at Brooklyn College, told one of his best students, who was going to do graduate work at Indiana, to look me up. It was Zella. In fact, Witkin told her to look up two geneticists, Tracy Sonneborn and me. She visited us both, in that order, and married me. If Tracy had been a bachelor, might she have married him instead?

When we got married Zella had not had much time to learn in detail about my research work. After a brief honeymoon we went to New York and happened to visit the Zoology Department at Columbia on the day of the weekly colloquium. The speaker was a graduate student who was presenting a recent study on bacterial mutations. He made an apologetic remark to the effect that had he known that Professor Luria would be there he would not have dared discuss that subject. On the subway that was taking us to her parents' home, Zella turned to me with some annoyance in her voice: "Why didn't you tell me that you were famous?"

4

The Science Path:

II. *The High Reaches*

The infirm glory of the positive hour . . .
T. S. ELIOT, *Ash Wednesday*

I have mentioned that the development of bacterial genetics was an important step in the rise of molecular biology. The story of molecular biology, although many times told, is such an exciting one in itself that I do not really need an excuse to recount it here, at least in brief outline form. It will provide a background into which the reader can fit the various topics with which my research has dealt during the past forty years. It will also, I hope, convey some of the intellectual ferment in the midst of which we have been working, an excitement comparable only to that of physics in the preceding forty years.

An eminent biochemist is reported to have defined molecular biology as the practice of biochemistry without a license. Some classical geneticist may have maintained that molecular biology is the study of genetics upon the wrong organisms. They both would be wrong and right at the same time. Molecular biology deals with questions of molecular structure, and therefore is biochemistry; but it is not the classical biochemistry that emerged earlier in the twentieth century out of the concerns of medical, agricultural, and industrial researchers. Molecular biology is genetics because it deals with genes, their functions, and their products; but, in contrast with classical genetics, it has dealt mainly with organisms such as bacteria and viruses rather than peas, maize, or fruit flies, whose study had established the classical rules of genetics, the transmission of hereditary traits from one generation to the next.

Essentially, molecular biology is a research program that attempts to interpret the activities of organisms and their cells in terms of the structure and activity of those classes of molecules— mainly proteins and nucleic acids—that are their specific constituents, the basis of their individuality. Information about the structure and activity of these molecules has come from a combination of physical, chemical, and biological approaches, attacking the problem at the various levels of individual molecules, of isolated cells, and of the organism as a whole.

The exploration of molecular structure started early in this century. In 1915 two British physicists, William Bragg and his son Lawrence, shared a Nobel Prize for their invention of x-ray spectroscopy, which can reveal the arrangement of molecules and atoms within crystals of a given substance. This extremely powerful approach to the structure of molecules, revealing the actual positions and distances of the atoms within molecules, was soon applied, despite enormous technical difficulties, to biologically interesting molecules, especially to proteins. A protein molecule may contain ten thousand atoms, a hundred times more than the small molecules studied by the Braggs. Yet biochemists needed to know their precise structure. Especially, they wanted to know how the molecular structure of a protein, an enzyme, for example, accounts for its unique function as specific catalyst of a chemical reaction. How do the various atoms of the protein molecule participate in the events of the chemical reaction promoted by that enzyme?

Fifty years passed between the award of a Nobel Prize to the Braggs and the first report by David Phillips, another British scientist, of a reasonably satisfactory answer to the above question. Phillips deciphered the complete molecular structure of an enzyme, showing which atoms or groups of atoms participate in the catalytic action of that enzyme on a specific chemical reaction. Even then, what Phillips had achieved was not a general answer:

it was a wholly satisfying description of one enzyme in its detailed atomic structure; but it applied to that protein and that protein only. The same was true of other structural studies of protein. Each protein is a riddle unto itself and its structure has to be unraveled, not according to any general scheme, but on its own terms. As an analogy think of tennis matches, which consist of serves, returns, volleys, etc.; having seen one match you cannot predict the sequence of strokes in another. Likewise, a knowledge of the constituent atoms in a protein does not allow one to predict its structure.

By the late 1940s biochemists had fairly well established the idea that all proteins—and there may be a thousand or more different proteins in a single cell, each present in hundreds of copies—consist of chemical chains made up of building blocks called *amino acids,* twenty different ones. The order of these building blocks in the chains, the length of the chains (often a hundred or even thousand amino acids), and the shape that the chains finally take up when they compact into their functional form is unique for each protein. Moreover, the shape is dictated only by the order of the amino acids in the chains. As in sculptures done in wrought iron, the same material in twenty different varieties is used to produce an infinite variety of forms. But in the case of proteins there is no sculptor to fashion them: the wrought iron fashions itself according to its own internal directions.

The great physical chemist Linus Pauling brought some "discipline" into the chaotic field of protein structure by identifying the molecular forces that help compact the protein chains, and in this way he predicted some of the simplest arrangements to be expected. Yet still today it is impossible to predict completely the properties of a giant protein from the sequence of its component amino acids; and x-ray analysis may take months or years for each protein.

It is not surprising for molecular variety to be the dominant feature of proteins. In a living cell the molecules of each protein perform a specific task; each protein must be unique and functionally adequate for a unique chemical function. The perfecting of proteins for their tasks is achieved by the continuous action of natural selection—the driving force in evolution. Since in the cells of living organisms all functions are carried out by proteins, it is on proteins that natural selection operates at the molecular level. Those organisms with better proteins will tend to prosper, that is, to have more descendants. Hence the great variety of the molecular structure of proteins is the result of selection of proteins for more efficient chemical function. This variety makes the task of the protein chemist exceedingly hard. If molecular biology had had to await the one-by-one unraveling of the structure of proteins it might have taken a hundred years to learn what we now know.

Fortunately, not all biological molecules are as idiosyncratic as proteins. In fact, the most important one, the DNA molecule, turned out to have a good sensible structure, very uniform as well as informative. The history of the identification of DNA with the genetic material of cells has been frequently told. Like the stock of an oil company with rich but still untapped resources, the rating of DNA in the marketplace of biological research fluctuated widely for many years. Most geneticists were inclined to believe DNA was the stuff that genes were made of: it was present in the cell nucleus where genes are kept, and its amount was reasonably constant from cell to cell in a given organism, as it should be if it represented the genetic material. Some biochemists were more skeptical; their analysis indicated that DNA was "too simple" in composition, made up of only four units or building blocks (nucleotides), which were called A, G, C, T from their initials. How could four units provide variety enough for the thousands of genes in a cell?

It was a bacteriologist, Oswald Avery, himself a biochemist turned geneticist by the force of his own findings, who delivered what ultimately proved to be the decisive blow for DNA. Avery was a short, bald, and benign gentleman with mischievously twinkling eyes. When his work led him to the study of DNA he was already illustrious for his contributions to the biology of the pneumonia bacillus. I first met him in 1943, when he had for years been studying a phenomenon discovered earlier by the British bacteri-

ologist Fred Griffith: an extract from a normal strain of pneumo-
coccus, as the pneumonia bacillus is called, added to cells of a
mutant strain could "transform" them to the normal form again.
Most exciting, if extracts of several different strains were tested,
each transformed the mutant into its own image; that is, the trans-
forming agent or principle, whatever it was, was specific. It
looked, at least to Avery's prepared mind, as if in each extract
there were genes of the normal bacteria from which it had been
taken, and such genes could enter the mutant bacteria and transform them. Avery believed it was so; he whispered it might be so,
cautiously but with delighted excitement. He and his co-workers
were seeking to identify the active principle in the extract. The
more they purified it the more DNA it contained and the less of
anything else. To make a long story short, DNA seemed to be it.

I won't go into the question, already belabored by historians of
science, of why Avery's discovery did not immediately convince
everyone. I myself, an early believer, was guilty some years later
of a rash suggestion that bacteriophage genetic material was in the
protein component, a scientific gaffe that sometimes still gives me
a pang of shame like the memory of some rude or gauche behavior. Almost immediately, however, Hershey came to the rescue of
DNA (and of me). In a set of experiments justly celebrated for their
elegant simplicity, he and his colleague Martha Chase demon-
strated that when a bacteriophage particle, which is composed of
protein and DNA, attacks a bacterium, the protein is left outside
and the DNA enters the bacterium, multiplies, and gives rise to
more phage. In bacteriophage, as in Avery's bacteria, as in every
living organism, we now are certain that the genes are DNA.
(Some viruses manage with genes made of another kind of nucleic
acid called RNA.)

The importance of the discoveries that identified as DNA the
genetic material of bacteria first, then of phage, and ultimately of
all organisms was that they make the problem of the gene into a
straightforward problem of chemistry (while still remaining fully
a problem of genetics). The structure of DNA at the molecular
level was not yet known, but at least chemists and geneticists

knew they were dealing with a specific chemical substance. Even more important, if a single substance, DNA, is the material of the genes, thousands of different ones in each organism, this substance must be able to exist in a remarkable range of different forms, one for each gene. The thought was staggering, the opportunities to find an answer uncertain but alluring.

In 1946 James Watson came to my virus class at Indiana University as a graduate student, a bit peeved at having been turned down by the California Institute of Technology. (Too young, maybe; he was not yet eighteen. Also Cal Tech perhaps took a dim view of the two-year undergraduate program he had taken at the University of Chicago.) Indiana accepted Jim as a zoologist because he was a bird watcher and could conduct bird walks. When he came to my lab in January 1947 I had just developed a successful attack on a new kind of response of phage to ultraviolet light, which I'll describe a bit later. I gave Jim the problem of studying the same phenomenon using x-rays instead of ultraviolet light, a problem that became his doctoral thesis. But Jim was unsatisfied by my circuitous ways of approaching what we both saw as the central problem, the gene. He was much more impatient than I, and when he learned of Pauling's models of protein structure, he began dreaming of DNA structure and the structure of genes. But he had to learn some solid biochemistry before he could go any further; or at least I so believed. And good biochemistry was something I could not teach him. The reader may recall that several years earlier Pauling had warned me not to do biochemistry unless I knew lots of chemistry, and I was not ready to follow the old saw: he who can, does; he who cannot, teaches. So I developed a plan: send Watson to Copenhagen after he completes his doctorate. There, I believed, Herman Kalckar would teach him biochemistry and arrange for him to learn the x-ray technique of the Braggs and maybe apply it to study the molecular structure of DNA. I arranged it all—only to end in sorrow. In *The Double Helix* Watson has recounted better than I can do here his Copenhagen adventure: Kalckar's distracting preoccupations, Jim's failure to make contact with the x-ray people, and his dismal feeling of being the brightest one around. He also wrote of the second step of his travels: how I happened to meet John Kendrew, the master x-ray crystallographer, in Ann Arbor and brought up with him the idea of sending Jim to Cambridge. Kendrew, not a man given to noisy effusions, answered more or less in the same way as Fermi had done when he was asked about my going to Rome: "It sounds reasonable." Like an arrow released from a crossbow or a prisoner paroled from Alcatraz, Jim rushed from Copenhagen to Cambridge and settled there, without awaiting the approval of the august committee that had awarded him his two-year fellowship. The story of the bureaucratic shenanigans that followed has been told.

At any rate, Jim won and stayed happily in Cambridge, presumably because there he might not be the brightest one. Soon he met Francis Crick. Francis had that wonderful quality of good physicists who turn to biology or to real estate: they are certain of their own ability to think at least a bit further than most other people in the new field—and they generally do. Francis, who up to that point may never have heard of DNA, was infected by Watson's fever. They thought and argued and built hypothetical models of DNA molecules—until the day they'd done it: a reasonable structure that filled all the known chemical properties of DNA! As Watson and Crick coyly wrote in their first published report, it "had not escaped [their] attention" that the proposed structure did something more: it suggested the way DNA might be copied, an essential feature if DNA is the stuff of the genes, since each gene must be copied every time a cell becomes two.

This brings us to the heart of the problem. DNA molecules are exceedingly long chains or strings, each made up chemically of only four different kinds of small units—A, G, T, C—which may follow one another in any order. For a convenient (but inadequate) musical analogy think of a score consisting of only four different notes, all of equivalent time value. The melody may not be very exciting but it can be distinctive. DNA consists of two chains held together by a peculiar interaction between their units: whenever one chain has A the other has T, A and T being held

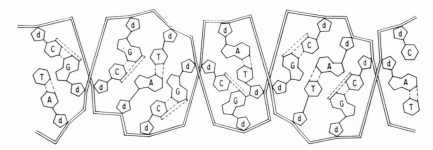

A distorted drawing of a short section of a DNA double helix, showing the helical backbones and some of the sequence of pairs of bases. A and T are held together by two bonds; G and C are held together by three bonds; d stands for deoxyribose.

together fairly strongly by bonds between their atoms. Likewise, G is always opposite to C and held to it. The technical expression is that the two chains of a DNA molecule have "complementary sequences" of units. In our musical analogy, there would be two fiddles, both playing on a four-note scale. When one fiddle plays A the other plays T and vice versa; the same for notes G and C— a very simple counterpoint.

The arrangement of units A, T, G, C in complementary pairs is related to the way DNA molecules replicate, that is, how one molecule becomes two. Starting at one point of a double-helix molecule, the two chains separate and each one directs the assembly, one unit at a time, of a new chain according to the rule that a T is put in the new chain opposite any A, a C opposite any G, a G opposite C, and an A opposite T. This is what had not escaped Watson and Crick: a double helix, with two separable, mutually complementary chains, is a natural arrangement for producing two similar double helices from one: just have the chains separate and each chain will direct the building of a new complementary chain. Molecular biologists, using the convenient lingo of computers, say that each DNA chain has a certain amount of "information" encoded in the sequence of its units A, G, T, C. This information is used to direct the assembly of a complementary chain. The two chains, of course, have similar amounts of information: if you

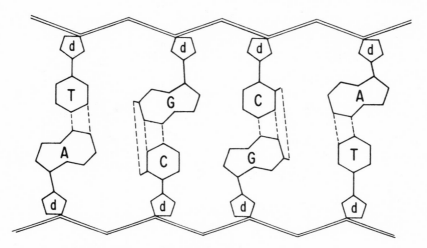

A short segment of DNA drawn without the helical structure.

know the sequence of one chain you can directly infer the sequence of the other.

If DNA is the substance of the genes, it must do more than make more copies of itself. Each gene must in some way affect some property of the organism. As we already mentioned, the genes do their work by directing the synthesis of specific proteins. The discovery of how genes preside over synthesis of proteins, how the "information" of a gene contained in the sequence of ACTG symbols is translated into the information of a protein—a specific sequence of twenty different amino acids in various orders and numbers—was one of the triumphs of modern biology. In this triumph a major role was played by biochemists and geneticists working with bacteria and bacteriophage. Being myself the one who first gave bacteria their due place in the world of genetics I felt especially pleased with the role they played in the rise of molecular biology, somewhat like a father seeing his children become successful.

The next step was to go a bit further into understanding what we call a gene. Classical genetics had identified genes as "objects" located in single-file sequence along certain microscopic threads called chromosomes in the cell nucleus. When Watson and Crick

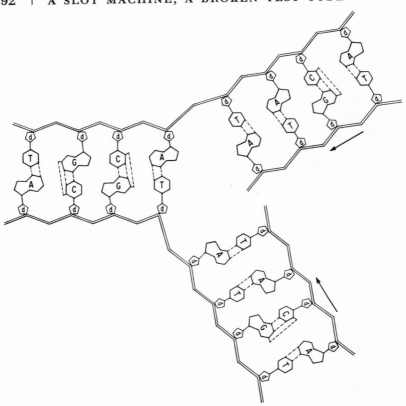

A segment of DNA (drawn as in Figure E) undergoing replication. Each DNA chain serves as a template for lining up the appropriate units, which are then joined together into chains by specific catalysts. The arrows show the direction in which the new chains are growing as the "growing fork" moves to the left.

clarified the structure of DNA, our view of genes changed, from beads on a string to stretches of a chemical ribbon. Genes were stretches of DNA double helix. This knowledge raised new problems: How are the individual genes marked off in DNA? Where does each gene start and end?

One needed a different kind of tool to dissect DNA into genes; that tool proved to be genetic analysis of bacteria. The DNA of a bacterium is a single, naked DNA molecule, so long that if it were stretched out instead of being coiled in the bacterial cell it would be a thousand times longer than the cell itself. In an analogy suggested by Seymour Benzer, a bacterium is like one of those lacquer boxes full of long noodles served in Chinese restaurants; in the bacterium the noodles are DNA. Soon after I had got bacterial genetics going with fluctuation-test experiments, two American geneticists, Edward Tatum and Joshua Lederberg, discovered that some bacteria can mate; they pair together so that genetic material can pass from one to the other. When the two bacteria in a mating pair differ by several hereditary characters, out of the mating there emerge some descendants that are hybrids, that is, having new combinations of characteristics derived from the two parents.

Soon a Franco-British team, working out of Paris and London, showed that when a bacterial mating pair is formed a stretch of DNA actually passes from one member of the pair—the donor—to the other—the recipient—like a thread passing through the eye of a needle. This DNA thread carries genes in a precise order. By stopping the process at various times, one can determine which genes enter first, which next, and so on. In this way geneticists can establish the order of genes in the bacterial DNA. For the bacterium *Escherichia coli,* the workhorse of geneticists, we now know the relative positions of about one thousand genes, probably one third or so of the total gene patrimony of that organism!

The most important event is what follows when a piece of DNA, with one or more genes, enters from a donor cell to a recipient cell. These genes line up very precisely with the corresponding genes already present in the cell; then one or more exchanges happen, so that a stretch of DNA from the donor, containing one or more genes, or even only a piece of a gene, comes to replace the corresponding piece of DNA in the recipient. This process, called *recombination,* is the key to the reshuffling of genetic material. Recombination takes place not only between genes, which are stretches of hundreds or thousands of units in DNA, but even between two adjacent units. Such reshuffling is not unique to bacteria. It occurs, for example, among genes in chromosomes of plants or animals whenever sex cells are produced, and they give rise to the enormously diverse combinations of genes that appear with each generation in a population of human beings.

At the other end of the biological world, gene recombination also happens in bacteriophage. Soon after I found the first mutations of phage, Al Hershey and his student Raquel Rotman found that when two mutated phages infected the same bacterium their genes had a chance to undergo exchanges, fully comparable to the exchanges just described for the genes of bacteria as well as those of humans or any plant or animal. Recombination and the consequent production of novel combinations of genes is a general property of DNA. Of course, like any other cellular event, recombination requires the catalytic action of certain enzymes, because in the exchanging of parts of DNA chains chemical bonds are done and undone.

Now that we have a better idea of what a gene is, let us return to the question of gene action. How is the information of a specific gene used to direct the making of a specific protein? We know already that a gene is a stretch of DNA with a specific sequence of units (AGCT in some order) in one chain and the complementary sequence in the other chain. A protein is a single chain of amino acids, twenty different ones. The problem is to explain how the sequence of four DNA units directs the ordering of the twenty protein units. Our earlier musical analogy will be helpful. Consider a violin score made up solely of triplets of four notes only. There are sixty-four different triplets: ATG, AGT, GAT, CTA ... We arrange the score in such a way that when a certain triplet appears in the violin score some other instrument, say a bassoon, plays one specific note out of a twenty-note score (let's say, written in Greek letters). For example, when the fiddle plays the triplet GCT the bassoon lets go with his note beta. This is a peculiar counterpoint: it is the counterpoint of the *genetic code*. To each set of triplets of DNA units there corresponds one specific amino acid in the protein. Sometimes different triplets specify the same amino acid. Also, a few triplets serve as signal to stop or start.

The genetic code has another remarkable quality. It is not only uniform in all cells of a given organism, but it is universal; the triplet–amino acid correspondence is the same in bacteria as in all plants and animals, including humans. This is really a marvelous thing, the essence of the unity of living organisms. All organisms have their program inscribed in the same alphabet, and they all decipher it by the same rules. Apparently, since the early days when organisms appeared on Earth, there has never been a tower of Babel to create a confusion of molecular language. Our cells have kept their ancestral molecular wisdom, even when we went astray in our multiple ways.

The chemical details of how the language of DNA—the violin sound of triplets—is translated into the language of protein—the twenty notes of the bassoon—need not concern us here. It may be left for biochemists and contrapuntists to worry about. The reader may, however, be interested in an important feature of gene action, and that is the exquisite efficiency by which it responds to the needs of the cells. Individual genes are continuously turned on, slowed down, or turned off in response to appropriate chemical signals in much the same way that electric bulbs can be turned on, off, or regulated by a dimmer switch. The unraveling of the regulation of gene activity in bacteria was the stupendous feat of two French scientists, François Jacob and Jacques Monod, the dramatic culmination of many years of patient work and brilliant insight. Each gene or group of genes, they concluded, has next to it a set of signal points—themselves short sequences of DNA— which are recognized by regulating proteins whose presence at the signal points turns the genes on or off. These regulatory proteins stick to the signal points or get off them depending on the presence and amounts of the compounds that are affected by gene action. For example, when a certain sugar is added to the liquid in which bacteria are growing, some sugar molecules enter the bacteria and combine with one of the regulating proteins. Then this protein, coming off a signal point of the DNA, turns on the gene that makes the enzyme that utilizes that sugar!

This beautiful story is now well understood for bacteria. Matters, however, are more complicated in cells of animals and plants. For example, we do not yet understand how cells of liver, or brain, or muscle of an animal, although they have the same genes, become permanently programmed to make different proteins; nor do we understand how a normal cell becomes a cancer cell, unable to behave normally within the body. We still have a long way to go.

Molecular biology as I have outlined it here says nothing about an important point, the stability of the gene itself. But a variety of tests have made it clear that by and large genes are very stable. Mutations are rare, and in fact the DNA chains are not broken down and reassembled. They are passed intact from one cell to its daughter cells.

Yet as early as 1946 I made a finding that was destined to open up a new insight on how the stability of DNA is achieved. I had long known that bacteriophage, when exposed to ultraviolet light, was killed in a straightforward way, the number of "kills" being directly related to the amount of light used. But Max Delbrück had noticed certain unexplained irregularities. I decided to look into this because I smelled some interesting possibilities. Sure enough, the cause of the trouble turned out to be something quite unexpected. What I discovered was that when two or more "dead" phage entered the same bacterial cell, they often became alive again and produced normal live progeny. This was the first example of resuscitation or *reactivation* of cells or organisms that had been damaged by radiation. I interpreted the reactivation, correctly, as a result of genetic recombination. Two or more phages, if they were damaged in different genes, could by genetic exchanges like those recently discovered by Hershey and Rotman reconstitute an undamaged, completely normal phage.

And so I put Jim Watson, my first graduate student at Indiana, to repeat the experiments using x-rays instead of ultraviolet rays as the killer radiation. His results came out as I expected: with x-rays there was much less reactivation of dead phage than with ultraviolet light, because x-rays not only affect the DNA units chemically, like ultraviolet light, but can also break the chains, and broken chains are not expected to rejoin.

The discovery of reactivation of irradiated phage immediately started a flurry of activity in the study of repair of radiation damage. It turned out that the repair of damaged phage by mutual help that I had discovered was only one special case of DNA repair. Cells of all types, not just bacteria, have biochemical mechanisms that repair, more or less efficiently, the damage produced on their DNA by ultraviolet light. In retrospect it seems reasonable to expect that organisms should have evolved defenses against an agent as dangerous and ubiquitous as ultraviolet light.

The repair mechanisms require the functioning of several genes. Human individuals who are genetically defective in one or another of these genes are said to be afflicted with *xeroderma pigmentosum,* a hereditary condition in which even moderate exposure to strong sunlight leads to skin discoloration and ultimately to skin cancer. It is a bit ironical that the path to understanding a not uncommon human illness should have started from the exploration of an observation on bacteriophage. And yet, would a frontal attack on the pathology of *xeroderma* have led equally fast to the discovery of its genetic cause?

Some years later a peculiar correspondence took place, one of the few occasions when a question of priority arose in the phage group. Delbrück, in a review on phage, gave me primary credit for the reactivation discovery, while giving Hershey only secondary credit for the discovery of genetic recombination in phage because the latter had been observed first in Delbrück's lab. Hershey wondered at the reason for the difference; Max replied that for recombination he had suggested the correct interpretation without proving it. For reactivation, he had the wrong interpretation, while I had proposed and proved the correct one. I did not know whether to be pleased or upset. I was bothered by the question of priorities. I especially feared the incident might hurt the mutual respect among Delbrück, Hershey, and me. Fortunately, my fears were unjustified and no ill feelings remained.

A scientist's ego is in there fighting, but fighting against the secrets of nature rather than against other scientists. Rivalries are tempered by mutual professional respect, enhanced by personal trust as well as by admiration for the quality of the work. Personal frustrations arising from lack of success or what appears to be lack of adequate recognition may embitter personal relations, but such frustrations do not engender ideological or scholastic splits as they do in more abstract disciplines. In a science that is forging vigorously ahead there is not much space for divisions. Those whose priority is work proceed apace; those who nourish grudges may find themselves left behind.

The events that culminate in bacteriophage multiplication all take place inside bacterial cells. The DNA of the phage enters a cell, its genes start functioning, and more phage is made. What happens during this time to the DNA of the bacterium? I started wondering about this at about the same time that biochemists such as Seymour Cohen and Al Hershey were beginning to explore the chemistry of phage-infected bacteria. My nonbiochemical approach was simple but informative. What my student Mary Human and I did was to take bacteria at various times after phage had infected them and observe microscopically what happened to the masses of DNA normally visible in the cells. Most kinds of phage, we found, caused a more or less complete disintegration of the bacterial DNA. Soon thereafter the biochemists showed that the DNA of the bacterium was actually broken down to its single units by enzymes produced by the phage DNA. The units are then reused to build the phage DNA. Breaking the bacterial DNA is evidently an economical strategy on the part of the phage. Why waste what can be used? The invading phage is the victor, and to it belong the spoils of victory. But things do not always go well for the phage DNA itself. And this brings me to another story.

While I was studying the breakup of DNA in phage-infected bacteria, I came upon a peculiar class of bacterial mutants. When infected by a certain phage the mutant cells were killed but seemed to produce no phage. This seemed mysterious. Was the phage lost, or did it produce some abnormal type of descendants? One day the test tube containing the phage-sensitive bacterial culture I was going to use happened to break. I have never been a very neat laboratory worker, and this time the breakage proved to be a lucky break. Rather than giving up my experiment, I got from my colleague Gio Bertani a sample of completely different bacteria, called *Shigella,* which we had reason to believe would work just as well. In fact they worked only too well. By the next day the mystery was cracked. My mutant bacteria had not failed to produce phage; they had produced a modified phage that refused to grow in its usual bacterial host, but grew perfectly well in Bertani's bacteria (which belonged to a different species). I had discovered the first instance of the phenomenon of *restriction* and *modification.* Phage that had grown in my mutant came out modified so that it could not multiply in any related bacteria, but could grow in different ones. In other words, the mutant allowed the phage to grow but modified it so that it could not grow except in *Shigella.* The *E. coli* bacteria restricted the modified phage.

Soon similar phenomena were discovered with other phages and bacteria by Bertani working together with Jean Weigle. Then Werner Arber and Weigle discovered that restriction was actually an enzymatic attack of the entering phage DNA. The DNA was broken to pieces unless it had previously been "marked," modified in a special identifying way. A useful analogy is that of the need for a valid ticket to enter a theater (except that fortunately a spectator with the wrong ticket is usually not cut to pieces). Essentially, each strain of bacteria has a set of two enzymes specific for that strain: one enzyme modifies chemically a certain sequence of DNA units; the other chops up any DNA in which that sequence is not modified.

This was really an astonishing situation. Why should bacteria develop specific enzymes to break DNA that comes from close relatives which happen to differ in some marks on the DNA? And why should bacteria that are very close relatives have completely different DNA-marking enzymes and DNA-cutting enzymes? An extreme instance of unfriendliness, which we do not yet understand. Whatever the biological significance of the R/M (restriction —modification) phenomenon may be, its consequences for molecular biology have been revolutionary. The restriction enzymes that cut DNA at specific sequences have become the tool of recombinant DNA technology.

The story goes like this. The restriction enzymes cut DNA at specific sequences of units, usually four, five, or six units long. For example, a certain enzyme may cut DNA when it has on one strand ACTGT and on the other strand TGTCA. The enzyme cuts both strands provided the sequence is unmodified, that is, is not marked chemically on A or C. DNA molecules, say, one thousand units long will generally have one or more sequences like the one listed above. When the DNA molecules are exposed to the enzyme in a test tube, the enzyme will cut them all at those same sequences. Another restriction enzyme will attack some other sequence. An appropriate mixture of restriction enzymes can be used to chop the DNA of any cells into many fragments whose end sequences are exactly known.

Imagine that a scientist wants to introduce into a bacterium a fragment of human DNA presumed to contain a cancer gene. He will use one or more of the restriction enzymes to cut the DNA from human cancer cells into fragments and also to cut an appropriate bacterial DNA into similar pieces. Then he mixes the two sets of fragments and adds to the mixture a sealing enzyme that rejoins the pieces together. Some piece containing the cancer gene will join up with the bacterial DNA. Then the bacterial DNA can be made (as in the Avery experiment) to enter intact bacteria, where the cancer gene can become part of the bacterial gene string and can be further isolated and identified.

This is just one example of the manipulations that restriction enzymes have made possible. A comparable experiment has enabled my colleague Robert Weinberg to isolate and purify for the first time an "oncogene," one of the genes that are responsible for the transformation of normal cells into cancer cells. Weinberg extracted DNA from human cancer cells, broke it into pieces, caused it to enter normal mouse cells in culture, and found that many of these became cancerous. Normal human DNA did not cause such changes. Then Weinberg, in a second round of experiments, managed to isolate and purify the human oncogene DNA from the mouse cells.

We have come a long way from my broken-test-tube experiment of 1952. The original finding has grown, passing through many hands and minds before reaching into medicine and cancer. My finding was completely serendipitous. I was trying to explain a minor observation and the answer proved to be totally unexpected, not reasoned out in advance. The discovery itself was not much of a feat: the restriction phenomenon was there for the asking. If I had not discovered it, someone else would soon have done so. My fluctuation-test work, on the other hand, was essentially unique. If I had not thought of it, bacterial mutations would certainly have been discovered soon in some other way, but that specific experiment, although fully purposeful and decisive, might well never have been invented because it would not have been needed. Science's path is essentially opportunistic. It aims at solving problems, not at doing good or bad experiments. If a problem happens to be solved clumsily, the elegant solution may never be looked for. This is not so, I believe, in mathematics or analytical philosophy, where a good deal of effort is expended in refining the precision and simplicity and elegance of solutions.

Since I have mentioned the practical areas of the technology that evolved from the restriction-modification phenomenon, I should add a few words about another, very different experience that also led to practical success. In 1953 I was asked to be a consultant for a major chemical company. The idea was to set up a search for drugs effective against virus diseases, of which at that time there was none on the market. I was not an expert on human pathogenic viruses, although my *General Virology,* which had just appeared, may have given the company an exaggerated opinion of my expertise. Also they may have thought that where experts had failed a non-expert had a chance. During my first interview with "management" I was asked how long it would take to have a product ready for sale. It was a silly question; to say something, I replied about ten years.

The program I set up for them was a good one, probably the best in the country. It was also a pleasant diversion. In spring or summer two of my consultees and I would take off at five, drive to a sailboat landing with a load of hot soup or stew and cold martinis, and spend an evening on the water—a pleasant fallout from industrial corruption.

Sooner than I expected we found a lead, followed it as hungry dogs follow an elusive hare, and developed it into a series of products. One of these proved to be useful in medicine. In 1963—right on my deadline—the product was licensed for sale. In 1967 I was let go as consultant. That industrial association helped pay my share of support for my mother in her last years of life after my father's death. It also taught me some interesting organic chemistry, most of which I have since forgotten. And it made clear to me the basic differences between industrial and academic research. The university is a world of scholarship and trust, where the reward for success is intellectual recognition. Industry is a world of contracts and insecurity, where pay is the reward for work, and success may make one expendable. I have seen industrial scientists being told at noontime that they are fired and must be out by five. More disturbing, I have seen managers deciding on purely commercial grounds whether scientific projects of great merit should be continued or terminated. Maybe the university, for all its limitations, approximates what an ideal intellectual community should be—a microcosm where shared purpose and mutual respect counterbalance the centrifugal momentum of individual passions and drives.

5

The Science Path:

III. *On a Gentler Slope*

> Two roads diverged in a wood, and I—
> I took the one less traveled by,
> And that has made all the difference.
> ROBERT FROST, "The Road Not Taken"

In the years that followed the work on restriction my students and I explored several paths and directions, some dead ends, others fruitful. As molecular biology became more biochemical, my own work on bacteriophage became less central to the field as a whole. When a field suddenly expands, or rather explodes, one has to make a decision whether to force oneself to the forefront, at the risk of overextending one's abilities, or to find a more practicable field—a gentler slope—appropriate to one's taste and competence. One may find gold or strike oil even away from the center of the explored fields. One line of research, initiated in the 1950s, led me into a completely new direction of research, the direction that still occupies me now and which I therefore must trace in some detail.

I have mentioned that my first experiments on the restriction phenomenon were done using a bacterium called *Shigella*. This is a dysentery bacillus: fortunately I was using a nonvirulent strain that was as innocuous as the usual *E. coli*. Since the same phage could multiply in both kinds of bacteria, I wondered whether the cells of *E. coli* and those of *Shigella* could mate with each other just as cells of *E. coli* can mate among themselves. This was not idle curiosity. Since *E. coli* is a normal intestinal resident and many strains of *Shigella* are pathogenic, production of hybrids between the two might confuse laboratory diagnosis: the hybrids might look like *E. coli* and yet be pathogenic, and vice versa. I soon found that *E. coli* could in fact mate with practically any strain of dysentery bacilli. If such matings did occur in the human gut, some of the hybrids would present a clear and present danger of confusion in the hospital laboratory. One of them was in fact a present danger to me. Late on a Friday afternoon in 1956, eager to get home to a drink and dinner, I accidentally swallowed a tiny blob of the bacterial culture. Drink and dinner and all day Saturday were O.K. Sunday morning I was in Chicago, talking to the Illinois Cancer Society, when the bacterium struck—the typical dysentery delay. All I remember of the trip back is the lavatory of an Ozark Airlines DC-3. If any fellow passenger needed the facility, tough luck.

Professional experts in diagnostic bacteriology soon took over the work on hybrid pathogens, with ultimately useful but unspectacular results. But I had some unexpected fallout. In 1956, a Japanese bacteriologist, Hisao Uetake, read my report on the hybrid experiments and arranged to join my laboratory at Urbana. Hisao is a splendid fellow, an excellent bacteriologist, politely stubborn. Whenever I said something wrong he came the next day with evidence neatly written in English and Japanese. Since I was in charge he would listen to me, but never for a moment would he defer to my authority. I found this kind of relation totally satisfying.

Uetake introduced our lab to an intriguing biological system that immediately caught my fancy. He and some of his Japanese colleagues had discovered a series of bacteriophages that, when they infected the bacterial cells, produced specific changes in the properties of the bacterial surface, altering the complex sugars that are part of the cell surface. In other words, bacteriophage infection transformed the bacterial cells.

The bacteria were of the genus called *Salmonella,* the cause of many food poisonings including the dreaded typhoid fever. The cells of *Salmonella* have on their surface a substance—a complex sugar or polysaccharide—made up of many different sugar molecules. Each *Salmonella* strain has a different polysaccharide. Epidemiologists believe that these differences have originated by natural selection: mutant strains with different complex sugars can infect human beings resistant to the original strain, and can then be transmitted to other victims. The *Salmonella* polysaccharides are powerful antigens, that is, substances which when injected into an animal stimulate the production of powerful antisera. An antiserum contains proteins, called antibodies, that combine specifically with the antigen that has elicited their production. The antibodies help the *Salmonella*-infected patient to overcome the infection. In the test tube the antisera serve as identifying reagents for recognizing the various *Salmonella* strains and for tracing the sources of epidemics.

Usually the antigens of *Salmonella* are very stable; mutations of the genes responsible for their synthesis occur only rarely. Uetake found that *Salmonella* cells, when exposed to certain bacteriophages, lose some of their antigens and acquire new ones. Uetake and I soon convinced ourselves that this change of antigen by bacteriophage was not a mutation but a true conversion: within a few minutes, each infected cell began to produce the new antigen, while the old antigen disappeared. Since the polysaccharides are normally synthesized by bacterial enzymes, we concluded that the entering phage DNA was either making some new enzymes or activating some latent enzymes of the bacterium. Because these antigen-converting bacteriophages allow most of the bacterial cells to survive, the phage DNA remained present and functional and converted the bacteria to a new antigenic type.

The idea of a phage bringing into a bacterium the genes for new cellular components was exciting in several respects, including possibilities for cancer research. Could the cellular changes that characterize the transformation of a normal cell to a cancer cell be due to the functioning of genes on a virus? I remember making this suggestion to my friend George Klein, a student of whose had recently found a new antigen appearing in cells made cancerous by a virus of monkeys.

Uetake and I were not biochemists: the search for the possible phage enzymes that converted the bacterial antigens was a task beyond our forces. The chemistry of complex polysaccharides is one of the most difficult branches of organic chemistry. Even more forbidding was the study of enzymes that make these polysaccharides, since these enzymes are usually insoluble in water. I was not going to tackle the enzymology of polysaccharide synthesis—it was a task for a card-carrying biochemist, and a very good one. And, although I had been elected to the august American Society of Biological Chemists, that election had not made me a biochemist overnight.

That was the time of my move from Illinois to M.I.T. Uetake returned to Japan, promising to send his right-hand man, Takahiro Uchida, to continue the *Salmonella* work. And then, a few months after my arrival at M.I.T., I had a real break. A young biochemist who had been in some of my classes at Illinois joined our M.I.T. faculty. Phillips Robbins at thirty or so looked like an undergraduate (he still does at fifty). He sang in choruses; always wore hat and overshoes when the sky was cloudy; was not allowed to drink in his home but enjoyed a scotch in mine; he later claimed I had corrupted him. Under his boyish appearance there are a powerful and concentrated mind, great scientific curiosity, and a superb biochemical competence.

Phil had just completed a major biochemical feat and was now searching for a new system worth exploring. (The reader may wonder about the meaning of such a "search for a system," which is a common operational way in research. One defines a problem that seems significant in its implications and worth exploring; then one looks for a system—an organism, a material, a set of observations—that offers a promising point of attack. This is not unlike the way mountain climbers approach the climbing of some still unreached peak.) Phil was especially interested in complex sugars, a class of substances present in all cells, especially on cell surfaces. Their importance had become more and more evident as biochemists studied how cells communicate with each other, how hormones act on the cell surface, how antibodies, the first defense line against diseases, work on pathogenic bacteria. Robbins wanted to know how cells synthesize complex sugars or polysaccharides from simple sugars. There must be some information, some chemical wisdom, that dictates, for example, that sugar X be first attached to some protein, then sugar Y on top of sugar X, then Z on top of Y, all in a specific order and with specific chemical links.

Here I was, with a perfect ready-made system the like of which Phil would never have dreamed of: a set of *Salmonella* bacteria whose polysaccharides were specifically changed when one or another phage attacked them. Phil caught fire and started to work. Soon Uchida arrived from Japan bringing the know-how, the patience, and the hard-working habits needed to initiate Phil into the mysteries of phage and bacteria. Phil went on from there with only occasional suggestions from us. In a few years he and his students had solved not only the specific problem of antigen conversion but the more general one of how complex polysaccharides of cell membranes are built step-by-step by enzymes located within the bacterial membrane itself. It was a brilliant, elegant piece of science, whose story belongs to Phil's autobiography if he ever undertakes to write one.

But Phil's feat did something for me: it made me curious about membranes. I began to wonder about the enzymes in the cell membrane—how they get there and how they work. Membranes have a fatty layer within them, and proteins that function in membranes must "like" fat. There was already quite a body of knowledge about some of these topics, more than I could learn from talking to Phil. I found a more congenial way: I persuaded Phil to join me in organizing a series of small international seminars for people interested in bacterial cell surfaces. With some funds from the National Science Foundation we organized what we called the Microdermatology Project, and met in Boston, in France, and in Canada. These were fruitful meetings that established connections and cooperation among scientists from six or seven countries.

Also we got to know each other personally and had fun together. Sometimes in the evening we had music—Anne-Marie Staub singing with George Klein at the piano, with Michael Heidelberger and his inseparable clarinet. Michael, the dean of American immunologists, to whom I owed my first encouragement to apply for a Guggenheim fellowship, is truly a miracle man. At this writing, age ninety-six, he still carries out personally a research program that would be the envy of many young colleagues. I wish my remembrance of his clarinet playing at the Royaumont Abbey to be a word of thanks and admiration for Michael Heidelberger.

Besides the companionship and the music, the Microdermatology seminars gave me what I needed: an initiation into the world of membranes, which I was eager to explore.

I should explain that I was not only looking for knowledge; I was looking for an escape. By the time I am speaking of, 1962–1963, the molecular biology of bacteria and bacteriophage was reaching a double climax. The number of young practitioners was increasing by leaps and bounds. Phage research meetings attracted two or three hundred people instead of a dozen or so as ten years earlier. The field was crowded; research findings were beginning to be circulated by phone rather than by publication. One had to be an eager seeker of "last-minute news" to function effectively; and I have never been that kind of scientist. I need to have time and leisure to work at my own pace. I often found the frantic activity of my young colleagues somewhat ludicrous. Maybe I was just aging. Max Delbrück had already escaped, starting a quiet, underpopulated research program on the physiology of the fungus *Phycomyces*.

Also, the field of my competence—the genetics of bacteria and phage—had more or less peaked in these years. The great work of François Jacob and Jacques Monod on the regulation of gene action, the work of Sydney Brenner and Francis Crick on the genetic code, and the unraveling of protein synthesis by Marshall Nirenberg all had taken place within a few years. For a while thereafter it looked as if research in molecular biology consisted in putting together little pieces of a large puzzle whose overall features were already evident. This work was often extremely elegant, developing the subtleties of genetic analysis to extreme refinement. But it was not for me. I liked to dig into unplowed fields; and I did not have the analytical interest to solve the puzzles of which molecular biology now consisted. The young men and women coming into the field were the outgrowth of our own work of the preceding decades: they came well prepared in those subjects that we, unprepared, had to create as we went along.

That is why I wanted a new field. Out of my collaboration with Phil Robbins and out of the Microdermatology meetings had come the stimulus to work on membranes. But the field was a hard one. The functional components of membranes are proteins that are among those most difficult to study. So I turned to a class of proteins called "colicins," which seemed to provide an easier route.

Colicins had been discovered in the 1920s by André Gratia. They are proteins readily soluble in water that are produced by certain bacteria, and they kill other bacteria of similar kinds. They proved to be of no use as antibacterial drugs, however, and interest in them soon petered out. But in 1963 Mayasano Nomura, a Japanese scientist later to be renowned for his work on the protein-making machinery of cells, had shown that there are three types of colicins, each of which kills bacteria in one of three different ways. Nomura proposed that these colicins kill bacteria by damaging the membrane of the bacterial cell. This was a good lead. How did a water-soluble colicin get into or through the fatty layers of the membrane? And once there, what chemical action did it perform?

For me to take up work on colicins was not a completely new departure. Colicins have certain features in common with bacteriophages. The genes that direct the synthesis of colicins are located in special genetic elements or minichromosomes, called "plasmids"—and production of colicin from plasmid genes is controlled in the same way as that of phage from phage-carrying bacteria. When I went to Paris on leave from MIT in 1963, I was ready to explore the colicin problem. I knew that when colicin E1 attacked a bacterium it stopped the essential synthetic processes. I knew also that one colicin molecule seemed to be enough to kill one cell. Where did the cell membrane come in? All cells must pump some needed substances from the outside fluid to their inside in order to live; this pumping is done by proteins located in the cell membrane. My first question was, what would colicin do to the pumping process?

I was settled in a small laboratory in Monod's department at the Institut Pasteur. The institute was then at the peak of success in molecular biology. Jacques Monod and François Jacob had recently established the principles of regulation of gene action and were refining their approach both by genetic and biochemical experiments. They and their mentor and colleague André Lwoff held scientific and intellectual court to a bright constellation of biologists coming from the world over. Personally, these three musketeers of French biology were as different as three friends can be: Lwoff courtly and ironical, Jacob friendly yet guarded and self-sufficient, Monod spirited and open to intellectual give and take. Jacques Monod became a close friend of mine. Lwoff and Jacob, however generous and friendly, were not as prone to close personal ties.

Jacques had exactly that touch of histrionics that one wants in an artist or in a friend—the willingness to open and even parade one's inner self a bit. I liked his existentialist bent that matched my own, and I liked his generosity, his willingness to make people feel what he felt toward them, positive or negative as it might be. I loved the way his mind soared in the pleasure of conversation, and I admired the courage he had shown in the Resistance and later. I enjoyed his book *Chance and Necessity* without sharing its conclusions, just as I delighted in his way of prefacing some preposterous statement with the words *"Je suis absolument convaincu . . ."** The year 1963–1964 would have been splendid for me even if it had led to nothing else than cementing my friendship with Jacques Monod.

So there I was at the Pasteur Institute. I was already too "emi-

Chance and Necessity (New York: Knopf, 1971).

nent" to be attached to anybody but still much too ignorant to do any biochemistry on my own. I had to work out a strategy. I got a colicin-producing bacterial culture, prepared some colicin, and then went next door to Adam Kepes. Adam is a specialist in the biochemistry of the transport mechanisms or "pumps" by which bacteria concentrate food into their cells. He is a perfectionist, continuously devising ways of doing things better and more precisely, a talent that seems to go well with his somewhat perverse view of the universe, a Hungarian's sense that complexity is a more common and more appealing attribute of reality than apparent simplicity. The line "Things are seldom what they seem" might be my friend Adam's motto—and he is often right, whereas I have always been and remain a lover of the simple.

Adam gave me the advice and regents I needed, and I went to work. I soon found that my colicin, as I expected, made the bacterial cells incapable of accumulating the substances they needed. The colicin, in other words, had blocked the function of transport proteins of the membrane. This was all very exciting; yet, although after my return from Paris the colicin work became a major activity in my laboratory, it took several years before we developed a satisfactory picture of what was going on. Several students and associates, Kay Fields, Anton Jetten, Charles Plate, and Joan Suit, joined me and enjoyed work on a problem that had not yet become popular. Everything we found was new and also taught us more about the secrets of the bacterial membrane.

What we discovered was that cell killing by the colicin was caused by a specific, unique damage. A molecule of colicin was enough to stop the flow of energy on which membrane proteins depend for their work of transporting foods into the cell. Using an electrical analogy, one might say that in a bacterium the flow of energy derived from food follows two circuits connected in parallel, one feeding the internal chemical processes, the other feeding the membrane processes. Colicin breaks the second circuit, depriving the membrane of usable energy. This was a pleasant result, although not a major contribution to science. But this finding roused in some fellow microbiologists a renewed interest in the biology of membranes. Some of them may have thought that if Luria, who is no biochemist, can get to membrane biochemistry through his colicin, this must not be as hard as it seems.

At any rate we went ahead, and in a few more years we got further into the secret of colicin action. The most exciting finding was the proof that the colicin molecules destroyed the electrical charge difference, that is, the electrical potential that exists between the outside and the inside of normal bacterial cells, and in fact of all living cells. "Shorting" of the electrical potential by colicin was sufficient to explain the energy blocking of the transport proteins, since this electrical potential provides the energy for transport.

Next we had to find out how colicin actually operates on the membrane. While Michael Weiss, a rabbinical student turned scientist, was working on the electrical potential story, Stanley Schein, a former M.I.T. undergraduate working by then on membrane biophysics in New York, had the idea of testing colicin, not on living bacteria but on artificial membranes made of the fatty stuff of membranes but without any protein. He borrowed some colicin from me, then forgot about it for a year or so, and one day he appeared to announce the colicin worked. It made his artificial lipid membranes permeable to substances such as sodium or potassium ions, to which they are normally impermeable. In other words, the colicin made channels in membranes through which the ions could pass. In our lab Celik Kayalar, a Turkish postdoctoral fellow, confirmed that colicin produced channels in artificial membranes and, going further, showed that then channels would allow passage of a large variety of substances—the same small molecules whose entry or exit in and out of cells treated with colicin we could demonstrate.

We had it: our colicin acted by making channels through which ions and small molecules can escape. Since precise concentrations of ions are responsible for maintaining the electrical potential across the membrane, the channels explained why this potential disappears under colicin action, and also why the membrane proteins that depend on that potential for their work become nonfunctional.

Everyone knows that in research there are no final answers, only insights that allow one to formulate new questions. At the present writing the hot question is how a colicin molecule changes shape when it associates with a membrane and produces a channel. This is not just an idiosyncratic curiosity. The study of membrane biology has progressed enormously in the last ten years. The action of certain hormones and especially the signaling between nerve cells involve associations between proteins and membranes and the functioning of transmembrane channels. These systems, however, are more difficult to approach by direct experiments than the action of colicin. Colicin may turn out, therefore, to provide an informative model for the study of transmembrane protein channels, vindicating my hunch of twenty years ago.

Looking backward to that fateful train trip from Turin to Rome from the vantage point of today, I see a satisfactory measure of intellectual continuity in my research work of forty-five years. Curiosity about a single colicin molecule making a channel in a bacterial membrane is not unlike curiosity about a single phage killing a culture of bacteria or about a single quantum of x-rays killing a phage; and the questions about the mechanisms of these biological events are also of the same nature. Along the way some of the achievements have been the products of purposeful pursuit, while others have been serendipitous. But the path has been reasonably straightforward, without a restless search for change or stubborn persistence in blind alleys. The harvest has been greater than I had reason to expect, a reward of earnestness more than anything else. Sometimes I wonder whether a life in science is more or less useful than a life in medicine such as I rejected. And then I realize how hard it is to define usefulness, and stop wondering.

6

The Science Path:
IV. *Looking Back*

> For she was the maker of the song she sang.
> The ever-hooded, tragic-gestured sea
> Was merely a place by which she walked to sing.
> WALLACE STEVENS, "The Idea of Order at Key West"

The preceding chapter ended with a backward glance at my life in science that conveyed a feeling of complacency if not smugness. What I found in science turned out to be congruent with what I was looking for when I started, plus many undreamed-of extra benefits. I was pursuing the goddess biology, not in her traditional abode of a grove luxuriant with plant and animal life, but in the unexplored sanctuary of her physical secrets. I was an intruder, an uninitiated, clumsy intruder. Biology responded to my advances by giving me confidence, rewarding my attentions, and helping me build a personal life happier than I had expected. Doubts and ambivalence persist, of course, mixed with a sense of achievement, in fact prompted by an occasional surge of self-satisfaction. The tension between self-doubt and the drive to perform is an aspect of myself I shall explore later. Here I comment only on my personal attitude about science as an enterprise, an attitude rooted in my forty-five years as a practitioner.

What I have liked most in science has been the problem-solving activity and the sense of order that this activity generates. I like seeing patterns emerge, answers dovetail to create an intellectually simple and satisfying picture. This is probably why, as I'll mention later, I was fascinated by "ideas of order" in Wallace Stevens's poetry and also why I have little taste for descriptive science, be it celestial astronomy or nature study. That is also why I tend, unjustly, to be impatient with social scientists, who struggle to make sense of large bodies of observational and experimental data not yet reducible to neat little nuggets of knowledge. And it is also why in my own field I am not an eager seeker of information. I like to operate with only a fraction of the enormous accumulation of knowledge. When I open a new issue of a scientific journal I do not scan the table of contents looking for exciting novelty; on the contrary, I hope that there will be nothing in it that I must read. I once mentioned this fear of input to Al Hershey, who replied that everyone felt more or less as I did, but I was the only one arrogant enough to admit it. Maybe so.

My avoidance of superfluous scientific input is not simply a resistance to effort. For the problem-solving kind of scientist like me science is truly, in the words of Peter Medawar, "the art of the soluble." When one tries to solve an intriguing problem one wants to be left alone. No one appreciates the kibitzer who suggests words for a crossword puzzle or tells one how to play a bridge hand. Scientists, like game players, prefer to devise their own strategies, even though these depend on an assimilated, shared body of knowledge.

Medawar's definition implies something more than the search for solutions to scientific puzzles. It emphasizes a most important feature of scientific research, the sense of what will work and what won't, which problems are likely to yield to and which will rebuff your efforts. Proclaiming some grand scientific goal—such as finding a cure for cancer or creating a better variety of corn plants —and then trying to go at it like a ram battering against a wall is alien to the methodology of science. Patient pathways of simple soluble steps are the effective way. The problem-solving approach has been congenial to me. Its most satisfying moments are those that lead to "strong inferences," that is, predictions that will be strongly supported or sharply rejected by a clear-cut experimental step. This was true, for example, of the predictions by Sydney Brenner and Francis Crick that the genetic code—the translation of nucleic-acid sequence into protein sequence—was "read" three units at a time starting from a fixed starting point. It was equally true of my own prediction that bacterial mutations occurring during growth of bacteria would generate groups of mutant siblings, as explained in Chapter 3. These are stellar moments in research, the times when one's thinking seems suddenly to mesh precisely with the structure of the phenomenon under study.

Significant advances in science often have a peculiar quality: they contradict obvious, commonsense opinions. This was true of Copernicus's heliocentric theory of the solar system as well as of Darwin's theory of evolution by natural selection. It was true, in a minor way, of my own conclusion that bacterial mutants resistant to a phage or an antibiotic originated by mutation and not by the action of an external agent. Once I was trying to explain this conclusion to a well-known bacteriologist. "I don't know what you mean," he replied. "The resistant bacteria come up after I add the antibiotic, hence they must be produced by the antibiotic." I was tempted to reply that since the sun comes up after my alarm clock rings, it must do so in response to the sound. Sudden visions that lead to clear-cut predictions are not, unfortunately, the most common sources of advances in science. My own experience is instructive in this regard. Of my three major contributions to biology, one, the discovery of bacterial mutations, was truly an intellectual illumination; another, repair of radiation damage, came out of a methodical search; and the third, the restriction-modification phenomenon, was due to pure chance. This does not mean that a scientist does not have deep, novel insights all the time: only that most of them turn out in the solving of lesser problems, and some even lead nowhere.

Though scientists (certainly this one) wish to be left alone with their problem solving, this is true only with respect to external, unwelcome inputs, what I would call noise inputs. It is not true in the laboratory, where most work these days is teamwork, where (at least in the United States) professors and assistants and students perform more or less as equals, where ideas are freely exchanged. The concept of the "team" led by a "leader," a favorite theme of science writers, is inapplicable to the way most serious laboratories work. The leader is simply the one whose prestige, based on previous accomplishments, attracts the financial backing needed for the research.

In fact, science is an immensely supportive activity, which to me has been one of its strongest attractions. The support that science offers is both intellectual—the sharing of knowledge—and emotional—the sharing of purpose. The reassurance a physicist gets from knowing that every colleague the world over believes in the correctness of Maxwell's or Boltzmann's equations, or a biologist from knowing that all biologists know Darwin's theory of evolution and the structure of the DNA molecule, is not just intellectually reassuring; it is also emotionally satisfying because it implies a sharing of knowledge and membership in a segment of humanity that speaks and thinks in a common language. In fact, the world of science may be the only existing participatory democracy.

Except for a few emotionally disturbed individuals, people in science do not cheat. Anyone reporting a falsified result is certain to be promptly caught if the experiment is of any significance, since the experiment will immediately be repeated. If it is insignificant, the false result will be ignored and bring little benefit to the perpetrator. Science does not select or mold specially honest people: it simply places them in a situation where cheating does not pay. Cheating in science, when it occurs, must be the product of a peculiar psychopathology, similar to that of the compulsive gambler. Both gambler and cheater court disaster and find in this courtship, in risking their fortune or their status, a perverse but exciting pleasure. Normal persons usually do not cheat, in science or in life, because they are participants in a communal compact of virtue. The attractiveness of natural science as a social activity is that its framework of factual observations and freely discussed interpretations provides a reassuring buttress to the individual virtue of its practitioners. I am not sure, however, that I agree with

Jacob Bronowski, who suggested that the internal ethics of science may rub off onto other areas of a scientist's activity. For all I know, scientists may lie to the IRS or to their spouses just as frequently or as infrequently as everybody else.

Jacques Monod in his book *Chance and Necessity* spoke of an "ethics of knowledge" and proposed it as a model for ethical behavior. He was misunderstood by some commentators as proclaiming the pursuit of rational knowledge at every level as an absolute principle. The real meaning of Monod's assertion was, I believe, that the pursuit of scientific knowledge and more generally the pursuit of knowledge is the outcome of an ethical choice: a commitment to rationality. It is never a commitment to give cold, analytical reason top billing over emotions such as compassion or justice. Monod himself, first as a member of the French Resistance and later as a champion of the rebellious Paris students in 1968, behaved with glorious spontaneity, always choosing human solidarity over cool aloofness. In human affairs, the knowledge that matters is the consciousness of right and wrong, the commitment to justice.

A further gratification of scientific research derives from the nonauthoritarian structure of science. Authority is the enemy of science since progress is predicated on a continuous dialectical surpassing of earlier achievements. Very few scientists, however much they may have achieved, have become idols as actors or politicians have. Even truly great scientists are challenged when they imprudently step on unsure ground. At a dinner in Cambridge, England, when the conversation turned to a recent, rather wild statement by the great philosopher-mathematician Bertrand Russell, I asked: "How could Professor Russell say something like that?" One of the physicists present replied: "You know, Luria, Bertie is not very bright." A typical college high-table quip it was, of course, and a rude one; but also a sign that among scientists criticism, fair or unfair, spares no one.

This anecdote may feed the popular delusion that science, especially in recent years, is rife with aggression and cutthroat competition; that scientists live in a perpetual race for priority and recognition, cutting each other down at every occasion. There is, in fact, keen competition for achievement and success, in science as in any other field. It would be surprising if this were not so, given the kind of work involved—the search for significant answers to problems of which many are aware—and also given the kind of personality that science attracts—intense, concentrated, driven by challenges. But the extent of the competition can easily be exaggerated. Seldom do scientists race with each other in hostile secrecy or, worse, in pursuit of a Nobel Prize. More frequently, several scientists working at the cutting edge of a rapidly moving field reach findings that overlap and are often published side by side, generally by agreement.

Even when they compete and disagree with each other, most scientists do not sustain fundamental philosophical disagreements in their subject matter. Nothing like the theoretical controversies that permeate the humanities or the social sciences exist in chemistry or biology. As I have said, scientists depend on the solidity of a shared framework upon which they build their current explorations. They do not continuously question their premises. What changes is the set of opportunities available for further work, and these are open to all. Only rarely in the history of science have true revolutions occurred—the Copernican and the Darwinian being perhaps the major ones—resulting in the opening up of new paradigms for scientific experience. Such revolutions are those that substitute a rational analysis of objective reality for a common-sense picture bolstered by religious authority.

Today, controversy flourishes only in the outfields of science, on such matters as the origin of the universe or the origin of life. I confess to a lack of enthusiasm, in fact a lack of interest, in the "big problems" of the universe or of the early Earth or of the concentration of carbon dioxide in the upper atmosphere. The kind of research needed to explore these problems is too indirect and too loaded with weak inferences to satisfy my taste. I was delighted to read recently in a memoir of Max Delbrück that Max once announced: "[I will] no longer read any paper on prebiotic evolution until someone comes up with a recipe which says: do this and do that, and in three months things will crawl in there." I also recall Fermi's cool attitude toward great cosmological theories. One day in Rome, possibly joking a bit, he said that like all grand theories the general theory of relativity did not really explain or predict any important physical phenomena.

Like Delbrück and like the majority of practitioners of empirical science, I am a reductionist, that is, one who concentrates on mechanisms and unit components rather than on complex systems in their entirety. Reductionist biologists generally attempt to interpret biological phenomena in chemical and physical terms. Holistic biologists concentrate on the study of organisms and groups of organisms as integral wholes. The distinction between holism and reductionism has been a subject of controversy among philosophers of biology, some of whom have even described reductionism as an aggressive, male-dominant attitude toward nature while seeing holism as a benevolent attitude, respectful of a supposed wholeness of nature itself. This negative view of reductionism actually implies a suspicious, distrustful attitude toward modern science as a whole.

My rather simple-minded opinion of the holism vs. reductionism controversy is that different scientists (irrespective of sex) look for different things in their work. Some ask for mechanistic explanations, others for broad comprehensive schemes. The further a branch of science progresses toward a comprehensive intellectual structure, the less meaningful the distinction becomes between the mechanical-reductionist and the integrative-holistic approaches. In physics the distinction has practically disappeared: research on the most intimate details of the atomic nucleus, on the macroscopic properties of matter, and on the physics of the cosmos have become fused into a single enterprise. At the other end of the spectrum, in the social sciences, the challenge of broad hypotheses based on relatively few solid factual data fulfills both a heuristic purpose and the need for interim systematization.

I guess my discomfort with holistic science reflects in part my separation from professional naturalists, who are the protagonists of holism in biology. My antipathy toward sports, ingrained since childhood, insured that there was something forbidding to me in the appearance of the sun-etched, bearded giants in jeans and sailing clogs who used to populate nature-study laboratories and beaches at Woods Hole (before a crowd of tennis-playing biochemists came to take their place). As a dedicated worshiper of the indoors, I feel challenged and threatened by the display of physical vigor that seems to go hand in hand with love of nature and outdoor life. I get ill on a fishing boat, and refuse to pick up a crab with my bare fingers.

Perhaps my lack of love of nature, my interest in problems rather than in objects, makes me less than a "compleat scientist." I have respected and admired those colleagues whose scientific work seems to fill their life and pervade every minute of their wakeful time—perhaps their dreams as well. In an extreme form this concentration on science makes one expect a similar concentration in others. An anecdote is told about the great German mathematician David Hilbert, who one day seeing a young colleague in tears (his wife had left him) put his arm around the young man's shoulders and said comfortingly: *"Es wird convergieren, es wird convergieren!"* (It will converge.) What else could make a mathematician cry than an integral that refused to converge?

I am not totally immersed in biology. Talk of science must relate to some activity of my own to give me pleasure; otherwise I tend to lose interest. I spend little social time with colleagues unless they are also friends who share my interests and concerns. Fortunately, my work situation has provided me an unusual opportunity for such sharing. In the M.I.T. Biology Department a group of men and women faculty members have informally coalesced into something like a professional family. Together, at daily lunches that are the brightest hour in the working day, we talk, joke, plan, and discuss every graduate student, every course, every exam in a way that I suspect is unusual in a research-oriented university department. Our group is of course open to all members of our faculty, but it comprises mainly a core of regular participants jokingly referred to as the politburo. We are held together, I believe, not by any desire for power, but by a shared sense of purpose and achievement. We have built a spectacularly good department of biology, unusual in coupling an urgent concern for students with a powerful research drive. The lunch group includes those most concerned with the modulation of our program to improve its performance. We seek and enjoy the emotional warmth generated by our shared concern. As in a family, we even repeat old jokes for the pleasure of evoking in each other a familiar response. Then suddenly someone starts telling of a result, his or her own or one heard about at a recent meeting. Questions pop out, and soon the speaker is at the blackboard drawing, explaining, arguing, reconstructing the argument. Everyone stops eating, asks questions, suggests explanations. These impromptu sessions are truly moments of grace, when we share the human aspect of science as one would share the clear water of a cool spring.

Much as I enjoy close association with my colleagues within the work setting, I realize that few of my close personal friends are scientists. In the few exceptions, friendship has rested on affinities other than scientific. Since I have not consciously avoided social intercourse with fellow scientists, other reasons must have directed my choice of close friends. Perhaps my tendency to avoid overexposure to science underlies a reluctance to make evenings and holidays a continuation of scientific research. The weakness of my corporate identification is another factor: I dread professional meetings and have recently avoided them, being wary of the "class-reunion" atmosphere. I cannot automatically feel close to microbiologists *qua* microbiologists or to scientists *qua* scientists, just as I do not feel close to a Jew *qua* Jew.

By and large I am a lazy socializer. I do not eagerly seek parties or other social gatherings, although once I attend I enjoy myself and contribute to the general cheer. I may even become the life of the party if appropriate stimuli are at hand. I am not a stick-in-the-mud; I just have a high threshold for sociability. Rescuing me from potential social isolation has been Zella's warm, almost passionate interest in people, an interest that people readily reciprocate. Our social life, therefore, has for many years been filled largely with psychologists and other social scientists and professionals, often young, lively, keenly concerned with the many facets of the human experience—more so than natural scientists incline to be. Concern for people's emotional and social life also tends to generate interest in public affairs, especially politics. And politics plays a major role in my personal associations: not that I like social chat about politics—I detest it. But I need affinity in political opinions and, more important, I have a taste for active political involvement. As I look back at my adult life, all my truly close friends have been socialists, challenging in one way or another the premises of capitalist society and participating in political action. Such questioning and involvement are less common among natural scientists than other groups of intellectuals. The presumed devotion of scientists to an analytical approach to reality shelters them from commitments that are entered into by willful choice and entail emotional fervor.

I cannot leave these comments about my personal attitudes toward the science world without mentioning science-related areas about which I have reservations or perhaps prejudices. One such area is the history of science as a discipline, whose relevance to science has sometimes, I believe, been exaggerated. What matters in science is the body of findings and generalizations available today: a time-defined cross-section of the process of scientific discovery. I see the advance of science as self-erasing in the sense that only those elements survive that have become part of the active body of knowledge. The model of the DNA molecule worked out by Crick and Watson stands on its own merits; alternative models have been discarded and forgotten, no matter how vividly they might have been proposed. The repeatedly told story of how the DNA model was achieved, humanly fascinating as it may be, has little relevance to the operational content of science.

The self-erasing quality of natural science, as a body of usable knowledge that grows by incorporating valid discoveries and usable interpretations, makes it different from the social sciences, which deal with unsolved problems involving the intervention of the human will. What Pericles said to the Athenians in 431 B.C. or Danton to the French Convention in 1793 remains significant because the issues they dealt with—imperialism or revolution— are still open issues today. The comments of ancient politicians belong to political science. They may be as cogent as those of present-day political scientists.

Things are different in natural science. Significant findings become part of the body of science as objective statements and not as samples of the reasoning of their authors. The writings and personalities of Galileo or Lavoisier, as distinct from their discoveries, are not part of the living body of science no matter how fascinating they happen to be as history or literature.

Another science-related area that I find alien (or, more precisely, intimidating) is that of instrumentation and technology. Just as I have never learned about the operation of an automobile beyond the principle of the internal combustion engine, so I have found even laboratory instruments forbidding. Using a microanalytical balance sets my hands trembling, and a computer elicits from me the kind of avoidance behavior one exhibits at the sight of a police car on a highway. I recall my delight when, leaving my laboratory once late at night, and passing through the M.I.T. Computation Center, I saw through a glass partition a young man, evidently exasperated, slowly and systematically kicking one of the computer units. It was the human spirit asserting, however ineffectively, a liberating revolt against the machine.

I suspect my inferiority complex vis-à-vis gadgets and instruments is partly responsible for my vaguely uneasy feelings about technology. I do believe in the potential beneficial uses of technology wisely applied, but do not like the science-and-technology marriage celebrated by university presidents in search of funds and by technocrats in search of power. I recognize the need to "sell" science to the public through technology just as one must sell novels through advertisements, and yet I wish one could let science grow on its own momentum while carefully screening the technology that science makes possible. If I were a dictator—a weak, ineffectual dictator full of inner qualms—I would push agricultural rather than military technology; I would encourage radio communication for ships and other vehicles and would obstruct television; I would ban video games. . . . But I had better stop here before I start dreaming up a utopia.

7

Teacher and Bureaucrat

First I'll instruct thee in the rudiments,
And then wilt thou be perfecter than I.
CHRISTOPHER MARLOWE, *Doctor Faustus*

It still surprises me that I should have been, and still continue to be, a rather good teacher. I had few models of good teaching in high school, none in medical school. Later in Rome, where I listened to good physics teachers, I learned that teaching requires superb control of the subject matter as well as natural skills and personality. When I started teaching for a living—that was in Bloomington, Indiana, on January 2, 1943—I knew hardly any microbiology and what I knew was not what I was supposed to teach. I remember being taken to task by my department head, Leland McClung, for asking in the "baby" bacteriology class the following question: how many bacteria are there in a colony of *Escherichia coli?* The answer required a couple of "Fermi guesses," that is, rough estimates of size and numbers (about 1 mm³ per colony, 1 μm³ per bacterium, hence about one billion bacteria). This is a mental exercise familiar to physicists but alien to traditional biology teaching.

Despite the few lessons in phonetics I had had, my English was still shaky and my self-confidence even shakier. I doubt I was much of a hit with the students, although the campus newspaper reporter who interviewed me called me "tall, dark-haired, and handsome" and was ready to be asked for a date.

Teaching, of course, meant learning. But only years later, when

I had the opportunity to decide for myself, even in undergraduate courses, what to teach and what to leave out, did I feel comfortable in the classroom. Little by little I discovered that much of the traditional subject matter that cluttered the undergraduate texts was there because no one had thought of deleting it. Also, textbook publishers and writers love facts and names, the part of biology I dislike. I have a nasty suspicion that a good deal of traditional subject matter is kept in textbooks because it provides convenient if meaningless quiz questions.

The year 1946–1947 was a crucial one in my growth as a teacher. Upon returning to Indiana from my year in Cold Spring Harbor, spurred by my interest in bacteriophage, I created a course on the biology of viruses. Since there was no text, no precedent, and no canon, I created a structure by selecting topics that made biological or physical sense. It was a success; in fact, it captured the eighteen-year-old Jim Watson in his first semester as a graduate student. In that year, too, unfortunately for that year only, we had at Indiana Roger Stanier, a marvelous teacher of bacterial biochemistry, a superb lecturer, and an arrogant and uncompromising intellectual. Roger was from British Columbia, but English in spirit, and though vocally anti-puritan, emotionally a knot of puritan revolts and inhibitions—a delightfully neurotic man. As in Dante's *Inferno* Farinata was contemptuous of Hell, so did Roger hold all Indiana in contempt. From him I began to learn that biochemistry was not just chemistry, but biology. I learned about the power of an integrated view of metabolism and of the subtle interplay between organisms and their environment. Most important, I learned that bacteriology could be as much fun as genetics, if a different kind of fun.

The following year, Irwin Gunsalus, another first-class biochemist with a powerful personality, very different from Roger although as dedicated to science, came to Indiana. Gunny and I decided to invent a course in microbial physiology. Again no text, no precedents: a free-for-all. We put in it whatever pleased us. It is a source of satisfaction to me that the scheme we developed in that year 1947–1948 has become and still remains today the common structure of good modern microbiology courses.

Both Gunny and I remember an argument we had one day in the garrretlike student laboratory at Indiana, an argument that had the students aghast and ended with my haughtily asserting: "I know more genetics than you know biochemistry." This superficially meaningless statement was significant as a sign of the times. What I probably meant—and we later agreed—was that the biochemistry of metabolism, which was then the substance of microbial biochemistry, was not the central part of biochemistry. The new biochemistry had to come from genetics: the biochemistry of biosynthesis, gene action, regulation—what we now call molecular biology. I may add that both Gunny's work and that of my own laboratory have witnessed the predicted fusion of genetics and biochemistry.

Gunny and I continued to teach bacterial physiology together for several years, first at Indiana and then at the University of Illinois. I also continued teaching a virology course, out of which grew my *General Virology*. An otherwise favorable reviewer wrote in a British journal that the title suggested not a book on viruses but a biography of "some forgotten hero of the Crimean War"—an example of the cryptic wit of our British colleagues. The Crimean War must have been the first occasion for the British elite to joke about the names of Italian generals, their allies in that preposterous little conflict.

Teaching, in my experience, is especially pleasant when done not in isolation (as is usual in many institutions) but as part of a coordinated and collective educational plan within a department. It has been my good fortune, at the University of Illinois and even more so at M.I.T., to belong to departments where teaching is meticulously planned in terms of student needs and interests, the content and sequence of courses being constantly and even heatedly debated and revised.

Personally, I like best teaching good-sized undergraduate classes. When in a proper mood I give them a fine show, conveying my own excitement without overwhelming the students with facts and figures. I generally warn the class that any numerical example

I may use is invented to illustrate some principle. The calculation is what matters. My general biology students at M.I.T. seem to enjoy my mannerisms, complain of poor chalkboard writing, and are willing to speak up. I love it when I manage to get a true discourse going in a class of one hundred students, encouraging the shy ones without suppressing the eager. Spontaneous jokes and anecdotes, used sparingly, help relax a tired class and reestablish lost contact.

Graduate classes, even seminars, I never cared for. The relatively few things I know well at any one time can fill two or three sessions; then I have to use an enormous amount of effort to prepare for discussion on other topics. Because of my lack of generalized curiosity I find it difficult to study and master a subject just in order to lead a once-in-a-lifetime discussion. At the graduate level, serious teaching happens in the laboratory, either in private conversation or in group meetings, among equals or semiequals. Good graduate students are pros, if still at various levels of experience, and should be treated as such. Each one is making a unique contribution to learning within the group. One unusual teaching venture, if such it can be called, was a discussion group in literature I led for several years for some graduate students in biology. To its purpose and the pleasure it gave me I shall return in the next chapter.

That I like teaching does not mean that I have a missionary attitude toward spreading the gospel of knowledge. For example, I would not have been able, as Max Delbrück was, to initiate at Cold Spring Harbor the phage-teaching program that grew into an entire new pattern of research-oriented teaching—short, intense practical courses with running discussions. I participated in the phage course there, but lacked the organizational drive that was needed to create such an enterprise from scratch. More significant, I believe, has been my reluctance to enter the relation of almost intimacy with the students that such teaching generates and which Max evidently enjoyed. Max's attitude was Dionysian; a group of students became almost immediately a party, and his path through generations of them was like a movable feast. My attitude is saturnine. Far from creating parties around me I tend to get bored and restless at students' parties. The truth may be that Max could enjoy people more because he was more sure of himself; I keep myself apart because my insecurity makes close association a threat.

When I stopped doing experiments with my own hands—partly because other concerns had become too distracting to allow concentrated work at the bench, and partly because new techniques had made my own rather limited skills obsolete—teaching became even more important to me. Especially in microbiology, in which experiments tend to last for a few hours and be completed in a single day, the day's structure is provided by the routine of planning, setting up, and performing experiments, often one each day. Deprived of this routine I would have felt lost except for the alternative routine of class preparation, lectures, examinations, and grading. Even now, the end of each teaching term leaves a vacuum in my days. That is also why I too often accept invitations to lecture at other institutions: they provide deadlines for organizing my thoughts in a communicable way—a form of teaching. There is nothing I dread as much as being without a task and a deadline. I need being under pressure; I enjoy it.

Thirty-five years of research work are recorded in my mind on a time ribbon on which faces and voices of my research students and associates remain imprinted. They are too many for all to be remembered here, but a few sketches and anecdotes may help describe my relation with them.

I'll start with Jim Watson, the first and most successful of my graduate students, who came on the last class of my virology course to tell me he was going to do his thesis work with me. He then disappeared, only to reemerge weeks later recovering from a spontaneous pneumothorax. He did then and still does look frail, although he is, as the saying goes, strong as an ox. Once, after he had given a public lecture in Cologne, the director of the Cologne Institute received a letter from an indignant lady taking him to task for making a man lecture "who was obviously near death."

Jim's lecturing is in fact often inaudible, although it can be very stimulating. When he was being considered for a faculty position at Harvard, the chairman of the committee that was to choose him wrote Fritz Lipmann, the eminent biochemist, expressing reservations about Jim's whispering performance. Fritz wrote back, scribbling right on the letter of inquiry: "Since he has plenty to say people will get close." Jim did go to Harvard. I was touched when he dedicated to me his superb treatise *Molecular Biology of the Gene.* * By the time the third edition appeared, however, Jim was married and Betty Watson rightfully displaced me from the dedication page.

A pair of early students who came to me in 1949, Robert De Mars and George Streisinger, both now successful scientists, provided a strange contrast. George was, and had been since the age of fifteen, a dedicated geneticist, and later became an eminent one. Buoyant and fond of good living, he wanted new experiences and was firmly determined to enjoy them. Many years later he and I traveled to Japan together; he loved every moment of it, while I was miserable all the time, bored by the environment and exhausted by the strain of conversation across linguistic and cultural barriers. Bob De Mars, now a well-known cell biologist, was in some respects the opposite of George: morose, self-critical, and a bit cynical. Both George and Bob have become somewhat distant from me, geographically as well as personally. I found this progressive distancing of student from teacher quite normal, especially in the case of a self-sufficient, dynamic personality like George Streisinger. But I have regretted the loss of contact with De Mars, because I had felt close to him when we were together.

Coming to M.I.T. times, I think first of Stanley Hattman, a soulful giant from City College who alone among my students never would call me by my first name. Even in writing he continued to address me as "Boss" until he became a full professor at the University of Rochester. Stan loved to speak German, married a beautiful German wife, produced three gorgeous daughters, and

*New York: Benjamin, 1965.

periodically sends me reprints of his publications with enclosed pictures of his huge bearded self proudly surrounded by his four beauties. How different was June Rotman, also a student at the same time. A Swarthmore product, smart, elegant, businesslike, she hated Boston, swore to get her Ph.D. in three years, and did so, working in a concentrated and precise way and writing a superb thesis. She was the only graduate student of mine, woman or man, who always came to work "dressed" rather than in rags. And as a professor she still dresses well. In an unusual touch for a student, after coming to our home for the first time, June wrote my wife a note complimenting her on our furnishings. I mention this because such unexpected touches sometimes reveal as much as would several years of day-by-day contacts in the laboratory.

Another student and still a close friend is Kay Fields, who was my first and valuable collaborator in the research I mentioned in Chapter 5. Bright, fiercely independent, always eager for new and difficult problems, Kay had more inclination than others of my students to be personally close to professors, probably disliking the hierarchic barriers of academia. I have always personally found some distancing between professors and students quite valuable emotionally, when I was a student as well as later as a professor.

I'll single out one more Ph.D. student, my latest and probably the last (since graduate students do not flock to nearly retired professors). Michael Weiss, a Yeshiva graduate who cares for everything except clothes, is a computer buff, and runs marathons in order to lose superfluous waistline inches. Mike is also a Hebrew scholar and something of a rabbi. He and I became involved in a peculiar excursion into Hebrew philology when a Brooklyn rabbi sent me the following inquiry: The Talmud says that in the sea dolphins mate with humans; is there something in molecular biology to suggest that dolphin DNA and human DNA are compatible with each other, so that hybrids might be produced? Being accustomed to crackpot inquiries, I replied with a few platitudes, suggesting that the Talmud may have had a moral or social lesson to impart, etc. A few days later I showed the rabbi's letter to Mike, who never leaves his curiosity unsatisfied. He promptly went to the Widener Library, spent a few evenings perusing Talmud editions and commentaries, and came back with a philological gem. The Jerusalem Talmud says "mated *with* humans" (which is nonsense), but the Babylonian Talmud says *"like* humans" (which is true). Then Mike discovered that the source of the mix-up must have been none less than Rashi, the great eleventh-century commentator. Probably by mistake (one Hebrew letter difference), Rashi wrote "with" instead of "like" in his transcription of the Talmud, and in his commentary changed "dolphins" to "sirens." He apparently thought the Talmud was referring to the ancient myth that sirens came from matings between humans and fish or dolphins, whereas the Talmud was simply teaching sound zoology.

Life in the laboratory is evidently not all work. The mood depends on the personalities of the participants, students as well as more experienced researchers, who often remain for several years before venturing off on their own. Gio Bertani, an Italian biologist who later founded an outstanding department of microbial genetics in Stockholm, brought to my laboratory his rigorous training in genetics that I never had had myself. Unusually silent and unemotional for an Italian, one day he announced that he and one of my students had just been married during lunchtime. They were both back at work. Bertani's career—education in Italy and Switzerland, scientific research in the U.S., head of a department in Sweden—illustrates the international quality of science. At least in periods of expansion there are no national barriers to the careers of those who make effective contributions. And those administrators who know how to take advantage of the mobility of scientists reap the fruit of their wisdom.

Mobility is important not only in geography but also across the borders between disciplines. A good example is that of Edwin Lennox, a young physicist who left a faculty position to join my laboratory and turned into a biologist. Ed spoke with the softest Georgia accent and drove a black Cadillac limousine transporting his and his wife's numerous progeny. Ed's influence was especially valuable because of the physicist's habit of demanding rigor and clarity of reasoning, even when one would have preferred to indulge in obscurity and sloppy thinking. In this Ed reminded me of Max Delbrück, also a stickler for clear thinking.

As the years passed and my research group grew in size, especially after I came to M.I.T., my actual participation in experiments decreased, an almost irreversible process since new techniques and procedures that one has not mastered come into being all the time. One continues to provide leadership and direction, but students actually learn from senior members of the research group. Of several of my associates who performed this function I shall mention only one: Joan Suit, a distinguished microbial geneticist in her own right. She left a faculty position at another university when she came to Boston for family reasons and decided to join my laboratory rather than seek another teaching assignment, although M.I.T. had no faculty position to offer. She has been more or less in full charge of my laboratory, doing her own research, educating students, and following their day-by-day work. I consider it an injustice that the academic system of our teaching institutions does not adequately recognize the contribution made by such research supervisors.

Thinking of all the people in my laboratory, with whom I have spent such a great part of my days and shared so much over the past forty years, I ask myself what they and I have learned from our association, what bonds and shared values we have established with each other. I cannot claim that we have developed an integrated viewpoint or attitude toward research, or even closer personal relationships. My ties vary in strength and persistence from one individual to another. I believe that all my students and associates would agree that ours was at all times a high-quality operation, functioning energetically at the forefront of biological progress. I believe they all learned from me to write good scientific English—some of them have continued to send me their manuscripts to revise or rewrite. Many of them were not only better prepared but also smarter and more cut out for research than I believe myself to have been; yet their respect for me never failed, nor mine for them. Still I never established with students the intimate relations that some of my colleagues had with theirs. As

I mentioned earlier I am rather shy of intimacy; and close association with the very young is always difficult for me.

A lesson I learned was that in research one must leave people alone, especially good people. It was not an easy lesson to learn. At times, especially early in my career, I would be too eager or too impatient, interrupting a student in the midst of work or offering more suggestions than were needed. The better the students, the more important it is to leave them to themselves. Occasionally, the lazy ones need to be pushed or the neurotic ones reassured; I had some of both.

The reason for leaving good students alone is not, as some people believe, that excessive pressure to come up with results may lead to sloppy or even dishonest work. In almost fifty years in science I have never personally been faced with any instance of professional dishonesty. Such honesty is a product of mutual respect, in the same way that fidelity in marriage is. I do not recall ever having to insist with my students that an experimental result should be repeated enough times, and under ever stricter conditions, before being accepted and ultimately published. Once, when my student Jane Adams had come up with an exciting and pleasing set of results—the first demonstration that a bacteriophage could incorporate a piece of bacterial DNA instead of its own viral DNA—I jokingly asked her: "Did you concoct these nice data to make me happy?" She exploded into tears and fury. I realized that for a true scientist integrity is not a proper subject for jokes; and I apologized.

In 1972 I was asked to set up at M.I.T. a Center for Cancer Research. It was a direct extension of the field of molecular and cellular biology already flourishing in our department. The establishment of the National Cancer Program of N.I.H. made it easier financially to take what was a natural step. Cancer cell research had since the late 1950s centered on the pursuit of specific genes whose alterations can cause a normal cell to turn cancerous. Such oncogenes, discovered first in viruses, were suspected to exist in normal cells as well. By 1972 evidence for oncogenes had become stronger; more was known about the biochemical differences between normal and cancer cells; and the art of culturing cancer and normal cells had reached a high sophistication.

Among my colleagues was Phillips Robbins, who by then had turned to the study of the chemistry of cell surfaces, normal and cancerous. And there was a younger man, David Baltimore, who was studying cancer-producing viruses. I had followed and even nurtured Baltimore's career since he was a beginning graduate student, and some years earlier I had brought him back to our faculty. In his first year of graduate school, David told one of his professors: "I cannot attend your lectures because they are terrible." They were. Brilliant, hard-driving, arrogant, insensitive, even ruthless, David is in my opinion one of the leading biologists of his generation, always on center, always in depth, spreading his wings over wider and wider fields of research.

With Baltimore and Robbins (and, needless to say, Nancy Ahlquist in my office) I had the first nucleus of a Cancer Center. I needed money, a building, and more colleagues. The National Cancer Institute plus private foundations provided the money. The building was a coup. M.I.T. owned, on campus, a building leased to the Brigham chocolate factory, such a venerable Boston manufacturer that Sunday sale of Brigham candies was supposedly exempted from the Massachusetts blue laws. Inside the building half-naked men with long poles stirred chocolate in huge cauldrons—a scene recalling Blake's illustrations for Dante's *Inferno*. One glance at the plans of the building showed me that it was what I wanted: enormously strong columns twenty feet apart, lots of windows, and a desirable vicinity to the Biology Department. And the *New York Times* sidewalk box was right at the door. The Brigham chocolate company moved out and in the fall of 1973 we moved in.

I do not remember enjoying any single task in my life more than designing and supervising the remodeling of that building. I became expert in the two major functions of a laboratory director: a knowledge of plumbing and the art of coaxing physical plant people to do in a week what usually might take two months. Even the M.I.T. gardeners loved me and filled our doorway with colorful impatiens. When the construction was completed we had, instead of the chocolate Inferno, a research building that has since been copied several times by other institutions. The only complaint has come from Zella, who says that my office is too stark for my personality. Maybe it will do better for my successor.

Cancer research is incomplete without immunology. Just as we think of genes going wrong and cell surfaces giving or receiving the wrong signals to and from other cells in the body, so we also expect cancer cells to have new immunologically specific elements. For this job we captured Herman Eisen, an eminent immunologist. At the age of fifty he had had enough of being a department head in a medical school and wanted to get back to the lab bench. My three musketeers—Baltimore, Eisen, and Robbins—were the foundation on which our Center for Cancer Research was built. The discoveries that my colleagues in the center have made and the honors they have received—top among them David Baltimore's Nobel Prize—easily support my belief that we have at M.I.T. one of the best outfits in basic cancer research. We are rightly credited, among other advances, with Phillip Sharp's discovery of messenger RNA "splicing."

Contrary to everybody's expectations, Sharp discovered that in animal cells most chains of messenger RNA, which mediate between DNA and proteins, before being used as molds for making proteins are spliced as if they were strips of movie film: certain portions are eliminated and the cut ends spliced together. Because of this the sequence of units in proteins is different from the sequence in the corresponding genes: some portions of the gene are not represented in proteins. This discovery of an unexpected complexity in molecular genetics is likely to reveal new features in the genetic basis of certain diseases.

Another great first was Robert Weinberg's demonstration and isolation of oncogenes, the genes that in cancer cells are responsible for the cancerous state. Some of those genes differ from a corresponding normal gene in only one nucleotide out of over a thousand. How such a minor change creates an oncogene that converts a normal cell into a cancerous one is an exciting and potentially useful subject for research.

I feel extraordinarily pleased with the Cancer Center. I imagine my pleasure resembles that of the businessman who started a successful business, although in my case there is no significant financial reward. There is something selfish in such pleasures, just as there is something selfish, self-congratulatory in witnessing the development and successes of one's children.

Some of my colleagues are jolly, others somber; some are wide-ranging intellectuals, others narrow in their interests; some are occasionally pains in the neck, with impossible requests or unrealistic deadlines; all are dedicated team people. Like a team of good horses, they pull hard even if their styles of pulling differ. They all tell me that I am a good director, sensitive but no pushover. I accepted the task of directing the Cancer Center with some self-doubt, thinking I might be trying to get away from active science. But it simply broadened my interest. It even taught me a bit about leaking pipes and overflowing sinks and improperly wired machinery. I learned one lesson: a director should choose good people, spread responsibility around, but keep close tabs on what's going on.

It was not hard to add the direction of the Cancer Center to my previous activities: running my own laboratory and doing my teaching. I have wondered about certain academic administrators I have met (not at M.I.T.) who seem to need mountains of paperwork to keep themselves busy. Maybe they know of administrative tasks that no one told me about. My director's desk is usually uncluttered. I answer my own telephone (I can't stand waiting for a secretary to buzz me). I call few meetings and go to as few as possible. Am I neglecting my duties? Or have I discovered an administrator's heaven? Sometimes, alone in my office, I think all is well.

8

The Way of the Imagination

The substance of shadow, that bursts and explodes into sight.
D. H. LAWRENCE, "Lords of the Day and Night"

My upbringing aimed, or at least conspired, to make me an unartistic, unliterary, moderately religious bourgeois concerned mostly with economic success—possibly paying lip service to the arts but without serious emotional involvement. Artistic and literary emotions were something one just could not afford: they might interfere with getting ahead or even with fitting properly into the limited framework within which one's life was supposed to develop. The image of the artist holding a glass of absinthe and consorting with lost women, however titillating, was the specter of what good middle-class parents feared for their children. This was a class ideology, not peculiar to my family: an ideology according to which luxuries should be postponed until after economic success was gained. Intellectual and artistic pursuits were luxuries. Worse still, they were luxuries without the benefit of the prestige conferred by furs and jewels.

I have often asked myself how many of those attitudes I internalized, and to what extent my later interests in the world of the imagination have been shaped by my upbringing. I have even wondered to what extent these interests of mine, which now occupy a small but significant part of my intellectual and emotional life, may have developed out of a rebellion against the outlook of the world in which I grew.

Certainly it was with determination rather than inspiration

that I proceeded to make myself somewhat conversant with the arts and literature. I did so by acts of choice like those that earlier in this book I have defined as commitments. Specifically, they involved decisions that would test my ability to acquire some degree of proficiency in certain fields, without ignoring the possibility that such ventures might be unwise, possibly a source of failure and inner conflict. I was acting as if the world of literature or figurative art or music was there for me to grasp by an act of will.

In no area was the process of commitment as a deliberate choice so clear to me as in my approach to music. I have no musical ear nor, in fact, spontaneous, eager attraction to music. Even now I may go for days and even weeks without sitting down to listen to a record. But when I was about sixteen, noticing the pleasure that music, either practiced or listened to, gave to some of my friends who had been brought up in musical homes, I decided to start going to operas and concerts. I often dozed after the first hour; yet little by little, in a way that must be well known to music teachers, I began to develop a measure of connoisseurship, achieving some success in being able to tell Haydn from Mozart and Handel from Telemann, and, most importantly, enjoyed doing so. Because of the positive reinforcement provided by this limited success, my pleasure in serious music began to grow. My favorites are the eighteenth-century works, whose structure and order probably appeal to a certain rigid element in my personality. My admiration for Beethoven has always been mixed with some unease at his failure to control the display of strong emotions. Such display tends to embarrass me, and I resent it even more in Brahms and other late romantics (as I resent it in personal contacts except when it is an uncontrollable outburst). As for contemporary twelve-tone or atonal music, I have not had the time or patience to acquire the connoisseurship needed to enjoy it, although I sometimes can guess what a composer like my friend Arthur Berger wishes to convey in his compositions. In music as in other art forms I seem to like best what might be called a controlled spontaneity: old jazz songs by Bessie Smith more than modern jazz with its fashionable polish.

I was already in my twenties when I began to look seriously at painting, sculpture, and architecture. The city of Turin was not a center of art, being more famous, I believe, for its museum of Egyptian antiquities than for any collections of classical or more recent art. In my few trips to other cities at the time, I had little opportunity to do more than dutifully glance at such traditional landmarks as Michelangelo's Moses and the Piazza San Marco. In Turin itself I witnessed the rising of a few buildings styled after the contemporary functional fashion of the Dutch and German school. The contrast between these elegant and stark new buildings and the antique, Baroque-based Piedmontese architecture, and even more the contrast with the concrete-and-marble monstrosities of official Fascist architecture, gave rise to heated arguments, but the significance of the novelty in terms of modern artistic sensibilities was then lost on me.

The turning point came with a five-month stretch of army duty in Florence, an experience that any person ignorant of art should have. The very drabness of army life, the slightly degrading experience of forced communal living and irrelevant activities, heightened the value of the city of Dante and Giotto for me and for some of my fellow trainees. Most of them, like me, had sat in on high school courses on art history in a state of excruciating boredom. But in Florence as in only a very few other cities—Siena, Bruges—art is in such harmony with the natural scenery, both in setting and in content, that no matter how resistant I might have been my defenses were bound to break down.

My closest friend in the barracks had read Ruskin, and together we traced the sources of his ideas from Santa Croce to the Pitti, from the Uffizi to the Museo San Marco. Uncertain of my own responses, I wondered at first whether my interest was sincere. I was definitely making a commitment to a new area of experience, but my search for meaning in art was a reasoned, deliberate effort to gain competence and expertise, not the quest for fulfillment of an emotional need. One day, however, something more stirring happened. From the cloister of San Marco I climbed the flight of steps that lead to the upper floor, to what had been Savonarola's dwelling place. Pushing open the door on the landing, I found myself before Fra Angelico's *Annunciation.* Before I could analyze the elements of the painting—the adolescent Virgin bent forward in wonder and fear; the Archangel reverent and almost courting—I was hit by a sudden, spontaneous emotion such as no visual impression had produced in me before. The impact was so strong as to amount almost to a loss of aesthetic virginity, an emotion deep enough to frighten and exhilarate me at the same time —like falling in love at first sight.

I have visited the Annunciation many times since, and looked at its details, and searched again for that first emotion. But one does not fall in love at first sight twice with the same person. Yet the emotion was not just an accident, a coincidence of mood and object and surroundings. Its significance was that it revealed to me my own capacity for aesthetic response.

Since then a number of works of art have evoked in me similarly powerful, immediate reactions: Brancusi's seal, whose mass of polished gray marble immobilizes the tension of a body in motion; the Holbein portraits in the Frick collection—Thomas More gazing into eternity and Thomas Cromwell rooted to earth. In architecture too I recall some strong immediate responses, for example, to the Mazarin Chapel by the Seine in Paris and to the clustered skyscrapers of Rockefeller Center in New York.

Perhaps works like these excite me because they possess a mixture of order and power, a sense that here human beings have achieved some unique and yet accessible height. Perhaps these works of art appeal to me because they have a finality comparable to that of Maxwell's or Einstein's equations. Fusion of parts into a meaningful total can be present in any work irrespective of subject. I find it in a Picasso ceramic of dancing figures that hangs in my home's stairway more than in his Guernica painting. I find it in Arp's sculpture more than in Henry Moore's; and in Mozart more than in Brahms.

The pleasure I find in elements of order and conciseness in art may, I suspect, be a reflection of a constricted, limited element in my personality, which I shall explore more fully later. It may also be a reaction against the bourgeois décor that surrounded my childhood. My preference for Bauhaus in architecture and interior decoration, the pleasure I get from cubist elements in painting and sculpture, and my dislike for "antiques" (except certain uncomfortable, plain wooden New England chairs) all have in common a desire for order and linearity. Hence also my relative insensitivity to Eastern art: the delightful but insignificant Persian miniatures or the Japanese textiles and paintings. My artistic sensibility, cultivated relatively late in life, has remained predominantly Western. I wonder whether this may reflect the strong consciousness of European history that was central to my education. The content of Western art can be grasped much more easily than that of art works based on a different cultural tradition.

There are exceptions, however, to my coldness to Eastern art: the glorious manuscript Korans, which I never fail to visit in the British Museum, and the sculptures of India, whose attraction, however, is diminished by the surfeit of copies: goddesses in large numbers are bound to call to mind chorus girls. As I write this, I think of another object of my admiration, the Assyrian bas-reliefs of Ashurbanipal and other Assyrian kings also in the British Museum. Their stylized ranges of rulers and warriors and chariots and horses, for some reason, give me a pleasure that requires no concern with their historical or geographic distance. Even the absurdly curled royal beards fascinate me. Right next door are the Greek sculptures from the Parthenon. But Greek sculpture leaves me cold; it seems never to transcend its physical subjects.

I do not wish to convey the impression that the arts play a major emotional role in my life. They don't. I believe, however, that my reaction to the visual arts is somewhat more immediate than, for example, my response to music. And any measure of immediacy is valuable to a self-analyzing, self-dissecting mind that tends to dilute emotions by questioning their spontaneity.

From interest in art to the practice of art is a relatively small step. I did take such a step, tentatively and almost shamefacedly, more than once, and always found it hard going. I never really enjoyed the process of "doing." My pleasure was spoiled by concern with the outcome. Such concern is appropriate when I work in science, which is my professional trade; there it is not only appropriate but helpful, preventing idle flights of fancy. I imagine the same is true of the artist for whom art is the central activity. But for the amateur who is trying to get pleasure out of drawing or painting or modeling, fear of failure or overconcern for success can inhibit the joy of performance.

A relatively late attempt to learn to play the piano in my teens was a dismal failure of will and skill. It never came close to giving me pleasure, let alone competence. I drew and painted a little for a while around my fortieth year, but only in rare instances did I get pleasure from the result of my efforts. In Paris, when I was already fifty, I decided to try my hand at sculpting. I had become more and more fond of sculpture, and for some reason it attracted me more than painting as a possible hobby. In Piera Rossi I found an excellent teacher—a bright, energetic woman, several of whose works now surround me at home. Working in clay and wood, I made some progress, and after returning home continued to sculpt on and off for a few years. But a new twist developed, which together with my reluctance to engage in long-range tasks caused me to give up sculpting. Paradoxically, what blocked me was a small initial measure of success. Both I and my teachers thought that some of my pieces of stone work were rather good for a beginning amateur. After that, my attempts were marred, both in execution and in outcome, by a new concern for achievement; and the pleasure was gone from sculpting.

That was the end of my excursion into creative art—a not completely useless excursion because it gave me a keener feeling for the elements of sculpture and of visual art in general. As I shall point out again later, the same streak of perfectionism that blocked me in sculpting tends to weaken all my commitments, not only to art but to other areas of activity, including scientific work. To the extent that perfectionism makes me avoid a task for fear of potential failure, it interferes emotionally with the conscious commitment to task performance. The ambivalence is psychologically interesting, but troublesome in practice.

Inevitably, in the intellectual life of a person like me who is not an artist, literature plays a role greater than other varieties of artistic experience. I do not wish, however, to imply that I am an expert in literature any more than in music or art. I only wish to recapture the development of my literary tastes and preferences in the course of my changing life experiences and shifts of languages.

Since childhood I have been an avid reader, and was a reasonably selective one by the age of twenty, rather late for a well-educated European youth. I studied Latin, Greek, and French in school, the first two not adequately enough to provide reading pleasure. I had private lessons, first in English, later in German, enough to read adequately even before English became my everyday language. I suspect that the experience of reading in several languages contributed to my taste by making me more conscious of form than I would otherwise have been. This taste, which makes me give almost as much weight to the form of what I read as to the content, has helped to save me from trash literature. All told, I must have read no more than a dozen mysteries in my life, and I have never been able to finish any science-fiction book. Sexually explicit writing is often appealing to me, but not the mechanical, hard-core variety.

I mentioned earlier that the first emotional stirring from the reading of novels came to me from the German neo-romantics: Wassermann, the Zweigs, Feuchtwanger, Heinrich and Thomas Mann. I vividly recall the impact of the Stefan Zweig stories *Amok* and *Letter from an Unknown Woman,* which I read first in German. Both stories deal with extreme distortions of romantic love. Zweig has been ignored or dismissed by American critics (though there has been a recent revival of sorts), but one who read him in German cannot, even fifty years later, recall the *Letter from an Unknown Woman,* and words like *"Ich habe dich geliebt, nie hast du mich gekannt"* ("I loved you, but you never knew me"), without a delicious shiver of romantic anguish.

My approach to serious literature was not easy. I remember reading Kafka's *Trial* in about 1930, puzzling about its significance in the same way as I would later puzzle over Joyce or a Pollock painting. One evening, as we argued among friends about *The Trial,* one of them just out of law school cut short the argument by saying: *"The Trial* is simply an accurate description of the Italian judicial system!" A quip with some truth in it. And not about the Italian system alone.

My reading experiences, in those years and later, need to be seen in the light of my school background, with its mixture of faults and merits. The educational approach to literature in the Italian high school was historical and fragmentary. No book was read in its entirety. Apart from a few excursions into foreign literature—one Shakespeare and one Molière play in translation, plus a random sample of French poems and prose—we read fragments of all major and minor Italian authors from the thirteenth to the nineteenth century, including an ample dose of Dante. This preparation gave us a solid foundation in the relation of literature to history; but it was a poor introduction to the art of reading and enjoying books, to searching for their inner structure and integral unity.

The feature of my schooling that in retrospect I value most is one that modern American educational theory rejects: the practice of memorizing poetry and, occasionally also, significant prose fragments. Poems by Dante, Ariosto, Leopardi, Carducci, and others that I learned by heart between the ages of ten and seventeen, as well as some poems memorized while studying French, are still singing in my head. I even recite them while showering. They provide not only pleasure when recalled but also a framework within which other metrics can resonate. Perhaps more important still, memorization of significant poems gives serious students a treasure of word associations that enrich the context of their language and conversation. I feel that the wealth of overtones in British prose, at least up to the early part of the present century, reflected a store of literature internalized and probably memorized in good British and New England schools, a resource that is denied to most present-day American writers (except those who happen to be professional humanists).

Be this as it may, when I left Italy for Paris I had an opportunity for a sudden broadening of literary experience. The first revelation was Baudelaire, whose poems had for obvious reasons been absent from our French classes in high school. An artist friend who lived in Paris gave me a copy of *Les Fleurs du Mal.* There I found many new sensations: golden words of sensuality that celebrate beauty in an almost tangible way, whether in woman's flesh, in jewels, in ships, or in sunsets; fervent revolt against the hypocrisies of society; and an assertion of the dignity of the damned that reminded me of the great figures of Dante's *Inferno.* Little by little, Baudelaire's lines memorized themselves, so to speak, in my mind—lines like *"J'eusse aimé vivre auprès d'une jeune géante,"* which seem to suggest a variety of liberating, transcending experiences.

My Paris years brought me other literary acquaintances: Balzac, Flaubert, Stendhal. The integrity of vision of these writers was a relief after the Italian novels of D'Annunzio and his Fascist followers. Stendhal especially became a favorite. I admire the vitality, the modernity of his characters—Julien Sorel, Lucien Leuwen, and even more that of his women, Mme. Rênal, Mathilde, and best of all the Duchesse Sanseverina. The single-minded concentration of these characters on the fulfillment of their emotional wills has for me an almost heroic quality—they are bigger than life. They seem to be living in an emotional world larger than that of the heroes of Balzac or Flaubert. I never could overcome the feeling that Flaubert's characters do not quite deserve the attention of such a great writer. Stendhal's novels remain among the books to which I return time and again.

Gide must still have been the favorite fare of young Frenchmen in the late 1930s, although the vogue of the *Nourritures Terrestres* had probably passed. Yet I did not read his books during my first Paris stay. Even later he never was a favorite author, probably because of the ambiguity and exhibitionism that permeate his work. Sartre and Camus, whom I discovered many years later, made a greater impact on me because of their existentialist philosophy, which seems to me an apt one for a scientist, as I mention elsewhere in this book. I was intrigued by Camus's psychological dissection of guilt and innocence in *The Stranger* (everyone is innocent) and *The Fall* (no one is innocent), although his characters have less depth than those who struggle with similar problems in Dostoevsky. Sartre's novels, lacking in a sense of humor, interested me less than his plays and essays, where his existential philosophy is more directly evident.

My move to the United States opened to me a new literary world, although I had read earlier some English and American books in translation. The American novels of the 1930s were a surprising introduction to the social and political currents of that period. I remember being shocked and terrified at discovering in Steinbeck's work and in that of other writers the extent of the tragedy that the great depression had wrought in the United States. Nothing resembling the disintegration of social groups that had taken place in America in the early 1930s had I ever seen. In a poor country like Italy, extreme endemic poverty existed and was the cause of great suffering; but its very chronic, centuries-old nature had generated some forms of community adjustment, an interpersonal network of families and family ties that made even the abject rural poverty to some extent tolerable. I also became conscious, both from reading and from direct observation, of the streak of violence running close to the surface in American society. Like everything else on this young continent, violence seemed to be "bigger and better" here than in old Europe. Not even in Fascist Italy had I observed the virulence of national prejudices, the violence of anti-communism, or the arrogance of capitalism already visible in those days. Nor had I been confronted with the menacing rudeness of New York City policemen or restaurant waiters. It was indeed a young, rough country!

The Oxford Shakespeare, still on the shelf next to me as I write, was one of the first books I purchased. Over the years I have read and reread the sonnets and the plays with growing enjoyment as my English-language acculturation grew. I believe, however, that I remain more interested in what Shakespeare's characters say than in what they are. They seem to me, even Lear or Hamlet, to be shallow human beings rather than complex thinkers. Perhaps the precision with which their human drives—power, pride, jealousy—are exposed robs them for me of some of their interest as individuals. Their introspections are moods rather than tortured searches.

My friendship with Kenneth Cameron when we were both teaching and rooming together in Bloomington made accessible to me a broader range of English literature. It was easier to choose what to read and to profit from it with the guidance of a professional and the availability of a well-stocked home library. Perhaps my most significant discovery was that of eighteenth-century literature. From the polemical writings of Swift and Defoe through the novels of Sterne and Fielding, I made the acquaintance of a century that seemed to be growing so civilized, so intellectually vigorous, even optimistic that it made one wish to have been born then (a squire, of course, not a dispossessed field hand). The same liberating winds that blew in the American and French revolutions seemed to me to have gathered in the English literature of that century.

I had not encountered anything like it in eighteenth-century Italian literature. That century had been literarily a fallow period and politically a reactionary one. Instead, I did make a welcome connection with eighteenth-century French literature, thanks to receiving from Jonathan Knight a collection of Diderot's selected works that he had just translated and published. A fellow microbiologist, Jonathan was a remarkable example of the British scientist who is also a first-class scholar in another, remote field.

Diderot gave me as much pleasure as Sterne or Fielding had. The human warmth that I missed in the Johnson-Boswell exchanges I found plentiful among the human beings created by Diderot in *Rameau's Nephew*. Diderot and Voltaire became favorites, read and reread for pleasure as well as reflection. I regret that a wonderful set of the complete writings and correspondence of Diderot, planned for nineteen volumes, which I had been receiving volume by volume from France, has remained unfinished at the thirteenth volume because the publisher went bankrupt.

One usually tries to discover themes in what one reads. Good-humored, commonsense confidence in rationality, and a philosophy of optimism are those that appealed to me in Diderot's writings. This thematic approach I used in what was to be my only venture in literary teaching. For five years, while I was the adviser to biology graduate students at M.I.T., I used to invite the newly arrived students to join me at my home for a Sunday-night literary seminar. One purpose was to encourage these young people to continue to read broadly and purposefully even after entering graduate school in science; another to explore with them the possible relevance of biological concepts to humanistic studies. Each year we adopted a broad theme—inner conflict, human frailty, good and evil—and read books that would range from Greek tragedy to Dante, Sterne, Voltaire, Constant, and down to Kafka, Joyce, Proust, Hesse, or the Bhagavad Gita, as our mood and current *Weltanschauung* dictated. It was an exciting venture, enhanced by the participation of Zella, who, of course, acted as psychologist in residence. I learned much from the students, some of whom had taken excellent literature courses in their college years.

This ended, unfortunately, when I undertook to set up and direct the Cancer Center at M.I.T. I had too many and too diverse things to do, since I had assumed this new task without dropping either my research or my normal teaching load. These were the core of my professional life, which I could not give up without risking dying of boredom as a full-time administrator. Something had to give, however, and that was the literature seminar. But recently I have started it again, this time not alone but jointly with my colleague Frank Solomon, who after a distinguished past as a writer has drifted into biochemistry. Our current program is mostly poetry, from Shelley to Eliot.

Some time ago I received a note from a former M.I.T. student who had been in one of my classes. She reminded me that when she had told me she was planning to spend the summer after graduation learning more biochemistry I suggested that instead she read Virginia Woolf. She claims that she did follow my advice, with the result that instead of chemistry she went into business administration. Shadows of Bloomsbury! Maybe she will be another John Maynard Keynes.

Until a few years ago my tastes in poetry were traditional if not altogether old-fashioned. Baudelaire and Rimbaud were the most modern among my favorite French poets, Whitman and Thomas Hardy among the English-language poets. I sampled modern poetry from its intellectual origins in Mallarmé and his English followers to Ungaretti and Montale, who had been totally unknown to me when I left Italy. But modern poetry had left me baffled and dissatisfied: too much concern for words, I felt, at the expense of immediacy of communication. Fortunately, in 1975 I had the chance of attending Diane Middlebrook's seminar on modern poetry. From this splendid and attractive teacher I learned to read modern poetry in a more intelligent way, repeating it aloud, searching for the relation of word sound to the underlying concepts. I don't know how much progress I made, but at least now I am able to enjoy reading some of the poetry of our times, learning to appreciate how the form of these poems fits the individual fury or irony or sensuality of the poet—as in the poetry of Auden or Adrienne Rich or Erica Jong, or in the more difficult work of T. S. Eliot and Theodore Roethke. I have come to understand why modern poetry has created new dimensions by freeing itself of the repertoire of conventions inherited from the classical and post-classical canons. Unfortunately, my septuagenarian brain is not what it was at ten or twenty, so that memorizing, which used to add to my enjoyment of poetry, is now out of the question.

A poet whose work attracts me strongly is Wallace Stevens, who seems to me to have been able to explore a range of aspects of sensibility, from music to philosophical meditation, in demanding but rewarding verses. The main themes of his poetry—the role of human action in giving meaning to the world around us, his "ideas of order," the conscious creation of the self through imagination, the search for a "supreme fiction"—strike in me the same chord that makes me like Dante, Blake, and Baudelaire. Perhaps it is a taste for the metaphysical, for the effort to see the human experience as intrinsically significant, whether in a religious or an artistic sense. Somehow I feel that Wallace Stevens's vision of the human spirit giving meaning to nature through art is akin to the scientist's vision of giving meaning to nature through science.

Yet the idea of order, the sense of meaning that emerges from the reading of poetry or the contemplation of a satisfying work of art, differs from the order and structure that one seeks in the exertions of science or even in the use of one's rational faculties in day-by-day tasks. The order that art seeks to define belongs neither to the domain of the strictly rational nor to its opposite, the sphere of the irrational (by which I mean the antirational, such as the interpretation of planetary conjunctions as omens in human affairs or of dreams as guides to the stock market). The organizing principles that emerge from the interaction of our artistic sensibility with the world in and around us are what I prefer to call the domain of the "unrational." It is the domain of the intuitive, of the movements that make up our emotions, artistic as well as social: love, pleasure, anger, hatred, and so on. Some of these elements may be embedded in our biological selves, others arise in communal life, from the first interactions of the child with its parents to the later ones with the community, including the multitude of objects, natural and man-made, that continuously impinge on our senses. It seems to me that the world of the imagination, the private domain of the unrational, is a distillation of the emotions and value judgments that an individual has felt and made, and which are predominantly products of social life. My resonance with Fra Angelico's *Annunciation* was not a mystic revelation. It was a sudden condensation of hundreds of inseparable accumulated elements, not rationally analyzable yet forming the background of my emotional response.

Rational, unrational, irrational—these three modes of thinking cover the spectrum of our mental processes. If the rational and the unrational are the most valuable—the content respectively of our task performance and of our emotional life—the irrational cannot be ignored or lightly dismissed. Sometimes it is misunderstood, as when one speaks of "irrational anger" or "irrational expectations," in cases when powerful emotions conflict with rational behavior.

Irrationality, I believe, is the misapplication and misunderstanding of the idea of power. It is what sells twenty million copies of astrological magazines each month in the United States; it is the illusion of finding in oneself or in certain objects the capacity to violate physical laws, as in extrasensory perception or telepathy. It is irrational to claim, as was claimed by a school of Russian scientists, the existence of a kind of radiation that does not behave as all radiation does; it is equally irrational to expect that prayer may have the power to bring rain or to make the stock market go up or down. The irrational creeps in everywhere, into our petty superstitions as well as into the creeds of the great religions. The story is told of a famous physicist on the wall of whose laboratory hung a horseshoe. A friend inquired: "You don't believe in that, do you?" "No," said the physicist, "but I am told it works even if you don't believe in it."

More seriously, I recall flying once at night from the West Coast to the Middle West after learning that my son, Dan, was ill with pneumonia. In the middle of the night I surprised myself by reciting the Hebrew prayers of my childhood. I was by then a convinced agnostic with a touch of antireligious persuasion. Yet under emotional stress I was making deals with the power of a God in whose existence I aggressively disbelieved. Something in my early upbringing had left an emotional trace that was reactivated under stress. I had briefly shifted from my commitment to rationality about religion to an irrational hope for external intervention. It was not a trust in magic; it was a reaching down in a moment of stress into the affective core remaining from my religious upbringing. Which leads me to examine my attitude toward religion.

I was raised in a religious, nonorthodox family. Our religion was, therefore, laced with all the compromises required by a middle-of-the-road approach. It did not provide either the stern reassurance of a strict orthodoxy or the release of a purely emotional cult. In my childhood, temple and prayers (in poorly understood Hebrew) played a theaterlike role, both drama and comedy. The religious holidays were the times of family reunion, the jolly uncle singing Hebrew songs while my father seriously celebrated the Passover seder and mother, aunts, and grandmother fought out the grudges carefully accumulated over the past year.

I was about twelve years old, I believe, when I started asking the fateful question: why should the Jewish religion be the right one just because I was born Jewish? It was the beginning of the assault of reason on the irrational world of the religious beliefs that I had absorbed. From then on I changed step by step from a Jewish believer into a vague deist and finally, around my twentieth year, into a determined atheist. The ceremonies of temple and home had less and less emotional appeal because of the conflict with the loss of religious belief. I began to see religion as the champion of the irrational, hence the enemy of science, attempting to substitute authority for understanding and delusion for reality. Later still, I saw religion as an instrument of social oppression.

Only when I matured into a more complex personality and, through art and literature, began to speculate on the role of the imagination and emotions in human experience, did I begin to understand better the role of the religious component in communal and personal life. Acquaintance with the liberal Protestant churches of America, their identification (in practice if not always in words) of divinity with an impulse toward individual serenity through community of purpose, first made me realize that organized religion provides an opportunity for fusion of human emotion and social action. In this form of religion, closer to the spirit of the Christ of the Gospels than to the stern theology of the Old Testament, the irrational, metaphysical elements of religion become vestigial and cease to interfere with rational interpretation of the physical world.

It was in the civil rights movement, first in the Middle West and later in Boston, that Zella and I saw liberal Christian ministers in action, wise and courageous and solidly in contact with reality, eager to provide opportunities for social action rather than just emotional release for guilt feelings. I recall an evening in Urbana, the evening after five black children had died in the bombing of a church in Birmingham. Anguished, Zella and I could not eat. She suggested we call Arnold, a Unitarian minister whom we barely knew. To my question "What can we do about it?" Arnold replied: "We can do something, right here. We have as much prejudice and discrimination in Urbana as in the South." By nine o'clock there was a meeting in our home, black and white men and women, many of them unknown to us as well as to one another until that day. It was the first meeting of the Champaign-Urbana Civil Rights Committee.

It was not only as a social force for good that I came to respect religion, but also as a medium for aesthetic experience. Whatever its origins and even its dogmatic content, religion is a product of the human imagination, a collective creation through which the yearning to interpret the human condition has traditionally found a major channel of expression. The poetry of Dante, of Blake, of T. S. Eliot is permeated with religious elements that are as essential to its aesthetic power as to that of the paintings of Fra Angelico or of the early Flemish artists. The religious tradition is the custodian of a substantial part of human history, both in its imagination and in its literary and artistic content.

I realize that the biblical literary tradition is waning in our predominantly secular society. But it remains a powerful communal force through which spiritual longings are often phrased, and continues to provide a wealth of shared images that help to express the anguish of individual consciousness. "When the voice that is great within us rises up" (as Wallace Stevens depicts the creative artistic impulse), it often speaks in the words of the prophets or of the Gospels. However irksome this may sound to the rigorously lay-minded, we are sensitive to emotions and aesthetic perceptions that are expressed through readily identifiable religious symbolism. Would Verdi's *Requiem* or T. S. Eliot's *Ash Wednesday* have the same impact if the authors had not been expressing themselves in terms of their Christian commitment?

Having thus mellowed in my views of religion, I did not, however, become a member of any specific religious organization nor did I soften in my objections to organized religion. More specifically, I never thought of returning to organized Judaism in America. My religious upbringing had little in common with the religious practice of the Jewish-American community, with its Eastern European background. My marriage did not bring me closer to the religious Jewish community since Zella, who is Jewish, came from a working-class family that viewed all religious practice as a middle-class pretense. And our son Dan was raised without religious education.

I generally object to institutions making claims on my loyalty or participation because of some abstract collective identification, be it religion, national origin, or profession. I have preferred to reserve my loyalties for individuals or groups of individuals in a freely chosen association. My upbringing as a Jew and my education as an Italian facilitate my intercourse with other Jews and other Italians (just as my fifteen years in the Middle West give me a bond with fellow Midwesterners), but it does not commit me to joining or supporting Jewish or Italian causes as such.

My softened attitude toward religious values has made me actually more intolerant of those features of organized religion that are directed to the satisfaction of irrational drives toward power. The bigotry of organized religion associated with unjust governments; the pernicious attempts to substitute the letter of so-called sacred texts for the observations of science; the use of such texts to justify inequality and oppression—these are the crimes of irrationality into which organized religion is constantly in danger of falling because of the ambiguity of its origins from a principle of authority. The association of organized religion with organized power in religious states, whether Arab or Jewish or Christian, seems to me incompatible both with the sane exercise of power and with the legitimate claims of religion as an expression of an ideal of human brotherhood.

Recently, a United States Federal Court was asked to determine (at substantial cost to taxpayers) the constitutionality of an Arkansas law ordering that equal time be devoted in the schools of that state to the study of "creation science" in addition to evolution. Creation science is the story—taken as factual—of the generation of the universe according to the Old Testament, the holy book of an ancient nomadic tribe called the Hebrews. That particular law was declared unconstitutional, but the effort to impose such teachings continues. The phenomenon is an interesting example of the use of religion by extremist groups in our society to gain control over education.

More distressing, at least to me, however, is what the wide support for such nonsense as creation science (as distinct from biblical scholarship) means in terms of the position of science in the culture of our supposedly scientific society. In fact, our society is permeated not by science, but by an exploitative distortion of science-based technology, as irrational as the irrational aspects of religion. Science itself, the sober evaluation of data, the restrained proposition of hypotheses, and the building of verifiable or at least disprovable theories, is probably as alien to the majority of people in American society as it was to the Hebrews of the Old Testament. Despite a plethora of science writers and reporters, the methods and beauty of science have remained concealed from the majority of the people. This majority includes those legislators, in Arkansas and elsewhere, who see no contradiction between a belief in a biblical universe six thousand years old and the presence of million-year-old oil deposits whose exploitation by special interests they are elected to protect.

The arts are the principal fields where imagination is productively at work, releasing our creative emotions from the fetters of factual reality. Imagination plays a significant part also in the practice of science, although here its sweep is constrained by the structure of the natural phenomena and their relationships. Since imagination is a necessary ingredient in the work of the scientist, we may ask: Is science itself an art? Does imagination contribute to it in the same way as to painting or musical composition or poetry? These questions are often, although not heatedly, debated among scientists themselves. I can only add whatever my own experience as a practicing scientist has suggested, as I reflected upon myself and observed other scientists in action.

To begin with, it may be worth repeating something that has already been asserted, that nothing could be further from the truth than the popular image of how scientists work: observing and measuring objects and phenomena more and more precisely; mechanically analyzing the data; deriving from them clear-cut hypotheses; performing critical tests of these hypotheses; and finally moving on to complex theories. In reality the scientist "plays" with continuously emerging patterns of data and ideas, just as a child plays with toys and learns from the play. Like the child, the scientist devises explanations and chooses among them not only for plausibility but also for aesthetic quality. He often agonizes over what to do next in the same way a painter may in the midst of work on a canvas. Sometimes a scientist agonizes not over the data he has but over those he does not have yet but needs in order to form a coherent picture. Hundreds of facts may bear on the interpretation of a new observation—is the available part of the pattern sufficient to set the new fragment into place? Sometimes, like the playing child, the scientist abandons a search. But sometimes the agony becomes ecstasy—the illumination that clarifies the structure of a problem. This was my ecstasy when I intuited the distribution of bacterial mutants from the seemingly irrelevant contemplation of a slot machine in action, or when I interpreted the revival of irradiated bacteriophage. But the imagination does not just enter into play at special starry moments. The entire work of the scientist, like that of the writer or the painter, is a succession of imaginative efforts—some vast, some narrower, and many that fall flat. Potent illuminations are rare, of course, and it is they that mark the advance of science: Watson and Crick unraveling the DNA double helix and discovering that their finding contained the explanation for the replication of the genetic material; Jacob and Monod unifying in the operon hypothesis the field of gene regulation.

In speaking of the aesthetic qualities of hypotheses, I mean that a hypothesis, besides being an interpretation of data, has some pleasing feature, usually a quality of simplicity or sweep, that satisfies the aesthetic sense of the scientist, even if it should turn out not to be true. A good hypothesis is one that makes strong predictions that can be tested and possibly disproved by clear-cut operations. But an elegant hypothesis also has a quality of unexpectedness, an element of surprise. An interesting example is that of the genetic code, the rules by which the information contained in the DNA of a gene in the form of a four-letter alphabet is translated into the sequence of amino acids—a twenty-letter alphabet—of the protein molecule. Many models, some clumsy, some simple, were suggested for how the genetic code operates. When the solution came, in the minds and the experiments of Sydney Brenner and Francis Crick, it turned out to be extremely elegant in its simplicity and immediate clarity and, once again, as for the double helix, pregnant with new insights. I remember that, after reading a two-page letter explaining the model, I gave an impromptu seminar to a group of M.I.T. students and was so excited that I got utterly confused in my explanations.

Closely related to the role of imagination in scientific research is the question of style. No two scientists, especially effective scientists, function identically, just as no two violinists play Bach's *Chaconne* in exactly the same way. I choose this example advisedly, since both violinist and scientist have limited freedom, the former being bound to the score, the latter to a factual context, but within the range of their freedom each performs with a unique personal style. Just as an experienced listener can tell which virtuoso is playing, so an experienced scientist can often tell which virtuoso is the author of an important scientific paper. Even in a small group with great affinities like ours, it is easy to identify the style and thinking of Delbrück, Hershey, or me.

The differences are not just in the writing, but in the thinking and in the quality of experimentation: from the terseness of Al Hershey's or Charles Yanofsky's work, to the almost whimsical quality in Seymour Benzer's research and writing and lecturing; from the slightly baroque manner of Sol Spiegelman to the aggressive mode of Seymour Cohen. Each of these leading biologists is distinct in style because each is a unique self and projects that self into every aspect of his work.

What about me? Can I characterize my own style in a few words, as I have attempted for some of my friends? That is harder. Assuming that style of work is an expression of one's personality, a compound of drives, inhibitions, and compensatory mechanisms, I may say that my own style in work and scientific exposition is uneven, reflecting my own ready alternation of moods, from excited and aggressive to self-doubting and despondent. I may sometimes spin hypotheses seeking to explain a set of observations and then fail to follow through because of lack of confidence. Like most people who are predominantly verbal, I function best in conversations with colleagues or students; the interpersonal situation gives me self-confidence by providing a testing ground and probably by releasing a productive component of aggression. I may venture to say that a positive element in my scientific life has been a certain dose of resilience, almost doggedness, which has kept me going when the going was hard professionally or emotionally. The same doggedness, the willingness to keep busy, has made me fill my life with enough science-related tasks, such as teaching and writing, to tide me over the inevitable periods when inspiration or luck in research ebbed. I am a strong believer in the importance, for scientists, except possibly the most endowed ones, of being involved in teaching and to have always a book or article underway.

I was told over forty years ago that according to the great physicist Niels Bohr the individual differences in scientific success are ten percent ability and ninety percent willingness to overcome intellectual obstacles. There is some truth in this aphorism. Personal style is in part the way obstacles are faced and, sometimes, overcome.

Let me return to the relation of science to the arts. A major difference is what I may call the uniqueness feature. A work of art —Michelangelo's *Pietà* or Thomas Mann's *Death in Venice*— is clearly unique. It can be copied or imitated, but "it will not happen again." In science too a discovery, once made and recognized, cannot happen again, a self-evident fact that was elaborated by the biologist-philosopher Gunther Stent. But the level of uniqueness is different.

If Michelangelo had not sculpted the *Pietà,* that specific work of art would not exist; nor would *Death in Venice* have been written by someone other than Mann, or *The Tempest* by anyone but Shakespeare. Most scientific discoveries, however, belong to a continuous, collective process of exploration of nature rather than to a series of individual explosions of imagination. If a discovery is not made by X it will be made by Y. In fact, many discoveries have been made almost simultaneously by two or three scientists. They are usually made in different ways because of differences in mode of thinking, style, and imagination, that is, because of aesthetic elements. If Watson and Crick had not discovered the double helix structure for DNA it would probably have been discovered by someone else within a few weeks or months using the same experimental approach. The only difference would have been that *The Double Helix,* the book by Watson, would not have appeared. Likewise, if I had not discovered restriction and modification of bacteriophage they would have been discovered elsewhere within a few months.

Not all discoveries are like that. When Bohr proposed his model of the atom in 1910, it was a unique and daring construction of his imagination, which explained many previously inexplicable phenomena by proposing a dramatic departure from established principles of electrodynamics. Bohr's model was correct in one sense, wrong in another, but it opened the way for the final resolution that was to come fifteen years later. Probably no one else would have invented Bohr's atom, at least not in that way.

In a narrower field, my own proof of spontaneous bacterial mutations by the fluctuation test, as described in Chapter 3, would probably never have been produced had I not done so. It was a critical but unnecessary development that might well have been bypassed in the course of scientific progress. That is, the discovery of bacterial mutations would probably have come from some different, more straightforward experimental procedure and the idea of the fluctuation test might never have emerged.

In scientific work, imagination is restrained by experimental verification, which is a more exacting and immediate form of validation than the one available to works of art, whose success hinges on public and critical approval according to relatively broad criteria. The succession of styles and preferences in the course of the centuries, preserved in artistic and literary works, remains a living testimony to the history of human sensitivity and to the changes it has undergone. Science is not preserved in the same way. It remains alive as a body of knowledge that includes only the concepts and theories that have been sufficiently validated. Even in science the speed of acceptance of a new theory may depend on the dominant thought of a specific time. But no scientist (except historians of science) cares for a disproved discovery or a theory that has proved to be false. We still teach and admire Kepler's rules of planetary motions and Newton's laws of mechanics not because of their historical role but because they are still part of living science, and also because they are witness to exceptional soarings of the human mind, peaks of the scientific imagination at work.

In an effort to claim for art and for spontaneous intuition a heuristic superiority over the scientific approach to reality, Herbert Marcuse stated that "art can communicate a truth, an objectivity . . . not accessible to ordinary language and ordinary experience."* I disagree. The value of art is that it makes it possible to communicate emotions without claim to truth or objectivity, appealing only to a community of feeling and emotional experience. Science's claim to truth and objectivity appeals to a community of logical experience and experimental verification. Except for psychology, science does not deal with emotions, although it grows

*An Essay on Liberation (Boston: Beacon, 1969).

out of a process permeated with emotions. Art in turn can convey emotions because its language grows out of the world of ordinary experience.

I must add to my views of the world of art as the realm of imagination something about my attitude toward entertainment, including the theater, motion pictures, and related media. Theater I love, but mainly in terms of performances: to see a great actor create a part, even in a second-rate play, is what gives me pleasure. Unfortunately, if one lives in the United States away from New York, the treats are rare, and Zella and I almost never manage to catch a first-class play. In my Italian youth I saw the great actors of that time, Marte Abba, Ruggeri, Melato, and later, in Paris, Jouvet. I regret having missed all the great American actors.

Opera I prefer on records, where I can skip the fillers, but I could easily do without it. I loathe musical comedies. The few times I was induced to attend one I was soon asleep. As in opera, only more so, the preposterous mixture of speech and singing in musical comedy makes me acutely uncomfortable.

I like films, although I tend to get impatient or sleepy after about seventy or eighty minutes. Here too I care for great performances more than great stories. Garbo, Bergman, Signoret belong to the artists whose performances leave a permanent impact by creating characters about whom even after many years I still long to know more. Their acting seems to add a dimension to my understanding of human emotions. This feeling is not too different from the sense of gain I get from association with some great scientists: both have to do with exceptional reaches in different realms of achievement. But I can enjoy a good film even without any great actor.

As for the remaining source of entertainment, I must make a statement that is neither a boast nor a confession. I have never (but for a single exception) watched television. (The exception was a program in which eight American socialists spoke as a panel.)

It is not easy to explain why, since television became available, I should have deliberately avoided the tube. Evidently not from experience—I had none. Dan and Zella have been normal TV watchers and I have often had to make complex arrangements to accommodate my idiosyncrasy. Nor have I rejected TV in protest against what some people claim it does to children; other equally competent people say TV helps children's learning in many ways.

I have wondered if my avoidance of television is just a high-brow pose. But, knowing myself, I am sure that in that case my TV avoidance would have made me feel guilty, as I do feel whenever I catch myself putting on an act. I feel neither guilt nor pride about my TV behavior, just a sense of freedom from a potential addiction. My rejection extends also, but not so completely, to radio. (I do try to listen to reports of snowfall on winter mornings, usually missing them because I have no idea how to locate a news program before I have to leave for work.)

The best explanation I can give of my denial of TV is to call it an act of witness: a witness for privacy and against excess informational input, as well as superfluous entertainment. There is a perverse part of myself that seems to resist passive entertainment and time fillers. Up to the age of about twenty I used to play bridge or poker, but I have not played cards since, solely because of lack of interest. The unending repetitiousness of the playing process, deal after deal, bored me stiff. And, as a means to fill evenings in dull company, there are better ways than games to combat boredom.

My resentment or fear of inputs and canned entertainment has more to do, I believe, with something that I have already mentioned: my reluctance, whether in science or in other areas, to take in "facts" that I do not at present know how to use. I have colleagues who eagerly await the latest issues of scientific journals in order to devour them from cover to cover. My reaction, as I have said, is to hope that the issue will not contain anything that I should read. In general, I detest facts unless I can fit them into some framework of active involvement. At lectures and seminars I retain only what fits my research or my teaching. I daily scan the *New York Times,* but read only those articles that deal with whatever political or professional or financial issue I may currently be involved with. As a result, I am an altogether underinformed person, efficient, however, within my chosen interests. Television I don't need, and I therefore stand as a somewhat ridiculous witness against the passivity encouraged by the tube.

9

In the Political Arena

> Make us one new dream, us who forget,
> Out of the storm let us have one star.
> CARL SANDBURG, "Prayer after World War"

Looking back on the many years of my life, from adolescence through maturity and on to advancing old age, I wonder how my political self grew and acquired its definition. My life has spanned decades of turmoil probably unprecedented in the history of humankind. It has seen the liberal faith of our fathers and grandfathers in a forthcoming era of peace shattered by two world wars and by innumerable instances of naked exercise of brutal power. It has seen their faith in civilized human behavior destroyed by the organized brutality of totalitarian regimes. It has seen a supposedly dying colonial oppression replaced by an even more intolerable wave of racially motivated aggressive nationalism.

At the same time my life has seen, as against the flow of disappointments, the counterflow of the struggle for a more just world. Revolutions have destroyed remnants of feudal power and replaced them with more or less successful charters of popular sovereignty. Peaceful or military insurrections have freed many nations from colonial suzerainty. More important, throughout the century and despite many disappointments, the movement against all forms of oppression has continued, stronger in some countries or continents than in others. It is based on the solid belief that long-term political options are not the outcome of capricious, random events but are determined by economic relations among human beings and social classes and are therefore potentially modifiable.

Over the years there grew in me a vision of society as a non-homogeneous structure within which, at any one time, I could distinguish certain dominant features no matter how confusing and fragmented the general picture might appear to be. Most important, I came to be conscious of the existence of a principal cleavage line, a dichotomous subdivision of society in terms of economic status and power into what can roughly be defined as the domains of right and left. The dividing line may be clear at some points in time and space and blurred at others. More specifically, on one side of the line I saw the realm of the economic establishment, with all its ancillary groups and structures, tending to perpetuate existing power structures; on the other side the realm of socialism and radicalism, which envisages the need for fundamental changes in that structure. Between these two alternatives I chose the option of socialism.

My commitment to socialism is essentially a commitment to the idea of economic justice and equality, a commitment fed by anger at the gross inequalities visible in society. This commitment may also have emotional roots not immediately related to politics. The sight, throughout my childhood, of my parents' borderline economic status and the shakiness of their class identification ("We cannot afford politics," my mother would say) made me wish to be solidly on one side or the other of the dividing line between the economically secure and the insecure. But essentially my commitment to socialism is a social choice, a commitment to economic equality. I am a socialist because I wish to help build a society with less inequality and more material and personal fulfillment for a majority of people. I envisage a socialist society as one based on planning for greater equality: a society in which private ownership, which promotes wasteful competition and generates monopoly, is replaced by public ownership and socially planned production and distribution. In a socialist society, planning for economic growth and progressive decrease of economic inequality would be experimental in scope and rate, involving a variety of forms of group participation and permitting maximum personal freedom consistent with the overall economic goals.

How is democratic socialism to be built? The move to socialism will inevitably entail a struggle, whose nature, however, may be different in different countries. In France or West Germany, for example, the existence of powerful anticapitalist parties, socialist or communist, may lead to a gradual shift as elected representatives of the left gain hold of more power in the government and carry out a more or less smooth shift from private to public ownership of the means of production. In the United States, in the absence of a politically unified and powerful left, different paths may evolve. For example, American capitalism may go through a period of corporatism: the capitalists may create centralized structures directed to maximizing profits, not by growth and equity distribution but by elimination of whatever bargaining power the workers have gained. Such corporatist structures, failing to provide an acceptable economic level of growth and equity, may generate massive opposition and be vulnerable to takeover by some energetic group of socialist planners. Thus socialism might come to America by a revolutionary takeover of institutions created to defend capitalism.

My political commitment is neither a fanatical allegiance to a set of political propositions nor a rationally based conclusion from study and meditation on the nature of human society. Rather, my commitment to political radicalism is a calculated existential choice that may be reinforced or weakened by practice but always remains self-questioning and subject to eroding doubt. It is, indeed, like Pascal's wager as to the existence of God, a wager made with trepidation and yet with deep seriousness. It is also not a commitment made once and for all in a static way. It has developed by steps, little by little, growing with a growing awareness of social injustice, with active involvement in political action rather than with any deep study of political science. In taking sides on political issues I never quite ignored the possibility that those on the opposite side might be right and I wrong. I have often anguished over this possibility. Yet the awareness of the element of relativism in the realm of human affairs has not hindered my political activity. Neither has it enabled me to overlook political differences in personal relations, as if politics were a game played by teams of aristocratic gentlemen who, like politicians in Victorian England, after a verbal debate enjoy a jolly weekend in some country manor.

The awareness of a society split by a more or less clear cleavage line between right and left, and especially the impatience with passive acceptance of social injustice, have inevitable consequences for matters ranging from personal relations to the nature and setting of one's work and the tensions by which one is driven. They need not make enemies of those who are on the other side of the line, nor necessarily make friends of those on the same side; but they provide a minimal criterion for meaningful association. It is impossible for a committed radical to have an intimate personal relation with a true conservative, even though the two may have complete trust in each other. Common political orientation shares with love certain qualities of openness and mutual trust. Like love, it does not by itself guarantee an easy personal relation. Not all fellow radicals are friends, just as not all conservatives are antagonists.

In our country a radical is often thought of as a wild-eyed terrorist, ready to demolish the next church in order to destroy religion or the next county courthouse to destroy the law. In reality, the churches that are bombed are usually black churches destroyed by Ku Klux Klansmen; and the only use I have had for a courthouse was to be married in the one of Monroe County, Indiana, by a kindly, exceedingly fat Republican judge. The radicals I know are often the gentlest human beings, like Howard Zinn or Daniel Berrigan. The violent image of radicals is on a par with the extreme leftist view of conservatives as gentlemen in pin-striped suits meeting at regular intervals to drink cocktails of metaphoric workers' blood. In truth, radicals and conservatives are like teams of horses pulling on opposite sides of the same structure. Someday, somewhere, something will give.

The question at hand is, how did my radical commitment develop? How and when and why did I become a radical, a relatively gentle one, without bombs in the pockets of my usually conservative clothes, armed only with a deep resentment of social injustice?

My background in Fascist Italy did not foster political rebellion. Yet before I was ten I had witnessed without comprehending it the truly revolutionary movement of the Turin working class. On our way to and from a summer place in the hills we passed by the Fiat factory, occupied and operated by its workers. Later we heard gunshots from the skirmishes between Blackshirts and Communist workers. This happened rarely in our neighborhood, of course, because most such battles took place when groups of *squadristi,* the toughs in the Fascist movement, went to seek quarrels in the workers' neighborhoods. It was *de rigueur* for middle-class adolescents, including my brother, to sport some Fascist emblem on their lapels or even carry a set of iron knuckles in their pockets, only to rush and hide these tokens of involvement at the first sign of danger. The whole scene had, as things often do in Italy, a farcical quality. But by the time many young and old people started seeing what was behind the anti-Communism of the Fascist movement, it was too late. Italian democracy had collapsed along with the abortive revolutionary movement.

After 1922 Fascists ruled the country. As I already mentioned, they did not rule the spirit of the nation. As the philosopher Norberto Bobbio was later to write, "it was a point of honor not to be mistaken for a Fascist." This was so, presumably, among intellectuals. It was so also, to some extent, among us very young. We discussed, while in our middle teens, whether it was preferrable to be "against" openly or to give the appearance of allegiance to the regime. Perhaps some of my school comrades were already reading political books, which the Fascist government never got around to destroying but only banished from the school curricula. While in high school I witnessed a quickly suppressed episode in which some kids, one class ahead of mine, printed on the school mimeograph and distributed anti-Fascist leaflets. The main culprit was expelled "from all public schools of the kingdom." Within the faculty the battle for and against the expulsion, as described twenty years later by my socialist teacher Augusto Monti whom I mentioned earlier in a book on Italian schools, saw honest men, whether members of the Fascist party or not, ranged against cowards. The cowards won.

I was rather oblivious of these happenings. Ours was the first group of students among whom anti-Fascism did not raise its standards, partly because responsible teachers avoided exposing us to politically provocative debates. Yet I apparently had in myself some spontaneous spark of class consciousness or hatred of oppression. Once, when I was twelve or thirteen, I went to our maid, whom my mother and grandmother had threatened to fire, and told her to stick to her guns: they were only trying to scare her. The silly girl, of course, repeated what I had told her, and there I was, accused of family and class betrayal. I suspect that I apologized, however unrepentant I remained—my first compromise.

Later years brought more significant conflicts. A few times, especially after 1935, I was approached by colleagues or other acquaintances who, as I realized only later, were trying to recruit me into one or another anti-Fascist group. I failed to respond, partly because I was too naïve and lacked a political framework that could accommodate these advances. Also, those feelers were usually couched in abstract philosophical terms, presumably inspired by a Marxist theory that was to me unfamiliar and alien. Then as later, my political interests if any tended to be practical rather than theoretical. If they had asked me first to help address envelopes or mimeograph leaflets I might have said yes, even though I would have been properly scared. But philosophical arguments about monism vs. dualism, idealism vs. materialism seemed to me at that time an exercise irrelevant to politics. The fault was perhaps of my schooling, which treated me to a feast of languages and mathematics and gave me only the shallowest background in philosophy and sociology.

Pulls in the other direction were not altogether absent. Fascism, for all its mixture of incompetence and oppression, was not wholly lacking in effective display: rallies, parades, symbols from ancient Rome were always around us; and a natural drive to communion generated at times an emotional response to this aesthetic appeal. I was usually skeptical, but I recall wavering once. It was in Rome, while visiting a mausoleum dedicated to the "Fascist martyrs," a few dozen early followers of Mussolini who had died in street battles. The carefully planned atmosphere of that memorial, its churchlike silence and soft music (Muzak had not yet invaded the markets) evoked in me a disturbing sense of veneration. I had to muster my distrust as a defense against seduction. Such episodes of internal, emotional flirtation with the all-pervading Fascist influence never went far, not even when, after completing my military service as a second lieutenant, I was obliged to accept transfer from the Army to the reserve of the Fascist militia. The alternative would have been to request not to be transferred, a gesture that would have been a public political assertion for which I clearly lacked both conviction and courage.

It was risky, although not too risky, to stand up and be counted. But no form of organizational activity against the regime was tolerated. The punishment for propaganda was twofold: a period in jail or "confinement"—exile in some godforsaken village, like the one that inspired Carlo Levi to write *Christ Stopped at Eboli* —and, after one was released, ostracism by "decent" former friends.* I recall one evening when a fellow student, Sion Segre, whom I did not know well, appeared at a concert after returning from a two-year stint in jail. He had been sentenced for bringing into Italy anti-Fascist leaflets and other propaganda materials. A few of us greeted him and sat with him, within a circle of empty seats; we did not feel it especially daring to sit with the jailbird. But his former closest friend, supposedly a staunch anti-Fascist, stayed away from him. Next day, he called to explain how hard it had been for *him* to stay away—to keep from doing what decency would have prescribed.

Strangely enough, it was during my service as an officer in the

*New York: Farrar, Straus, 1953.

Italian army that I became aware of the extent of anti-Fascist sentiment. While on duty in the Alps I was invited one evening to a dinner of young officers. When I got there I found out that the occasion was to celebrate the defeat of the Fascist militia at Guadalajara in the Spanish Civil War, a battle that tragically pitted Italian militiamen against Italian fighters in the International Brigades. The rejoicing was actually political: Mussolini's participation in the overthrow of democracy in Spain had been castigated.

Then and for years afterward, Spain remained the touchstone of political identification throughout the Western world, almost as if that ideal line I invoked above as the demarcation between right and left ran through the Spanish battlefront. We did not know or understand then that the Spanish tragedy was the rehearsal for the forthcoming struggle between different worlds. In Italy the war in Spain was officially labeled as the defense of Christian life against godless Communism, a formulation that has apparently not aged since and has been adapted to other situations in the following decades.

It was my move to France that gave me the opportunity for broader perspectives and more factual information. From the time of that move I date my serious concern for politics. Politically, France was still the France of the nineteenth century. Politics was debated as intensely as baseball is debated in American beer bars. There were cafés of the left and cafés of the right. I remember once going unknowingly into an Action Française restaurant and feeling like a black in a Klan club. Even physicists were split; the left and right physicists had their own separate seminars.

The intensity of discussion, the availability of political newspapers commenting on the news from every shade of the political spectrum, from Action Française to anarchism—none of them approaching the *New York Times* in journalistic competence but all superior to it in fervor—would have made it hard for an Italian exile to keep out of political involvement. And politics was not all in newspapers. I witnessed the May 1 march to the Père Lachaise cemetery, a million workers paying tribute to the martyred workers of 1871. These too were lessons in politics. And I was eager to be involved, realizing how much the years of Fascism had gone toward atrophying my faculty for independent thinking.

In Paris, I discovered, everyone but the French bought three, four, five newspapers each day, not searching for bits of political news as I do now when I read the *Times*, but comparing viewpoints and comments by some of the most eminent European intellectuals, then gathered in Paris as refugees from Fascism in its many forms.

Most of the recent refugees from Mussolini's anti-Semitism were not political. They sat in comfortable *rive droite* hotels bemoaning their past comforts. One, I recall—a peculiar type of refugee—ordered from Italy his favorite kind of sausage. But the younger exiles, like me, were avidly seeking a political education. I met Italians of the right and of the left. The former were Liberals, a name that in Italy stood for the conservative party, the party of the bourgeoisie that had been in power before Mussolini. The word did not have the connotations that it has in America, where a liberal is viewed as a defender of personal freedom—sometimes seen by conservatives as a disrupter of God-fearing society and by radicals as a compromiser in matters of social justice. Among leftists I met communists, socialists, republicans, in those days still occasionally in contact with each other under the influence of the Front Populaire movement. Such contacts were more or less incidental since my work kept me away from the circles where politics was a full-time if unremunerative occupation. But I read a lot. I read Croce, whose liberalism, couched in lush Neapolitan-school language, impressed me more for its style than for its politics. I read Marx and Engels, finding their economic analysis of society persuasive, their vision of a future classless society inspiring, their predictions of the future course of society naïve. Of Lenin's books those written in action were interesting, the philosophical disquisitions much less so.

From that time dates my political orientation as a somewhat unstructured radical. My initial commitment was shaky and uncertain, without a solid body of analytical knowledge to bolster it.

Ever since, my political commitment has been predominantly personal and emotional, not dependent on continuous reinforcing by factual information or historical analysis. It is not a fire that needs to be continuously stoked by indignation at the lies of conservatives or neo-conservatives or reinforced by denunciations in small-circulation newsletters. It is kept alive and reinforced mainly by the spectacle of injustice wherever it occurs, whether in the United States or the Soviet Union or Israel. I am enough of an *homo politicus* to realize that, since politics deals with human society, it does not deal with Truth or Facts but only truths as weighed on a relative scale and facts as witnessed by inevitably biased observers. Absolutes are incompatible with human consciousness, so that any commitment is a mechanism that enables us to act despite doubts and uncertainties. Without believing that I am right in the absolute, I can feel right strongly enough to oppose those whom I see as sources of injustice and causes of suffering. I suspect this was also the basis of the political philosophy of Sartre.

The world of refugee politics in Paris was a world of ideological parties, not of meaningful political action. The French political scene, however, presented in those post-Munich days ample sources of political education. The collapse of the Popular Front had brought the "Center" to power. For the first time I observed the so-called liberal center in action and began to learn how ambiguous liberal positions and centrist practices can be. Centrist politicians like Daladier and Bonnet were not defenders of the Popular Front reforms but watchdogs for the conservative capitalist class, which feared its own extremist right wing almost as much as it did the Communist left. There I first learned, I believe, to search for the line between right and left I mentioned earlier, following it as it wove among groups irrespective of their labels. I learned to ask, where do X or Y stand on certain issues and what do they do about it? I had entered France a political ignoramus; I left it a deeply political individual, a socialist—unattached, without party loyalties or allegiances, but existentially committed to a socialist orientation. However fragile my commitment was at first, it gave me self-respect as a member of society such as I had not felt in my Italian experience.

The move to the United States exacted another and more diffi-cult effort at political understanding. The great liberal republic did not resemble European democracies either in its political structure or its range of tolerance. While I was in Lisbon, waiting for my boat to sail, I was cryptically warned by a Portuguese chemist, a socialist who had spent two years in California: "Be careful when you talk about right or left in the States. The U.S. is not as easygoing as Fascist Italy or Portugal. Americans have no politics but take them seriously." He was right. One of the first things I heard of after arriving was the celebrated Bertrand Russell scandal of the previ-ous spring: the lunatic right-wing fringe of New York City had got a judge to rule that City College could not employ Russell, the great philosopher and mathematician, because he preached immorality (such as allowing children to see their parents without clothes on). Such know-nothing groups seemed to me more dangerous than the extremist groups of French politics, just as a bull blind with rage is more dangerous than a lion driven by hunger. The hunger of the American people seemed, anyway, to have been relatively well assuaged compared to that of my Italian compatriots. I remember my surprise when I read that the American working class was "fighting for bread and butter." Where I came from butter was a luxury and bread was often in short supply.

I arrived in New York in the midst of the 1940 presidential campaign. Like everyone I knew, I hoped that FDR would be reelected and be the leader who would stop and ultimately defeat Hitler. The campaign in itself was an education: two parties with similar programs on almost every big issue, representing different power centers within the establishment, plus a motley array of nonelectoral, purely ideological groups on the right and left. The Italian political-refugee crowd existed on the periphery of Ameri-can political life, liberal-conservatives being mostly Democrats, while a half dozen leftist groups bickered among themselves in continuous "united front" negotiation. In New York I met, among others, Randolfo Pacciardi, tall, handsome, somewhat narcissistic, the chief of the Republican party of Italy in exile. He had been a commander of Italian anti-Fascist volunteers in Spain and would later be a vice premier of postwar Italy. For his newspaper I wrote my first series of political articles, on the class structure of the Italian schools. I have forgotten both the name of the newspaper and the pseudonym I used; but I do recall (such is the power of the ego) that Gaetano Salvemini, the venerated leader of anti-Fascist intellectuals, told Pacciardi that my articles had settled the issue of the Italian school system. I also wrote a couple of articles on the historical roots (or absence of such) of Italian anti-Semitism, and in so doing learned about the writings of important nineteenth-century scholars, such as Carlo Cattaneo, whose names Fascism had blotted out. These articles were never published, however; I believe that by then Pacciardi's paper had collapsed for lack of funds.

Speaking of newspapers, discovering the *New York Times* was a pleasure for European refugees, irrespective of their political alignment. The appearance, more or less justified in fact, of olympian impartiality of this newspaper was a welcome change from the sectarianism of most newspapers of France. It also added somehow to the feeling that in the United States one was on more solid ground, in a country where a compact of truthfulness was at least possible. Later, of course, as I grew more sophisticated, I learned to be alert to the hidden agenda behind the impartiality of the American press—to see that the word "fit" in the *Times*'s slogan was a shield for conformity. The *Times* had, in fact, played a shameful role in the Russell affair. Yet, for over forty years, I have found any *Times*-less days disappointingly empty. And over those decades I never ceased to be grateful to newspapers like the *Times* and the Washington *Post* for their superb reporting, even on the most controversial issues.

For a while, my budding professional career put political activities in abeyance: Cold Spring Harbor and Nashville were not the most favorable arenas for politics, especially for a newcomer to this country. The war, and the fact that I was not in the army, made me reluctant to engage in political discussions with people who might have their children on the front and might resent my meddling. It was a reassuring sign that never in those war years even in Tennessee was I the target of snide or chauvinistic remarks. In Nashville I found a community, including its academic component, for which politics was a vague, irrelevant, rather distasteful segment of experience, except when it resonated with some almost archetypal slogans absorbed in childhood. There, my addiction to the *New York Times* was taken as an affectation or an innocent flaunting of deviance.

In Nashville my friend Max Delbrück and his wife, Manny, surprised me in a different way. Their attitude toward politics, especially class-oriented politics, was to consider it as a silly and even distasteful joke. Not that they were uninvolved in world events and the consequent human suffering. On the contrary, they were then and later eager helpers of persecuted individuals. I believe, in fact, that they have been among the largest contributors to Amnesty International. But the politics of right and left was not for them. Politicians of any color, and even I, seemed to them ludicrous. Max even teased me because in Nashville I bought the "liberal" newspaper rather than the more traditional "conservative" one. (They were owned, I believe, by the same publisher.) I came to respect Delbrück's point of view, although it could not be mine. The political commitment had become too important a part of my personality.

The fall of Mussolini in August 1943 found me in New York. Hopes ran high in the Italian refugee community and provided an occasion for parties, banquets, and even a private "united front" theatrical sketch. But the news of the German takeover in Italy soon squelched the hopes of imminent liberation. For me that was a crucial moment: I realized that I had become American in every sense except formal citizenship, and I had no wish to return to Italy. As I'll recount later when I explore the recesses of my sentimental life, the break was not only with Italy but also with emotional connections that until then I had believed to be viable. So, when I went back to Indiana that fall season (which was marred by the only life-threatening illness of my life—the revenge of a virus), I was a somewhat different man, eager to participate in every aspect of American life, politics included.

There was at Indiana University a group of faculty members holding a range of progressive positions and active mainly in campus politics. I found such activities rather unexciting: I had not yet grasped the significance of defending and promoting democracy at all possible levels. More interesting to me was an electoral campaign for a Democratic candidate for Congress. The idea came from my friend Kenneth Cameron. A Committee of Independent Voters came into being, waging its own campaign separately from that of the Democratic candidate himself. It succeeded in advertising the real issues, national and local, and acted as an effective gadfly in the entire state. Yet the candidate went down to defeat. The campaign itself was fun to watch. The effort although serious had interesting sidelights, including fundraising parties that roused a good deal of sexual excitement and activity —all for the good cause. On Election Day it turned out that the chairman of the Independent Voters Committee had forgotten to register to vote.

Such details apart, in observing the campaign I learned a lot about electoral politics: the multitude of issues, the role of professional party politicians, the importance of solid leadership, and the difficulty of trusting well-meaning but less committed members of a committee to perform their assigned tasks without constant prodding. I also realized the importance of choosing the issues on which to do battle. A group of progressive intellectuals, no matter how hard-working, has no chance of success except in situations when a campaign is wide open, with candidates close enough in strength so that a relatively small push can tip the balance. As I later learned, this principle applies to all sorts of issues, not only electoral ones: a small plus can be effective when approximately equal forces are opposing each other. I also learned, then and later, that electoral campaigns are not a suitable vehicle for long-term political organization of radical forces. Campaigns on emotional issues such as war or racial injustice yield more permanent results.

Yet my next exercise was again an electoral one. When we moved to Cold Spring Harbor in the fall of 1945, just after our marriage, Zella found out that an American Labor party candidate was the only opponent available to run for Congress against the Republican boss of solidly Republican Suffolk County, one of the bastions of conservatism in New York State. The ALP man had agreed to accept the Democratic nomination on condition that he did not have to give speeches or campaign in person. And no one was doing it for him. It was a splendid opportunity for us to slay the dragon, visit the countryside, and make new friends. So Zella (and I unofficially since I was not yet a citizen) got things moving.

We toured Long Island seeking votes in our ancient Dodge, which developed gear troubles every twenty miles or so. The only seriously organized labor in the county was at the state hospitals. There we met some wonderful Irish-Americans, who invited us to their homes, offered us beer and whiskey, helped us fix the car gears, and told us their sad tale of minimal wages and dreadful working conditions. We met shopkeepers fed up with the local county administration, and we met a peculiar group that had lived for decades in the shadow of the great estates of the island— servants, stable keepers, and gardeners. Many of them were filled with enough revolutionary spirit to vote Democratic. By the end of the summer, when we left to return to Indiana, we had canvassed the county and been well toasted with Italian wine and Irish whiskey. Came November, our candidate polled 37 percent of the vote, the highest Democratic vote ever in that district till then. And the seeds may have remained: since then that Congressional district has sent a Democrat to Congress eleven times.

This episode illustrates the flexibility of my political attitude. The ideological line between left and right weaves its path separating establishment from its opponents, irrespective of party labels. In the sixties, in Lexington, Massachusetts, I voted regularly for a distinguished Republican Congressman, Bradford Morse, who once said publicly, "I am the only Republican for whom Dr. Luria ever voted." Even that was not quite correct.

My experience with the hospital workers in Long Island had intrigued me enough so that after my return to Bloomington I decided to join the University Teachers' Union and see whether it could become a force for good in the university. Anyone who has not tried to organize a faculty union has missed the "infirm glory" of being looked upon with distrust by administrators and with embarrassment by colleagues. It is a rather pleasant feeling, especially if one is, as I was by then, comfortably if not aggressively confident in one's professional invulnerability. The Indiana University Teachers' Union never had more than twelve members, although our self-assurance made us look as if we were at least fifteen. Such self-assurance, of course, was not totally empty. We were closely tied to the local labor federation, mostly covering the building trades. We were also connected with the powerful State Federation of Teachers, attending their meetings and enjoying their confidence. I learned then to admire the surprising energy of the members of the schoolteaching profession. Never before or again did I participate in meetings where most members rose at five, took long walks, usually two-by-two, arguing about teaching methods and salary scales, and after several hard-working sessions stayed up till midnight arguing about everything under the sun. I suspect natural selection must be at work: only individuals with such energy would survive years of exposure to schoolchildren.

I believe our University Teachers' Union accomplished something in the way of salary raises and, more important, in terms of faculty gumption in facing the forthcoming McCarthy period in one of the most reactionary states of the union. It also accomplished my removal from Indiana to the University of Illinois. I was president of the Teachers' Union in 1950 when the State and County and Municipal Workers Union decided to organize the university workers. The Teachers' Union was asked to help and did so, to the extent of my giving a mild talk, which, taken out of context, was represented by the local newspaper not only as a clarion call to unionization but also as a denunciation of the university administration. An offer from the University of Illinois was then pending, and a call from my dean soon informed me that it could not be matched. No harm done—the unionization drive succeeded, the workers' union came into being. And Zella and I and Dan moved about 150 miles west to Urbana.

Before that move another campaign had attracted me, that of the ill-fated Progressive party of 1948. In the East the Progressive party was seen, as it certainly was, as a complex sum of influences, goals, and gripes. To us in the Middle West it seemed a genuine enough new political movement against the social retrenchment of the Truman years and the beginning Cold War, with its testing of atom bombs and the growing danger of nuclear war. As a delegate from Indiana I attended the Progressive party convention in Philadelphia in July, traveling from Cold Spring Harbor and, after the convention, spending the night in an apartment shared by five social workers, former girl friends of Zella's at Brooklyn College. If the convention was not much, the rest of the evening was cheerful. By that time it was clear that the movement had failed. It had failed to capture the imagination of moderate Americans, who contrary to expectation were not eager to recapture the sense of mission that had existed during the war. And it had failed because it had become a movement of the left, isolated from the mainstream of American politics.

I was a pollwatcher at the fall election, certified, however, by the Temperance party, since the Progressive party was not eligible in Indiana to appoint watchers. By 9 P.M. on election night it was evident that the Progressive party was crushingly beaten, so I adjourned to an all-night cocktail party—the end of my only experience in temperance. It was also the end of any illusion I might have had that a political party that sprang from a protest movement, without a solid constituency—be it in labor or farmers or any other economically coherent group—could perform the miracle of creating a mass third party in America. Traditional party politics, I realized, was too solidly controlled by the establishment to allow space for any but possibly some revolutionary new party. Yet such a party may not emerge for a long time, short of economic disaster or nuclear war—both rather undesirable developments.

Politics in my years at the University of Illinois was more of an institutional than a national activity. The firing of the university president was just one episode in a concerted campaign by the conservative forces in the state to take control of the university as a power base. A famous football player, Red Grange, by then a prominent Republican on the board of trustees, delivered the *coup-de-grâce* and President George Stoddard was out. (His successor was mainly distinguished by his calling all Jewish professors on the receiving line by some randomly chosen Jewish-sounding surname.)

Within the university the longer battle was for control of the chapter of the American Association of University Professors, a powerful organization that influenced all aspects of faculty policy, both on campus and in the state legislature. The chapter was at the time in the hands of the right, meaning a group of conservative, anti-Stoddard professors. At the crucial meeting, the right changed the agenda to put the voting first, in the reasonable expectation that many left members (including a group of physics professors) would arrive too late to vote. I therefore stood and filibustered for fifteen minutes, until our people came in and the election could take place. And indeed we won.

What I learned then is the importance of parliamentary procedure, or rather, the importance of being conversant with it and willing to use it effectively. Parliamentary procedure of the Anglo-American kind is utterly unknown, or at least unapplied or inapplicable in Latin countries. No one there would see why another fellow should talk first just because he had raised his hand first: each believes that what he has to say is clearly (to him) more urgently needed. No French or Italian chairperson of a meeting could ever be prevailed upon not to answer in person all questions that come up. One system is not necessarily better than the other: one makes for order, the other for spontaneity. The Anglo-American system gives everyone a feeling of fairness, even when manipulation is at its worst; the Latin system leaves everyone frustrated even when the issue is resolved.

I'll always remember a historic meeting in Mexico City, where an international committee was formulating a resolution on biological warfare. The American representatives were Roger Porter, a thoughtful and highly respected statesman of microbiology on the international scene, and I. The chairman was André Lwoff, the most eminent microbiologist of France, pillar of the Institut Pasteur, and Nobel laureate in 1965. The draft document had been written in a strange Anglo-Swedish language by an eminent Swedish scientist. Every attempt to modify and translate the document met the chairman's obvious conviction that only he knew enough English to do so. Moreover, at each session the Russian representatives reappeared with what looked like the same document, but with hidden insertions that had been rejected the previous day. Roger and I spent hours after each meeting reconstructing a readable document. Surprisingly, out of that chaos came a formal declaration outlawing biological warfare, a declaration that was later unanimously adopted at the United Nations. What counts is the result more than the procedure.

By the late 1950s McCarthyism in its least gentlemanly form was on the wane, but the nuclear danger was waxing. A new kind of struggle had to be fought. The U.S. and Soviet governments were testing nuclear bombs like mad, megatons of explosives and their by-products being released in the atmosphere. In the U.S. every protest by concerned groups met with the standard answer: the Government knows the facts and the consequences, you don't, so pipe down. It was time for counterforce action. The effective steps came from Linus Pauling, the famous chemist and antiwar leader. Pauling's driving personality, brilliant wit, piercing eyes, and ebullient self-assurance made him a natural leader, in science as in politics. In 1957 he drafted and circulated among scientists a statement that declared, in brief, that we knew as much about the effects of radiation and hydrogen bombs as did government scientists, that the tests were terribly dangerous, and that it was up to the government to prove us wrong.

I was one of the ten initial signatories of the Pauling statement. Within a few months it swept the country, collecting thousands of signatures even by scientists in government laboratories. And it worked. The campaign against testing grew; women in upstate New York got up in arms against milk polluted with radioactive elements that would find their way into the bones of children. The sign that the battle was officially engaged came when news of the opposition to testing by the Federation of Atomic Scientists moved from some occasional paragraphs on the inside pages of the *New York Times* to several front-page columns—a reliable barometer of establishment opinion.

The Pauling-statement campaign was the first example of efforts by professionally qualified citizens against the government technocracy and its claim to a monopoly of technical knowledge. Such a group speaking up on a technical issue carries a weight that larger but less expert groups often lack. The absence of a comparable technological issue at the start of the Vietnam War made it difficult to mobilize the same spectrum of forces. It is easier to rouse people to protest danger than immorality. It is also apparently easy to rouse the Immigration and Naturalization Service to action. Soon after the Pauling statement was released, one of their officers appeared at my home asking all sorts of questions, in what I interpreted as an attempt at intimidation.

Good-bye to the Midwest now, and to my apprenticeship in American politics at its rural roots. For a couple of years Boston and the country as a whole were calm. Most of us did not realize what time bombs, in Cuba and in Vietnam, the Eisenhower administration had set for its successors. When John Kennedy marched into Washington in 1961, like a plumed knight on a white courser followed by a troupe of academic donkeys dressed up as statesmen, we believed the country was on its way to a period of simple, honest grandeur. Three months later the Bay of Pigs invasion showed how wrong we had been. As I already mentioned in an earlier chapter, a full-page advertisement signed by sixty Cambridge professors (it was initiated, I believe, by some students of David Riesman's) was the first public denunciation of this operation for what it was—a cowardly, immoral action rather than just an incompetent fiasco. I recall being upset by the attitude of some colleagues in the few days of the invasion when the outcome was in the balance: let's wait and see how it ends—behavior like that of spectators at a street fight waiting to see who wins before taking sides.

Newspaper advertisements including large numbers of professor's signatures became a major, in fact the largest political activity of the Boston-area academics. I was actively involved in it. Over the years I developed, I believe, a good deal of expertise in the machinery of soliciting, gathering, and publicizing the names of individual members of university faculties in support of specific political positions or demands. This technique was used effectively in 1961 in the battle over civil defense, when the government, either in a fit of panic or in a deliberate move to rouse public opinion in preparation for military adventures, started pushing for a nationwide system of anti-nuclear shelters, complete with stored food and drink plus at least one gun to keep one's neighbors away. Into this potential Theban tragedy moved two hundred M.I.T. professors, denouncing this criminal folly in a *New York Times* ad, on the very day that Nelson Rockefeller as Governor of New York had conned his State Legislature into voting $100 million for shelters. The language of the *Times*'s article was even stronger than that of our ad. A most delightful byplay was that at about the same time one of the common brush fires in California completely destroyed the personal shelter of Willard Libby, one of the Commissioners of Atomic Energy and a major proponent of home shelters.

The shelter program died, partly at the hands of critics like us, partly at the hands of some hard-headed Congressmen who had no use for the vagaries of the Cambridge crowd that was running the White House. Having known some of that crowd before they joined the Best and the Brightest, I shared those Congressmen's misgivings.

Newspaper advertisements as a political technique have a number of features that make them particularly appropriate to an academic constituency. First, they do not require membership in an organization—academics hate to belong to anything but academies. In the advertisement technique no affiliation is involved. Each action requires a single individual decision to participate and to sign a statement exactly known, verifiably free of misplaced commas or split infinitives. Second, the operation is relatively inexpensive: during the Vietnam War one thousand names at ten dollars each filled a *New York Times* page. The cost is now twenty-five dollars, but salaries have also increased. In addition to their own great visibility, ads in major newspapers induce a spreading effect, since they are often reproduced in local papers by concerned citizens. Finally and most importantly, a timely advertisement may break the silence on some current issue and do so more forcefully than would an op-ed column. One might believe that the sporadic nature of the advertisement operation would be a disadvantage, but this is compensated for politically by the sense of urgency that each call for signatures puts on the participants. Of course, behind the concept of advertisements signed by professors there is the hopeful but unproved assumption that someone —among the public or in the government—cares what professors think and say. I for one am optimistic on that account. I believe there is a substantial though not vocal constituency that believes education is significantly coupled with good reasoning. I have even found such believers among elected officials.

In the academic community, and more generally in the liberal milieu, advertisements provide a welcome opportunity for some people to be, so to speak, counted without standing. The average liberal academic is uncommitted to political action, no matter how enlightened his or her intellectual positions may be. Commitment seems to vary in inverse proportion to the political significance of the issue. Whales, exhaust emissions, the Sierra Club—the pet bourgeois concerns—are politically the most neutral. Civil liberties, sexual equality, human rights follow in increasing levels of controversiality. Opposition to governmental policies—war, nuclear armaments, imperialist ventures—is the hardest for the average liberal to act upon. Newspaper advertisements provide an opportunity to do so, and a request for a signature can often put a person of liberal sentiments on the spot to act on his or her convictions.

The first advertisements opposing the Vietnam War were sponsored by an improvised *ad hoc* committee, meeting on short notice at the Harvard Faculty Club or at other places in and around Cambridge. Usually a phone call, prompted by a new escalation of the war, brought together a half-dozen people who, after some discussion, decided whether a public statement was desirable and feasible, and if so, what it should say. Soon it became clear that some continuity was needed: the *ad hoc* group became the Boston Area Faculty Group on Public Issues, whose acronym BAFGOPI, however awkward, acquired deserved notoriety. By most standards BAFGOPI was a singular organization, but its oddity was perfectly suitable to an academic enterprise. It had a post-office box, a checking account, and a chairman. During most of BAFGOPI's existence, this was Hilary Putnam, the Harvard philosopher, who claimed he had been chosen as chairman because of his Brahmin family name. When Hilary became more radicalized and lost interest in BAFGOPI, the group functioned without a chairman until its more or less temporary demise at the end of the Vietnam War. By then, however, the modus operandi of BAFGOPI was set. We had acquired a network, that most important resource for political activity. We could in a day or two activate the collection of signatures on a hundred or more campuses throughout the country or at least in its northern half.

I cannot even recall all the colleagues who took an active part in BAFGOPI work in the Boston area. Indispensable was Everett Mendelsohn, the science historian who seems to know everyone at Harvard and a substantial sample of people everywhere else.

Our ads were topical: "Stop the bombing" was the first and most concise one, early in 1965. Other ads addressed specific outrages or demanded withdrawal. They did not go into political analysis or suggest further study: they became an opportunity for members of the academic community (several thousand in some cases) to join in a public antiwar stand. Sometimes success became troublesome. One ad, for example, brought so many signatures that we could not check each one for authenticity. Thus we received and published the signature of the Archbishop of Baltimore, who wrote a kind note pointing out that his signature must have been a fake. We apologized.

Since BAFGOPI had no political policy or ideology, other colleagues throughout the country knew that they were called on simply to join in a specific action and were not coopted or manipulated for political purposes. Our ads were never revolutionary in content. We never called on soldiers to desert or on students to resist the draft, and for that reason BAFGOPI after 1968 was viewed with some impatience by some more radically committed colleagues. But we felt that it was more important to provide for a large number of colleagues the chance to stand up and be counted than to appeal to a small number of committed radicals who had, anyway, other means to be heard, especially within the student bodies. In fact, other less costly approaches to antiwar protest within universities became available. The teach-in technique, devised by a faculty-student group at the University of Michigan, proved effective and spread rapidly. These all-night-long sessions of speeches and debate were useful in crystallizing antiwar sentiment, but they tended to involve relatively few faculty members. At a BAFGOPI meeting, someone reported that the Michigan group proudly described itself as the "inventors of the Teach-In." "What about us?" he asked. "What can we boast of?" And someone replied, "We invented the *New York Times.*"

The *Times* was not our only outlet, both for strategic and financial reasons. The *The Washington Post,* which is sent to all members of Congress homes and offices every morning, was used for ads targeted specifically at Congress, for example in support of antiwar bills or opposition to the dispatch of troops. Ads in the *Boston Globe* had different purposes: to reach a wider range of our local colleagues and students as well as to encourage that venerable and wavering paper to take clearer editorial positions.

At one time this worked out well. I had written a couple of scientific op-ed pieces for Victor Zausmer, who was then managing editor of the *Globe*. Zella and I became friends with him and his wife, a charming Viennese woman. (Her eighty-year-old mother, in the grand tradition of bourgeois Vienna, had never cooked *anything* with her own hands.) At any rate, I asked Zausmer if I could edit a series of ten successive Sunday columns.

"O.K.," he said, "but not more than half on Vietnam. People don't want to hear about it anymore." This was in 1969. "Alas, alas, most certainly alas," I thought in Aeschylus's words.

My series right away seemed to be moving toward disaster. The first column had to be turned in on a Thursday. I had made the mistake of asking an extremely prominent, noncontroversial scientist to be the first author. On Tuesday I received (by dictation from Washington) the column—nonsensical, ungrammatical, unacceptable. Panic set in, which is often a source of fast action. And so I turned for help to a remarkable and venerable figure.

Some time earlier my wife had substituted for me on a delegation to the U.S. Attorney General pleading for dismissal of the case against Benjamin Spock and his "co-conspirators" in antiwar activities. She came back full of admiration for a fellow delegate, the historian Henry Steele Commager. When Commager was asked by a whippersnapper Assistant United States Attorney, "What are you doing here, Dr. Commager?" he replied, "We are here to write a page of American history," and proceeded to lecture the crowd of young lawyers about the meaning of the Bill of Rights.

I had asked Commager for a later *Globe* column, but in the crisis occasioned by the scientist's failure I called him in Amherst. "Any chance that your column is already written?" "No. When do you need it?" It was Tuesday evening. "Could I get it Thursday morning?" "It will be on the Peter Pan bus at 4 P.M. tomorrow." The column arrived, and it was a jewel. Obviously written by a great writer, without corrections or afterthoughts, it placed the Vietnam War where it belonged, as an outrage and a negation of American tradition. The *Globe* people liked it, the public liked it and responded to it, and 134 newspapers reprinted it. None of the next nine columns had a similar impact, but many of them were excellent, and the last, by Howard Zinn, was superb and enthusiastically received.

My friendship with Commager grew and with it my admiration for him. Once more I had a chance to provoke him into writing about Vietnam and he again responded in grand style. I was having dinner in San Diego in the spring of 1970 with the editor of the now defunct *Look* magazine. I asked him why *Look* had not published any strong denunciation of the war. "No one has come up with a good one," he replied. "Would you publish one by Commager?" "Of course." With a few phone calls to Amherst and New York a meeting was set up. The two parties agreed and the Commager article was soon ready. When it did not appear, I inquired of the editor. "It is too important to put in a routine issue, so I'm keeping it for the July 4th one." It came out, a superb piece of American history and a scathing indictment of the Vietnam War as a violation of the spirit of that history.

In Massachusetts it was relatively easy and rewarding to oppose the Vietnam War. The state's long history of concern for civil liberties and individual rights (despite the blemish of the Sacco and Vanzetti trial) made peace initiatives flourish somewhat more easily than, say, in California (where 75 percent of people to whom the Bill of Rights was shown in the street thought it was some sort of subversive document). In 1969 a Lexington minister and a Brookline state representative formulated what became known by their names as the Wells-Shea bill. The Reverend John Wells was a soft-spoken Southerner, very persuasive. When I once spoke in his church the contrast between our two accents and approaches must have been striking. James Shea was an intense, dedicated young man greatly respected in his constituency as well as in the State House. The Wells-Shea bill would have made it illegal to send any Massachusetts citizen to fight abroad in a war not formally declared by Congress. It was but a gesture, of course. What is remarkable is that the bill passed both houses of the Massachusetts Legislature and was signed into law by the Governor. I recall an afternoon when a few faculty members and several hundred students walked from M.I.T. to the State House, where we called on the Governor to come out and meet with us. The Governor appeared and was asked to instruct the State Attorney General to test the Wells-Shea law in federal court. This was later done. The courts, not surprisingly, denied the state's jurisdiction. Soon thereafter Don Shea, with whom I had shared a few seminars on the war before various student groups, died tragically by his own hand—a victim of his own exhaustion in working against the Vietnam War.

Governor Francis Sargent was a typical Boston Brahmin, lantern-jawed, almost as if acromegalic, a dedicated gentleman of a type I had met already on that venerable body, the board of trustees of the Massachusetts General Hospital. On a day in October 1969, a glorious New England fall day, Governor Sargent was the main speaker at a peace rally on the historical Lexington village green. He was hooted and insulted by a few rowdies, and rather than just ignoring them and talking only to the converted, he turned on his critics and lectured them into respectful silence. At the end of that afternoon, as I walked off the green with my neighbor Konrad Bloch, a Harvard biochemist, Nobel Prize recipient, and like myself a refugee from racial persecution in Europe, I remember asking him, "Aren't you and I lucky, both castoffs from our old countries, to be here today in this unique town, in this wonderful spot, on such an occasion?" The following morning I heard that I had been awarded a Nobel Prize. All this, and a Nobel Prize too!

My self-chosen role in the antiwar movement—as a mobilizer of faculty members and publicizer of protest—made it inadvisable for me to participate in more extreme antiwar actions even when I felt them to be justified. Identification with a totally uncompromising antiwar position would make me less useful by providing my "constituency," on the mailing list of BAFGOPI, with a ready excuse not to act. I had many discussions on this point, especially on the question of encouraging students not to respond to the draft. I approved of such actions in principle but did not join my colleagues in encouraging them publicly, although like many others I was pledged to succor draft resisters if they were prosecuted. Also, I am not a pacifist by commitment and could not endorse some of the pacifists' most extreme positions. My moderate position did not prevent me, of course, from participating in several marches and other protest actions, although I personally have no taste for physical presence at such affairs. I do politics best on the telephone, less well in the street or in a crowd, where I always feel physically uncomfortable. Once in 1970, when I wanted to join a Washington march and let myself be arrested at the Pentagon, Noam Chomsky warned me that even one night on a steel plank in a D.C. jail such as he had experienced would cause my poor twisted spine, an ailment I have suffered from since I was forty years old, to immobilize me for a month. So I did not go.

Opposition to the Vietnam War raised the more general issue of obedience or disobedience to the law. Most of us reasonably honest people may go through life without ever facing such conflict. We are aware that many laws are unjustly enforced, or unjust in their content, or even deliberately enacted in order to protect injustice; but seldom are we in a position that makes it desirable or urgent to violate a specific law. Our feelings—my own at least —have by and large been inspired by Socrates's action of refusing to escape from jail and avoid execution because to do so would violate a law which, although misapplied in his case, he deemed to be derived from legitimate authority. An unjust war shakes the foundations of Socrates's position because the slaughter of human beings for reasons of state challenges the legitimacy of the state's authority. During the First World War this was the position of religious pacifists as well as of leading American socialists like Eugene Debs. In the Second World War the situation was ambiguous. The horror of Hitler's Nazism and the threat it posed to the very structure of modern society gave the war a certain measure of validity: soldiers knew that at least some of the values for which they fought were worth fighting for. Western capitalism and Russian socialism held at least the promise of a better future after Nazism was obliterated.

But the Vietnam War was different. Resistance to illegitimate authority was a major if not always explicit element in the confrontations on university campuses, from Berkley and Columbia to M.I.T. and many others. Continuation of academic activity as usual during the Vietnam War, once the war was seen as a violation of national morality, was in truth an obscenity, but one hard to correct even within relatively liberal institutions. M.I.T. had its own upheavals, ranging from a day-long strike for peace on March 4, 1968, to an actual occupation of the president's office in 1969. The confrontation was rather mild compared to those at Columbia University, probably because of the relatively liberal attitude of the M.I.T. administration and the conservatism of the students. Some faculty members shared and encouraged the activists' initiatives; others like me tried to protect the activist students from being penalized for what were exceedingly trivial offenses compared to the obscenity of the war itself.

A special kind of protest, brilliant in its simplicity and integrity of purpose, was the one conducted by groups of religious individuals such as Daniel and Philip Berrigan. These two brothers, both Catholic priests, were indicted several times for a series of "outrages" such as the burning of draft-board files or spilling blood on them—the only innocently spilled blood in the entire war. The purpose of these actions was to dramatize the need to break unjustly applied laws.

My first, indirect connection with Dan Berrigan took place in 1965. One evening I was phoned by a gentleman who wanted my help on behalf of Dan Berrigan; as I had read in the papers, Berrigan had a few weeks earlier been exiled to Mexico by his bishop. My caller explained that a petition asking for his recall was being circulated among well-known Catholics, whereupon I offered him the names of many Catholics on BAFGOPI's list. He insisted he wanted my own signature; my friend Bob Cohen, a physicist at Boston University, had told him I was "the most prominent Catholic layman in the antiwar movement in Boston." After the misunderstanding was cleared up, I called Bob and told him that he and my wife (twenty years apart) were the only two Jews I knew who had believed me to be Catholic.

In the summer of 1970 Dan Berrigan was a fugitive from the law. For several months he remained in hiding, sought by the F.B.I., state troopers, and other arms of the government. His crime was the burning of draft files. One evening at suppertime I received a phone call. Dan Berrigan, whom I had never met, wished to meet me. I assumed he had heard of me because of

BAFGOPI. I went to meet him—a man of almost luminous integrity, transparent good will, and utter directness. I noticed in him the kind of serenity I have found also in other religious activists, a serenity that I believe comes from a confidence in commitments validated by religious faith. Berrigan just wanted to talk—about the war, BAFGOPI, and the situation in the universities. He is a poet, so we talked of poetry as well, especially of Denise Levertov's, which we both admired. It was a perfectly quiet evening, not marred by our knowing that one of us was risking arrest, and the other was courting trouble. The Vietnam War, and the moral obligation to resist it, had made a fugitive of a poet and possibly an accomplice of me.

A few weeks later, for a meeting in Wellfleet, I drafted a brief statement comparing Socrates's plight and choices to Dan Berrigan's. The latter could not cooperate with the law, because it was a law nullified by actions that had made the authority of the state illegitimate. Berrigan was upholding a morality that the actions of the state had forced upon him. His refusal to turn himself in was one more protest against those actions. Like all of us in the antiwar movement, Berrigan was not advocating victory for the Viet Cong or defeat for the U.S. army. He wanted to dramatize the horror of the war in order to bring it to an end. The issue was moral, not military. The statement I had drafted never became a newspaper ad: Dan Berrigan was arrested a few weeks later.

As the Vietnam War continued its evil course, spreading as well to Cambodia, ads and teach-ins as well as many other kinds of antiwar activities continued. The last major advertisement we published was not, however, only antiwar. It was directed against Richard Nixon, running for re-election in 1972. It was paid for by thousands of signers and published in many newspapers throughout the country in the last weeks of the campaign. As we know, it did not win the election for George McGovern. It was an interesting operation, however, with some fun in dealing with all sorts of newspaper editors. One of them, in Chicago, called me to say the ad could not go in because the head of his legal department had "reservations" about some statements concerning the President. Upon which I called Dun Gifford, a prominent and respectable Boston lawyer, who had helped get the anti-Nixon ad started. I asked him to be my lawyer for one day. Then I phoned the chap in Chicago and told him the head of his legal department should call the head of *my* legal department, at such and such number. Fifteen minutes later, without any more legal consultation, the ad was accepted—a tribute to effective name dropping.

The McGovern campaign made me notorious in an unexpected corner of the United States. I had been invited to give a technical talk at the University of Virginia in Charlottesville and, once there, someone asked me to talk to a few McGovern-for-President activists. I had a surprisingly large audience, including a reporter for the local newspaper, which on the following day carried a banner headline, "Socialist Speaker at the U. of V." The local McGovern people were pleased; they had not had so much publicity in the entire campaign.

After the end of the war and the American withdrawal from Indochina, meaningful political activity was for a while at a low ebb. Like the rest of the country, the academic world wished to forget Vietnam, or rather to believe smugly that this war had been an aberration in American history. The shaky myth of American innocence and good will had to be rescued from the teeth of reality. Any distasteful action of the Soviet Union became an excuse for American complacency. I never cared for the algebraic theory of political morality in which a minus ten grade for the Russian government and a minus five for the American becomes a plus five for our side. Other people's guilt has never seemed to me a proof of my innocence.

In 1973 the overthrow of the Allende government in Chile, engineered with the open approval and covert assistance of the U.S. government, served as a reminder that Chile, Vietnam, as well as Guatemala in 1954, were all episodes in a long-term policy of world domination that called for interventions, diplomatic or military, in the interests of American investments. After Allende's murder I had the sad honor one evening of introducing his widow to a Boston audience—a truly great woman in sorrow and dignity, most unlike our first ladies caparisoned in silks and jewels. I was also privileged to greet and welcome a wonderful Chilean popular singing group in exile, Chilapaiyun, before a Cambridge audience. In my introduction I tried to mix a few Spanish words, probably badly pronounced, since after the concert someone asked if I was Russian. Or was I being red-baited?

A peculiarity of politics in the post-Vietnam years has been the game of using the defense of human rights as a tool of foreign policy. In this game, one Russian dissident in jail may equal, for propaganda purposes, ten Palestinian Arabs killed or the slaughter of one thousand rebellious Salvadoran peasants. Semantics enters the picture: totalitarians are those oppressors we don't like, authoritarians those with whom we do business. Such use of human rights by the American government or by various political groups raises dilemmas for individuals, like me, who don't like oppression but fear the use of propaganda for Cold War purposes. For example, what does one do when physicist X is being arrested in the Soviet Union and one is asked to act on his behalf? My solution has been to protest by telegram or letter directly to Soviet authorities, but to refuse to sign appeals that are to be publicized in the United States, heating up Cold War emotions. I feel that I can speak strongly to my own government, where my opinion must in principle be listened to, and should speak softly to foreign governments if my plea is to have any effect at all. Particularly annoying to me is to be asked to sign or support some cause or statement in the capacity of a Nobel Prize recipient, as if that gave my opinion a greater value in any socio-political subject. I know enough Nobel laureates to realize that the value of their opinions ranges over about the same spectrum as that of any other moderately educated persons. I hope that when my political opinion is asked for it is because of my long-standing interest in politics, not because of the decision by a Swedish medical faculty to honor my research.

Old BAFGOPI, in mothballs since 1974, had to be revived again in 1982 to gather and convey to the Congress the feeling of our university colleagues about the situation in El Salvador, or rather in Central America, where military governments, established or propped up by the U.S. government, face the revolutionary insurgency of the oppressed peasantry. We felt that the policy of the Reagan administration might lead, deliberately or by mistaken calculation, to a new Vietnam, an adventure equally immoral and with the added danger of a nuclear confrontation over Cuba. We sent to each member of Congress a fact book on El Salvador and asked Congress to deny the military government military aid. After so many years of academic silence I was pleasantly surprised by the resourcefulness and energy of the academic community, at least around Boston, where literally thousands of signatures were collected repeatedly within a few weeks, sometimes in a matter of days. If this can be taken as a sign of the times —and the vigor of the anti-nuclear-weapons movement at this writing suggests it—one may trust that the U.S. government would have a hard time if it tried to set in motion another military venture. The harder task is to keep it from promoting wars by proxy.

Among the most interesting aspects of the situation, at least for me as a putative "prominent Catholic layman," is the dynamic role of the Catholic Church in antiwar politics. During the Vietnam War Zella and I were among those few who refused to pay part of our federal taxes, which forced the Internal Revenue Service to siphon the money out of our bank account. A minor gesture, which however assuaged our anger. Today, in 1982, the Archbishop of Seattle has publicly encouraged clergy and laymen to withhold one-half of their taxes in protest against the nuclear arms race. I feel humbly blessed.

There is one area of political concern about which I cannot write light-heartedly or without emotion, and that is the politics of Israel. I was first exposed to Zionism in my teens, in Italy. Zionism was then for some Italian Jews a way to affirm their anti-Fascism; cultivating a loyalty to an internationalist cause served to counter Fascist nationalism. Even then I had doubts, seeing the absurdity of fighting one nationalism with another, so that I never was a Zionist, either then or later in France or in the United States. Yet like many non-Zionist Jews I felt admiration for the technical and cultural achievements of the Israeli people, especially those of the socialist communities in the kibbutzim. These achievements I had the opportunity to observe at first hand on my visits to Israel, where I taught and lectured several times.

From the start, however, I was disturbed by the establishment of a Jewish state, rather than a multinational and racially blind state. It seemed absurd that a new country should constitutionally mark itself as sectarian by way of race or religion—even more absurd, in fact, when it was a country whose dominant national group had just emerged from the Holocaust. Unfortunately, in the present world of rampant and aggressive nationalisms the Holocaust itself has become, not a source of human solidarity and of revulsion against racial oppression, but, perversely, a justification for a new oppression, for a policy of distrust and antagonism. It is depressing to see the government of Israel act like the ruler of a power-driven master race, using military superiority for policies that border on the genocidal. Even more depressing is to realize, in conversation with educated and otherwise sensible Israelis, that the policy of their government mirrors the sentiments of a large segment of the Israeli people. One senses a widespread contempt for Palestinian Arabs individually and collectively—in fact, a contempt for all Arabs. Such racist contempt that tries to relegate its object to an almost subhuman status degrades morally those who nurture it.

The millennial pride of Jews in their own survival and accomplishments despite oppression has turned in Israel into a pride of technocratic achievement and into a delusion of superiority. One witnesses with anguish the Jewish state become, in the name of ensuring its own survival, one of the most cynical players in the rotten game of power politics. What Jewish philosophers and mystics called the Jewish spirit seems to have parted ways with the spirit of Israel.

Most recently Israeli troops caused untold sorrow and loss of life in Lebanon. A comical but disturbing personal note has been my excommunication by a trio of rabbis for publicly criticizing Israel's conduct. Organized American Jewry has lost all sense of measure in its support for the government of Israel.

Meanwhile, what started as a comic opera in the Falkland Islands developed into another real war, if a relatively minor one, between England and Argentina. And all over Central America, the slaughter continues as revolutions attempt to overthrow the local oligarchies. Born just before World War I, I am more than seventy years old, and have seen nothing but war and slaughter throughout my adult life. When I open my morning newspaper my heart sinks as the front-page news bring more of the same. Some days I cannot face it, and I turn first to the stock-market tables or even the book review in order to delay facing the gruesome reality. How long can the folly last? More important, how long can one maintain the measure of optimism, the degree of commitment without which meaningful involvement in public affairs cannot be sustained? I dread lest discouragement set in or, even worse, that I may come around to the Panglossian view that the world we live in is the best of all possible worlds. Then like Candide I may yield to the temptation to tend my own garden. Could I then preserve my self-respect?

I have explored in this chapter my political life as a citizen. A scientist, however, is exposed to political pressures also *qua* scientist, more so in the last several decades—since the atom bomb, and Sputnik, and recombinant DNA. Many of the ills as well as the boons of our world have come from science through its technological applications. It may be useful for me to discuss some areas where science and politics do intersect, if only to clarify how my political opinions as a citizen have influenced me, often restraining my involvement in the politics of science below the fervor that some of my radical colleagues would have expected. At times I have caught blame from the left as well as from the right, not because I wavered but rather because I tried to stick to a consistent, reasonable position. I was blamed by the right because I did not uphold sufficiently the interests of pure science; I was blamed by the left because I criticized activities that I considered either middle-class romantic or politically unsound and counterproductive. Let me give some examples.

In the mid-seventies the so-called recombinant DNA technology became an immediate possibility. One could foresee—and events have confirmed—that it would soon be possible to transfer genes from any one of many different organisms to bacteria or to other cells. These manipulations promised to reveal how genes function and how their function is controlled, for example by hormones. Such knowledge would help clarify problems of organic development, including the development of cancer. It could also lead to the production of clinically valuable materials. My own research in the forties and fifties had contributed some key steps in the series of development that made DNA technology possible, but by the 1970s I was not involved in that kind of work. The controversy that followed, and was particularly heated in Cambridge, exemplified in microcosm the issues that arise when an activity such as science interacts with society in a way that is seen as novel and threatening.

The first issue was safety: would recombinant DNA technology be dangerous? Would microscopic green monsters crawl out of Harvard to spread new diseases throughout Cambridge and ultimately the entire world? Would M.I.T. laboratories pour into the Charles River the germs of some new plague? The other issue was control. The government and a committee of experts were formulating national guidelines. But who should make the decision whether or not the research was to be done? The scientists? The government? The potential beneficiaries? The potential victims? The problems were serious, more so politically than scientifically; but the controversy was sometimes less than serious. The Cambridge City Council heard venerable Harvard professors in jeans and beads describe in passionate words the forthcoming horrors. These scientific critics were seconded by radical leaders in three-piece suits as well as by enraged citizens urged by populist sentiment. The council also heard scientists who explained the presumed innocence of the proposed work, often not realizing that hard-to-understand technical arguments baffled the council and the public.

I was knowledgeable enough to be aware that the dangers were vanishingly small; committed to science enough to see the dangers of turning the decision over to the hue-and-cry of public opinion, that is, of the newspapers and radio stations; skeptical enough of government's wisdom to see that government guidelines, useful as they would be when they came, would not reassure anyone at the local level. So I favored and supported the Cambridge solution: appointment of a representative group of citizens from all walks of life charged with recommending the conditions, including federal guidelines, under which recombinant DNA research could be done in Cambridge. The mixture of expertise— the scientists; of power—the government; and of town meeting democracy seemed the best compromise achievable, at least under capitalist democracy. I was sometimes the target of obloquy, from the populists as well as from the science purists. Both groups of course had their hidden agendas. The populists, by opposing what they considered an elitist solution, believed they were fighting "the system." Given the political realities, they were unwittingly undermining the relative independence of science from establishment control and fostering antiscientific sentiment among the public. The scientific purists, on the other hand, by rejecting the role of the public and the government in the decision-making process, were erecting a barrier of distrust that could do even greater harm to the scientific enterprise.

I differed from the populists because I did not and do not believe that one opens the way to socialism by fighting on idiosyncratic, middle-class issues bolstered by faulty information about hypothetical dangers. I differed from the purists, as well, in my less than uncritical attitude toward science. Despite my commitment to science as an intellectual pursuit, I have never internalized the view rather common among scientists that science is some kind of sacred priesthood before which all other interests and considerations must yield. I have known scientists who do in fact look upon science in the same way a truly religious Catholic would look upon life within the Church, as a dedication to a supreme, ideal set of values. There must be great comfort in believing that one belongs to an elite, not of birth or wealth, but of professional worth, a feeling of election or divine blessing—one admirably described by Thomas Mann in his trilogy, *Joseph and His Brothers.* * For scientists the sense of value is often reinforced by the coupling of scientific work with the comfortable expectation that it may actually benefit humanity. The priesthood of science has the privilege of being even harder to enter by conversion after a sinful life than is the Catholic Church. It provides a sort of absolution from responsibility for any controversial matters that may arise in the applications of science. It automatically takes science out of the domain of morality by proclaiming it to be intrinsically moral. For the believer in the absolute Good of science anything that goes wrong can only be the fault of the users of science, not of the producers of absolute Knowledge. While by and large I agree that moral issues usually arise because of society's unwise uses of technology, science is too close to technology to absolve itself of the obligation of respecting public concern. When Dominican friars conveyed the victims of the Inquisition to the "secular arm" for an *auto-da-fé,* did they thereby absolve their theology of responsibility for those burnings?

Years ago, in a lecture before the American Philosophical Society entitled *Slippery When Wet,* I explored, as many others have done, the question of scientists' responsibility or lack thereof for the uses to which technology is being put. I mildly concluded that scientists should at least feel responsible for informing their government and the public of potential dangers that might arise from the uses of science, just as they actively publicize potential benefits. Months later an eminent scientist (now dead) wrote me that he was sorry to have missed my lecture; he had read the printed version and wanted me to know that he "completely disagreed." I was reminded of the anecdote of the Texas newspaper editor

*New York: Knopf, 1948.

who, when a shower of bullets entered his office window, re-marked to his assistant, "I knew that editorial would be effective."

In some other political disputes about scientific or pseudoscientific research and its impact on contemporary society I played minor, peripheral roles, either because others were more competent in the area or because I did not find any satisfactory ground on which to make a useful stand. Such was the IQ controversy, which has been well summarized and in my opinion settled by Stephen Jay Gould in his book *The Mismeasure of Man.** The controversy started, as is well known, with the proclamation by Arthur Jensen, a professor of education, that "compensatory education . . . had failed." The intelligence quotient or IQ was inherited and unmodifiable by educational efforts, and therefore efforts to improve intellectual performance through education should be abandoned. The main "scientific" support for Jensen's conclusions about the heritability of IQ scores was data on identical twins by the late British psychologist Cyril Burt, data which later were shown to have been falsified.

On the surface the ensuing controversy was mainly a struggle among groups of educationists for power over the public schools. At a more intellectual level it assumed the character of a battle between elitists and populists in the educational field. It finally became a wider political battle, with ugly racist overtones hidden under the pretense of biological imperatives.

From their inception early in this century IQ and other psychological tests had been used for purposes of racial or class discrimination. In the 1920s and 1930s, such tests on immigrants had been used to conclude, for example, that Jews were intellectually inferior. (A team of geneticists had "proved" that pellagra was a genetic trait of poor Southern whites—this after the true cause of the disease, a nutritional deficiency in the vitamin niacin, had already been established.) The heritability of IQ (see Gould's book) is not supported by any stronger evidence than that of pellagra.

My own single public participation in the IQ fracas came in

*New York: Norton, 1981.

response to an initiative by Bernard Davis, an eminent bacteriologist and a recent convert to neoconservatism. Davis persuaded some dozen scientists from all parts of the world to join in a protest, published in the *New York Review of Books,* against an alleged threat that research funds might be denied to Arthur Jensen and others on his side. Seeing on Davis's manifesto the names of several people I respected, I couldn't refrain from writing to the *New York Review* that these people had been coopted or conned into protesting a nonexistent threat, thereby raising a red herring in a very unscientific way. In fact, the signers probably believed they were defending the right of scientists to pursue research, not realizing that they were defending a misuse of pseudoscience in the arena of social policy.

Similar issues were raised in the more recent controversy on sociobiology. Edward O. Wilson, a Harvard entomologist, ventured in his book *Sociobiology* a number of shaky speculations about the genetic determination of specific aspects of human behavior, possibly being unaware of the controversiality of this topic and of the somewhat naïve nature of his extrapolations.* His speculations and those of his epigones were roundly criticized by some psychologists and were, unfortunately, the ground for villainous physical attacks on Wilson himself. Possibly in response to such criticism and intolerable violence, Wilson deepened and enlarged the scope of his interest in human behavior, developing it into a field of increasing complexity on exceedingly weak grounds.

This was an interesting situation with strongly polarized positions. On the one side there were scientists like Wilson himself creating a flimsy biology of human behavior by analogy rather than by legitimate study of the performance of the human brain in such uniquely human activities as language, pattern recognition, concept formation, and so on. On the other side were his most extreme antagonists, some of them scientists, who claimed that all biological study of human behavior was intrinsically wrong and morally evil, presumably because it can be distorted for pur-

*Cambridge: Harvard University Press, 1975.

poses of oppression. To me the latter position is untenable. I do not believe in the absolute right of scientists to investigate whatever subject they want; but I trust that a true science of human behavior based on solid biological and psychological findings could be intellectually and socially valuable. I suspect that beneath the intransigent attitude of some of my fellow radicals, even of scientists, toward human brain research and its relation to behavior there is an underlying antiscience, even antirational bias that may be socially more dangerous than any erroneous scientific conclusions.

It is the antiscience attitude as well as the political naïveté of the environmentalist movement that has made me stay away from it, so much so as to gain me the reputation of being an admirer of pollution. The way I prefer to put it, the environment is a bourgeois prejudice, meaning that most concern for natural surroundings, natural foods, natural ways of life are expressions of middle-class narcissism. I strongly endorse removal of industrial pollution that threatens people's health and lives, but I am utterly impatient with suburbanites who complain of being polluted when they go into the city. I especially detest those environmentalists who smoke two packs of cigarettes a day while complaining of exhaust fumes.

The essence of such distortion is the inability or unwillingness of many people to think in rational, statistical terms about dangers and opportunities in the modern world. This is something that most scientists can do, and it may be a major reason for their social usefulness. I do not share the view that scientists are practitioners of a superior activity, occupying in the world of intellect the supreme position that philosophers would enjoy in Plato's ideal city. As I hope to have made clear to the reader, I feel gratitude and humility for having had the chance—for chance it was at least as much as choice—of becoming a scientist. I find satisfaction in making a living by doing exciting work, shared with intelligent people, with almost no drudgery, with some reasonable confidence of not hurting anyone (at least directly), and possibly producing something useful. The pride I derive from my commitment to science comes from having once made that commitment and having kept it despite occasional difficulties and crises.

I do not share the optimism of some scientists that science could by its own momentum solve the urgent problems of society. Scientific technology can never accomplish more than the purposes to which it is put, and the purposes are dictated by societal organization. I have no confidence that any social system based on unequal and unjust distribution of power—economic or military—can handle the problems of society effectively. But I do believe that the problems that beset society, including the proper use of science, could be solved by a world-wide reorganization of political systems based on a just distribution of wealth and opportunities.

Since I have expressed my reservations concerning the position of science as a superior human activity, I wish to avoid the possible misunderstanding that I might even slightly share with certain radical thinkers such as Herbert Marcuse or Theodore Roszak an antiscience bias, or at least a belief that something in science is intrinsically harmful and destructive. I always considered such ideas, even when held by radical philosophers, as romantic, middle-class longings for a simpler, more sheltered, and ultimately less shared world. As a political individual, however, my life in science has convinced me that science cannot claim either responsibility for nor absolution from the problems of society. The concerns of society, even those that originate from the advances of science, such as nuclear weapons and the depletion of essential materials, reflect structural ills that cause unwise applications of scientific knowledge. If the political will for reorganization were on the move throughout the world, then science, technology, art, and all other activities of the human mind would be the capital resources with which a better world could be built.

10

Emotions

Ah, but to play man number one,
To drive the dagger in his heart,
To lay his brain upon the board
And pick the acrid colors out,
To nail his thought across the door,
Its wings spread wide to rain and snow. . . .
WALLACE STEVENS, "The Man with the Blue Guitar"

At the beginning of this book, I suggested that an autobiography should be something of a confession. It need not be a confession of malignancy or wrongdoing; however ambiguous our personalities may be, the ambiguities are seldom as extreme as those of a Dr. Jekyll and a Mr. Hyde. Yet within each one of us there is a little Pandora's box filled with our impulses, good and evil, rational and irrational, a box from which escape, like whispers of wind, the sighs of emotions: smiles of pride, rumbles of self-satisfaction, wisps of irony, frowns of guilt, and shivers of fear. An autobiographer should dare to open the Pandora's box and exhibit its contents, which are the inner core of personality, the forces that modulate one's activity and one's attitudes toward oneself and toward others. Ideally, self-revelation should be as candid and direct as possible within the limits of self-respect and respect for others. It should be unembellished by vanity or irony or bravado. This, of course, is a hardly attainable goal. The process of self-exploration is itself an exercise in self-creation, from which the self emerges not only distorted but also in some measure transformed.

As I have done for other areas of activity, so also for the domain of my emotional life I shall attempt a developmental approach, searching for the roots of my emotional drives in the impressions of my formative years and in the memory of experiences that molded my commitments. If this search turns out to be incomplete and its output distorted, let it be my excuse that it is all that my memory and integrity can deliver. At this writing my self-image is a complex mixture of strength and weakness, selfishness and altruism, dedication and sloth. Although still an active person, I have started to settle down to a slower pace. Hence, I believe I can examine my own drives with a certain measure of equanimity, being less afraid that my effectiveness will be hampered by a too-lucid insight into myself.

As I recall my childhood I find in it roots for both strength and weakness. The upward social striving of my family fortunately directed us children not to commercial success but to intellectual pursuit. The family was intensely school-oriented, and my brother's successes in school were a major source of family pride. Being six years his junior I suffered secretly from envy, even more so when later my own successes always seemed to be measured with the yardstick of my brother's performance. Yet the fact that the family emphasized scholastic performance rather than sports or financial talent, in which I was deficient, contributed to my self-assurance, a feeling that was reinforced by academic success. There was also the influence of friends like Ugo Fano, who, coming from academic families, strengthened my desire to belong to the intellectual world.

In my younger years my mother provided another source of self-esteem. Handsome and somewhat domineering, even when she read poetry or stories to me she conveyed a sense of physical and intellectual elegance. I was in grammar school when an almost fatal illness changed her into a semi-invalid, permanently dependent on opiates. This condition not only deprived me of my most immediate source of delight, but created at home an atmosphere of illness: ailments of any sort were rewarded and handled more effectively than health. My brother, I believe, readily accepted that pattern, being frequently depressed in his youth and hampered in his professional growth. I remember that I consciously reacted against the ill-health paradigm. I wished to emphasize my health in contrast to my brother's complaints, but unfortunately every minor illness returned me to the fold. Unconsciously I was probably affected in my own self-image, believing myself weaker than I claimed to be.

The most regrettable consequence, helped perhaps by a tendency to laziness, was that while insisting on my own health I accepted the family influence when it came to physical exercise and sports. Since my brother's illnesses kept him away from physical-education courses, I too came to be considered inept for such courses and was excused from them. That was the beginning of a distressing and humiliating series of experiences in sports and physical fitness. When in my teens I tried sports like skiing or tennis, I found myself utterly clumsy, not only poorly coordinated (which might have been constitutional) but also unable or reluctant to make an effort to learn. Skiing was worst. I was afraid of abandoning myself to the slopes, unwilling to experience the thrill of speed and to exert the effort to control it. I had neither confidence nor courage. As I grew older I felt relieved of the obligation to participate in sports, and with time I came to think of physical exercise not only as irrelevant but as a form of narcissism. Yet I am aware that this attitude is insincere, stemming from a feeling of inferiority and aiming at compensating for it.

To this day, physical fear has remained a significant emotion. It has revealed itself in skiing and mountain climbing (which I reluctantly attempted a few times) and in many other situations demanding physical courage. Since childhood I experienced fear of the bully as well as discomfort in the company of more adult, more masculine schoolmates, a discomfort I felt later in bars and crowds, even friendly crowds sharing my own political persuasion. This fear has made me sensitive even to the smell of gymnasiums, the coarse effluvium of masculinity that probably rouses the energies of athletes while it nauseates me. It has made me uncomfortable in the presence of people whose personality suggests the possibility of physical violence. Perhaps for that reason I have always been more comfortable in the company of women than of men.

My self-image as a physical weakling surrounded by dangerous stronger men has not made me a coward in respect to nonphysical risks. I have been willing, even eager, to "stick my head up" for controversial or unpopular causes. Yet this sense of physical inadequacy has undoubtedly influenced my choice of physically safe situations in which conflicts are controlled or hidden. The appeal of academia may have resided in the shelter it affords against the threat or use of physical force. There are more subtle ways to settle accounts in the university.

As in sports, so also in mechanical skills my upbringing contributed toward making me deficient. In my parents' home it was considered dangerous as well as unjustified to fix things with one's own hands—a rather typical attitude of the European middle class. Now, I am a fairly adequate fixer around the house, but still an unskilled and untrained gadgeteer. Fortunately, as a biologist I can get along reasonably well with limited manual dexterity, but I admire those who can play with tools as an artist may play a fiddle. When my son, Dan, then twelve years old, was using the M.I.T. biology shop to prepare a science-fair project, he came to my office and announced: "Why should Bill [Strovink, the mechanic] not be paid better than you? I bet he is better at his work than you at yours." It was his first glimpse of the unjust pattern of rewards in society.

My mother's unwillingness to acknowledge openly her dependence on opiate drugs (as would have been possible without embarrassment since Italian law allowed prescription of morphia to addicts) gave our family life a Kafka-like quality, deriving from a shared shameful secret that ought not to be mentioned or discussed outside the house. I resented that secretiveness, especially in relations with my friends, which I would have liked to be fully open. My family's social attitude, their attempt to simulate an economic security that was not real, added ambiguity to my friendships. I was on my way to becoming cynical because of my inability to be straightforward.

Fortunately a number of good influences were present in the school and circles in which I moved. Teachers like the anti-Fascist Augusto Monti, whose powerful personality radiated integrity and whose teaching was a search for the roots of integrity in literature, played a big role. Acquaintance with young anti-Fascists made it clear to me that it was respectable to risk jail for an idea.

At a more directly personal level, an anecdote will illustrate one of the turning points in my moral development. I was walking one day with Vittorio Foa, a friend, who was later to distinguish himself in politics, first as a political prisoner in Mussolini's jails and then as a labor leader in postwar Italy. I was nineteen, he one or two years older. While talking of military service (then universal in Italy), I said that I expected my colonel uncle would arrange to have me declared physically unfit. Vittorio faced me and said: "To exempt yourself in that way would be dishonest. If you do, you should at least tell people that you *are* physically unfit, rather than boast of your dishonesty." It was a simple lesson in personal decency: using family influence was dishonest, and avoiding the stigma of physical unfitness was as well. In my cynical way of operating I had not even stopped to consider what the decent action would be. Like a sudden spark dispelling darkness, that episode showed me how far I had strayed from the way of integrity, admittedly in an environment—that of Fascist Italy—where for most people life was full of compromises. It made me reexamine my own standards and begin to develop a commitment to morality, not as an abstract concept of virtue but as a principle of commitment to just action. And at the next call for military service I refused my uncle's help and was inducted into the army.

Meanwhile my personal development had started on another path, the sentimental one. I believe I was then seeking in love affairs an emotional fulfillment that my family, resolutely unsentimental, had not provided. I was seeking love as an emotional and intellectual relief from what I saw as the drudgery of home life, and also as the possibility of a relation free of concealment and compromises.

My first significant love affair, rewarding at first, ended in dismal failure because of contrary demands. I was in love with love more than with my beloved. She, older and more mature, saw love as sexual and marital fulfillment, whereas I was sexually timid with women of my own social circle and totally unprepared even to consider marriage. Her consequent infidelities were totally justified, yet I suffered, a romantic bittersweet torment that left me more than ever eager for an ideal love.

Another romance marked me more deeply. This time my beloved, whom I shall call H., was a young scientist and artist, attractive, intelligent, sensitive. She was the daughter of an eminent professor, a connection that made her even more attractive because I looked upon academia as an ideal society. We loved each other, although my own feeling was again in part the sentimentalist's love for the emotion itself. Our relation lasted for some time, unfulfilled except at the emotional level. H.'s family opposed a marriage (which we never seriously considered), believing that I was after their money. My parents, on the other hand, were horrified at the thought of my marrying a Gentile. Even apart from these oppositions, it was an impossible love that should have ended sooner. But I was miserable and desperately needed H.'s presence and affection. Like the worst sentimentalist, who wishes to have the luxury of an emotion without paying for it, I kept the relationship going for years, even after I had left Italy. I lacked both the courage to break and the courage to fulfill the relation in marriage. The resolution to break it off came when, already in the United States, I had become a new and different person. I realized then that I had no more wish or motive to return to Italy when the war ended; and realized at the same time that the romantic attachment had lost its force. My love had died with the part of myself that had changed.

The years that followed were emotionally complex. They saw the onset of depressive symptoms, which were not unrelated, I believe, to the emotional crisis I had been through. On the positive side, I soon met and fell in love with Zella. This love developed along different lines from the sentimental dependence of my earlier affections. It was a real, robust, and physical relation, reinforced by her constant presence and by a congruence of opinions and attitudes. When we married, Zella was twenty-one, twelve years younger than I, already a woman with a remarkable mixture of strength, integrity, and reasonableness such as I have seldom encountered in anyone else. I believe that in almost four decades of marriage she has hardly ever told a lie to me or anyone else, even an innocent white lie. I personally feel that a sensible, innocent lie is sometimes preferable and even more believable than the truth; yet I cannot but admire Zella's truthfulness, or rather, inability to lie.

Mutual respect in our marriage has not sheltered us, of course, from occasional disagreement and grudges, soon resolved in open discussion and mutual trust. Our relationship has been a cheerful one, marked by bantering and playfulness even in times of stress or illness. We tried not to allow our professional worries to make us forget that family life came first. In fact, one contribution to our good marriage may have been our unwillingness to make our home life an appendage to our professional lives. We asked each other's advice and understanding when work was stressful. We tried to know enough of each other's work to be helpful, to rejoice in each other's successes and comfort each other's distress. But neither of us forced upon the other the day-by-day details of our work or the gossip of our institutions. Fortunately, our fields of work have been sufficiently different to arouse curiosity without impelling direct involvement.

Maintaining in marriage a core of privacy in matters of work may be a form of mutual respect—not forcing on one's partner an involvement that can only be derivative. Yet I confess to the suspicion that my quest for privacy, in this as in other areas, may have had a neurotic foundation. Since work stress was often for me a trigger for depression, I may have chosen to insulate my family from its tensions.

In recent years, when the danger of depression had been eliminated, Zella and I found more things to enjoy together. For many years we were a model couple in modern housekeeping. We alternated monthly in shopping and cooking and in assuming responsibility for other home chores. This exercise, which was in part an assertion of our shared feminist convictions, came to an end when worsening sciatica made it painful for me to stand at the stove. One evening early in our shared housekeeping venture while I was cooking for our guests (whom I had brought home with me) and Zella and they were chatting in the living room, I suddenly realized how many times over the years the reverse had been true: Zella working in the kitchen while I relaxed or entertained guests. The pang of guilt was not too painful, since I was finally doing something to atone for my sexist past.

Our only child, Daniel, might have had a happy, relaxed childhood and adolescence. A bright, lively boy with a knack for unexpected, impish turns of phrase, he unfortunately grew up in a bad period of my life. In my early thirties I started suffering from recurrent depressions, which did not hamper significantly my ability to work but made me tense and hypercritical, an attitude that unfortunately spilled over into my relationship with my boy. We loved each other but were often at odds, my inner tension turning into an impatient, commanding attitude toward him, while he reacted by provoking my criticism, arguing and sparring in order to control the situation. I believe that this made Dan a less secure, less relaxed child than he would otherwise have been. Zella's patient strength and Dan's trust in her saved him from becoming disturbed and helped make him a mature adult, an honest intellectual, courageous, dedicated to significant causes, and capable of enjoying the good things of life. Our relationship has grown emotionally closer and stronger with the years.

The story of my depressions, which caused much suffering to me and to my family, ought to be told in some detail, if only for purposes of medical history. Depressive episodes of various intensities and durations came at intervals of several months for three decades, demanding of me a staggering effort, while they lasted, to keep functioning at a more or less normal pace. Over twenty-five years, at different times and in different cities, by psychiatrists and psychologists, I was subjected to psychotherapy of various ilks, from Freudian psychoanalysis to less doctrinaire treatments. I was exposed over those years to what I saw then and see now as a series of intellectually vacuous interactions claiming to have therapeutic validity. Only my suffering and a sense of duty to seek treatment justified my willingness to persist. What seems to me unforgivable is that even when, in the 1960s, antidepressive medication became available it was either not prescribed for me or prescribed in preposterously small doses, fifty times smaller than was used by competent practitioners, as I later found out.

I might still be suffering under pointless treatment by some psychotherapist if a major depressive attack had not brought me into the hands of a competent psychiatrist. Three months of adequate doses of anti-depressant drugs followed by long-term lithium treatment have freed me of all symptoms of depression for the past ten years, adding a new dimension to my enjoyment of life and making my family life serene, relieved from the fear of impending depressions.

I do not wish to comment here on the bearing of my experience on the medical question of the physiological vs. behavioral basis of recurrent depression. But I do know that my experience is not unique. I already have saved several friends and colleagues from the misery of psychotherapy by directing them to competent treatment. I only wish to emphasize the extent of the harm that the bias and ignorance of certain therapists can do to depressive patients. For decades my life was plagued by an illness whose characteristics make it a source not only of pain but of guilt. Depressives feel that it should be up to themselves to overcome the depression, and psychotherapy increases the guilt when the therapist insists that depression is the surface manifestation of suppressed anger or unresolved conflicts.

These, then, are the sources of my personality as it developed over the years: parental family environment and my reaction to it; search for emotional fulfillment finally achieved in my own adult family; drive for professional achievement; and drive toward personal decency.

What have been the results? I can answer only in terms of my own self-image, which, like that of most people, is a compound of contradictions. My sense of being a striving, energetic, successful person is moderated by lingering doubts about my competence in science and in everyday life. I instinctively strive for control in interpersonal affairs, only to suffer guilt when I become aware of my own attempts to control others unfairly. The streak of perfectionism in my personality makes every slip painful; I recall, and feel pained in recalling, each social blunder, big or small, I have committed from adolescence until yesteryear, even after the curing of my depressions has made me less vulnerable to anguished self-criticism.

The effort to overcome the feeling of physical inadequacy has contributed to my desire to be in control; but the will to control, to feel powerful, has always remained ambiguous. In matters of money, for example, my attitude has oscillated between irrational miserliness, making me regret unnecessary expenses or resent minor overcharges, and pointless greed, causing me to waste time and money on the stock market. Presumably the latter activity serves to fulfill a wish for "adult" behavior.

A fortunate element in my personality has been a tendency to live in the present rather than looking nostalgically back to the past. I have not, unlike T. S. Eliot, regretted "the door [I] never opened into the rose garden." Rather, I have tried to live in the day-by-day reality. I do not long to reimmerse myself in the locales of my earlier experience, to return nostalgically to Italy or France or later residences to recapture my past. In fact, when I change place of residence I forget streets and buildings and people very rapidly. Like a migrating amoeba I pull up my pseudopods and roll on to the new setting.

The ability to live in the present has, I believe, served to counterbalance the self-doubt, the sense of personal inadequacy that my youthful experiences and my emotional upsets inevitably generated. I have learned that success depends in great part on concentrating whatever resources one has on the task at hand, without letting the feeling of inadequacy become an excuse for retreat. Concentration on realistic tasks was for me the expression of a commitment to effective activity. The resulting successes did generate a core of self-confidence that overcame the potentially stifling influences of childhood and later the effects of depression, a core of sturdiness that has stood me in good stead for seven decades.

Self-confidence need not be aggressive, but is not unrelated to aggressiveness. My aggressive tendencies have been mostly verbal, expressed in a prompt and sometimes cutting repartee, which makes for interesting conversation but does not enhance good will. Such verbal aggressiveness has occasionally been a source of embarrassment and of self-reproach because it suggests hostility and anger. Without being an angry person I have in me a reservoir of anger, which I try to channel in positive directions, particularly into political activity, where anger is profitably directed at social injustice. A modicum of anger is a valuable component in politics, where the issues are never fully black and white and emotion is needed to strengthen the will. Many sincere and committed liberals fail to be effective in political work because their commitment is not shored up by angry indignation toward social injustice.

Old age brings a thinning out of one's field of personal connections. Friends die, leaving behind memories of affinities and congruences. Being old myself, I bemoan their passing, but do not miss them. Their role in my life has been fulfilled; our interactions have been emotionally and intellectually meaningful. Max Delbrück, Jacques Monod, Jacob Bronowski, among those gone, are some who gave me their friendship and the reassurance of being treated as an equal. Such a reassurance, more than any measure of success, vouches for the validity of one's life's work. To the relentlessly introspective person, success alone would be a source of anguish if it were not validated by the approval of those one respects.

It would be much harder, I suspect, to write an autobiography were it not for the shared aspect of life, which gives it meaning. The story of one's life path acquires humane significance from the contacts with other human beings. Dante's allegory, seeking insight and understanding in the words of the dwellers of Hell, Purgatory, and Heaven, is also an allegory of life deeply shared. Even as one approaches the end of the journey, one hopes, like Dante, for one final stretch of meaningful toil.

Index

Acknowledgments

Grateful acknowledgment is made for permission to reprint:

Excerpt from "The Man with the Blue Guitar" and from "The Idea of Order at Key West" from *The Collected Poems of Wallace Stevens* by Wallace Stevens. Copyright 1936 by Wallace Stevens, renewed 1964 by Holly Stevens. Reprinted by permission of Alfred A. Knopf, Inc.

Excerpt from "The Waking" from *The Collected Works of Theodore Roethke* by Theodore Roethke. Copyright 1953 by Theodore Roethke. Reprinted by permission of Doubleday & Company, Inc., and Faber and Faber, London, Limited.

Excerpt from "Prayer After World War" in *Smoke and Steel* by Carl Sandburg. Copyright 1920 by Harcourt Brace Jovanovich, Inc.; renewed 1948 by Carl Sandburg.

Excerpt from "Ash-Wednesday" in *Collected Poems 1909-1962* by T.S. Eliot. Copyright 1936 by Harcourt Brace Jovanovich, Inc.; copyright © 1963, 1964 by T.S. Eliot. Reprinted by permission of Harcourt Brace Jovanovich, Inc. and Faber and Faber, London, Limited.

Excerpt from "The Road Not Taken" from *The Poetry of Robert Frost* edited by Edward Connery Lathem. Copyright 1916, © 1969 by Holt, Rinehart and Winston. Copyright 1944 by Robert Frost. Reprinted by permission of Holt, Rinehart and Winston, Publishers, Jonathan Cape Limited, and the Estate of Robert Frost.

Excerpt from "The Unknown" in *The Sorrow Dance* by Denise Levertov. Copyright © 1966 by Denise Levertov Goodman. Reprinted by permission of New Directions Publishing Corporation.

Excerpt from "Here He Comes Again" from *Listen to the Warm* by Rod McKuen. Copyright © 1967 by Rod McKuen. All rights reserved. Reprinted by permission.